Praise for *TransElectric*

"It's an extraordinary story of an exceptional human being. What a story! What a life!" —**Sir Elton John**

"Cidny Bullens, who has been a great friend and a high-order musician/singer/writer since we first met scuffling around Laurel Canyon in the early 1970s, has found home. I was moved by the union of honesty, compassion, and forgiveness in this fearless *TransElectric* book." —**T Bone Burnett**, Grammy-winning record producer, composer, and songwriter

"Cidny's courage and willingness to face the music he was making head-on touched the hearts of every musician on the sessions we worked on together all those years ago. I'm pleased that the kindhearted Cidny has finally become the rock 'n' roller he'd always dreamed of being. My one word for the book, which I couldn't put down, would be . . . courageous." —**Rodney Crowell**, Grammy-winning songwriter/producer and author of *Word for Word*

"A fierce, brilliant memoir of a remarkable rock 'n' roll life—heartbreaking, triumphant, funny, powerful, and deeply human. Cid Bullens writes with a songwriter's eye for emotional detail that will keep *TransElectric* playing in your head for a long, long time." —**John Mankiewicz**, executive producer of *The Big Lie* and *House of Cards*

"Runaway, rock star, wife, mother, man. Cidny is all these things, and now reveals himself as a wonderful author as well. Honest and emotional, Cidny's story is full of incredible highs and unimaginable lows that left me feeling uplifted and inspired. Cidny writes as boldly as he lives." —**Rob Roth**, director of Broadway's *Beauty and the Beast* and author of *WarholCapote*

"If you can find a better story, call me!" —**Mary Gauthier**, Grammy-nominated singer-songwriter and author of *Saved by a Song*

TransElectric

CIDNY BULLENS

CHICAGO
REVIEW
PRESS

Published by Chicago Review Press Incorporated
814 North Franklin Street
Chicago, Illinois 60610
ISBN 978-1-64160-790-2

Library of Congress Control Number: 2023930564

The names of some individuals have been changed to preserve privacy.

Interior design: Nord Compo

Printed in the United States of America
5 4 3 2 1

For my wife, Tanya Taylor Rubinstein,
without whom this book would not have been written.
You are the magic.

Electrical current runs all through rock 'n' roll. It was born out of the mud, and rumble, and backwash that remains after a great thunderstorm. Those of us who are lucky enough to be in rock 'n' roll, carry that electricity for our lifetime, forever able to call up the sweat and skin and fever that once consumed us. I have ridden the long arc of the lightning bolt to where I am now. It has taken my whole life to be able to look back and see that I have always been TransElectric.

Cidny Bullens
Nashville, Tennessee, 2022

CONTENTS

FOREWORD

CINDY HAD EVERYTHING GOING FOR HER. She had the songs, the voice, the guitar, the attitude, the look. It was a bit like Hilary Swank in *Boys Don't Cry*. That kind of tomboy look that was so sexy.

I would never have known that Cidny was so troubled with who he wanted to be—his identity. That night he told me that he wanted to transition to a man, I just cried and cried and cried. I finally kind of understood Cindy at that moment. And I thought, my God, you've lived this incredible life. You've been so many different characters. You've dealt with so much grief and sadness. Now you've come through it, you're in your sixties, and you've made this transition.

This is an amazing story. Bravo, Cidny.

—Sir Elton John

PROLOGUE

MY WIFE IS A WITCH. No really—she's a witch witch. She erects altars all over the house to various ancestors and saints. She casts spells and recites incantations. Half of our budget seems to go to candles and roses. Alchemy is a word that slips easily off her tongue. (There is no black magic in her repertoire, but there is a black cat.)

Tanya had been my solo show coach and director. I didn't know anything about her witchery when we started our personal relationship in early 2016. But she would tell me often, "I always know who someone is." Sometimes she scared me.

Months later in the tiny upstairs apartment of my duplex in Portland, Maine, in my rickety pine four-poster bed that had survived every move across town and across the country, every argument and act of love, every doubt and every dream I've awoken with since the beginning of my former marriage decades before, Tanya looked at me with her soft, loving eyes and said, "You are a cosmic rock star."

I looked at her quizzically, a shaft of sunlight dancing through the window on my half-naked new male body. I thought of myself as a failure, more than not. I had never reached that level of success I always imagined I would. I was a good, earnest, well-meaning person. But I had failed, in my mind, at my true calling. Then she smiled and said, "Yes. You're *my* cosmic rock star. Don't forget, I always know who someone is."

The sun shifted just slightly on my chest. My mind started wandering, landing on certain moments from my life—what was and what could have been. Who was that person so long ago who came ever so close to being a true rock star? Tanya, my witchy wife, sees only that person still—the essence of me. Time has a way of crusting over our youthful desires and our recollections of them, even as they lay smoldering still just under the surface. As I bend further down toward the lower right end of the arc of my life, could *I* remember the true essence of me? *Can* I remember?

This is the story of a rock 'n' roller, a mother, and a transgender man—all at the same time. Parallel lives that all just happen to be mine.

1

WALKIN' THROUGH
THIS WORLD

Some may walk on the wild side
Of course you can walk like a man
I'm walkin' through this world
As exactly who I am
You can't see me now
And you couldn't see me then
But I'll keep walkin' through this world
As exactly who I am

> *"Walkin' Through This World" by Cidny Bullens*
> *@2019 Red Dragonfly Music/BMI*

I WAS GOING TO BE MICK JAGGER. I looked like him. I moved like him. I could sing like him. "Are you Mick Jagger?" girls gushed when I sauntered past them, fifteen years old, in Harvard Square in the mid-'60s.

"His younger brother!" I'd shout back in a fake English accent.

"Cut your hair!" shouted men from their Pontiac GTOs and Chevy Camaros when they saw me walking past, my jeans low on my slim hips, the waves of my page boy haircut swinging just above my shoulders. In high school I got on stage for our talent show and lip-synced "(I Can't Get No) Satisfaction," and the crowd was on its feet, roaring with applause. Every girl wanted me to be her first kiss. I was going to be a star.

I wanted to be Mick Jagger because he was in the Rolling Stones. The Beatles were the music, but the Stones were the fire. I had so much energy inside of me; maybe it was my rage that I could only express with a pounding beat, a growl in my voice, the raw, raunchy soul of rock 'n' roll.

I'd been in L.A. for less than a year, pumping gas, sleeping on couches, auditioning for cover bands, and occasionally singing backup on a recording session. I showed up one night at my frequent hang, Cherokee Studios, on Fairfax Avenue in Hollywood, for the filming and live recording of Dr. John's new album. I wasn't invited. In fact, somebody tried to kick me out, but I didn't leave.

Studio A (the Big Room) was brimming over with record executives and A-List musicians and artists. At the end of the session, the band started jamming. A couple of the studio staff, plus owner Bruce Robb, who I knew, had already jumped on stage to join in.

Man, I wanna be a part of this, I thought. I glanced around the room hoping no one would notice, walked behind the temporary stage over to an empty drum set (there were two), and sat down. Though I wasn't a great drummer, drums were my passion as a kid. I easily slid into the twelve-bar beat. I turned my head to the right. What was an empty set a moment ago was now about to be occupied. Ringo Starr was watching me, smiling. He sat down and joined in. As his sticks hit the snare and the hi-hat, Ringo's head swayed from side to side, sending his legendary hair left and right, up and down, *exactly* like when I was thirteen and saw the Beatles for the first time on *The Ed Sullivan Show*.

I am playing drums WITH Ringo Starr! Holy crap! I looked in front of me. Now Eric Clapton was playing congas. Dr. John was just burning up the piano. Even then, as a young man, Dr. John, the Night Tripper, looked like a behatted, aging Louisiana snake-oil salesman. And here comes Joe Cocker, beer in hand, climbing up onto the stage. Barely able to stand, he grabbed a mic.

I was twenty-four years old and playing with the big boys. Nothing in my life had ever been safe, so why should I be scared of anything? Scared? *Hell no, I am exactly where I am supposed to be—right here, right now.* After a while, a guy bumped me off my drum set and sat down to play. *I'm here now.* I didn't even think. I walked up toward the front of the stage. Standing up proved too much for Joe Cocker, and he was helped back to a seat at his table. Somebody threw me his mic. Again, I didn't even think. I started improvising the blues on the spot. *Fuck it. I don't care. If they throw me out, so be it.*

"Four o'clock in the mornin', baby where you been," I sang, my voice deep and gritty. In that moment, that mic gave me power. Hearing my own voice carrying through the air, electrically charged, ignited all that was underneath my skin.

I was always angry. Angry that nobody knew who I really was. Angry that I could not *be* who I was. I don't remember what words I made up on that stage. I was always making up songs, but my rage at the world was real.

That night I sang with all my heart—nonsensical words, just sounds that sounded like words—guttural, from the bottom of my being. Maybe I was singing about how trapped I felt in this world. Or how frustrating it was when I tried to fit in. I couldn't and I didn't. So, I sang. My T-shirt soaked with sweat, when the song ended, I relinquished the mic.

Bob Ezrin, the record producer, was standing at the front of the stage. His eyes narrowed. He fingered for me to come over to him.

Oh shit, I thought, *I'm really in trouble this time*. Bob Ezrin and I had already met a few months before, there at Cherokee. He was a prominent producer who had worked with Alice Cooper, Lou Reed, Pink Floyd. I was there at Cherokee as much as possible, fetching coffee, hanging out with the studio owners, the Robb Brothers, recording a needed background vocal here and there—always observing, soaking it all in, trying to learn my trade. And I met a lot of people in the music business. I hesitantly walked to the front of the stage toward him.

He was staring at me. "I didn't know you could sing like that."

I shrugged.

"You just got yourself a deal kiddo."

"A deal?"

Bob Ezrin grinned. "A record deal. Al Teller wants to talk to you. United Artists. Don't go away."

I felt like I couldn't breathe. What was happening? Is what I'd dreamed about coming true? Maybe somebody was seeing me at last. Only they weren't.

"There's just one thing," Ezrin said, serious now. "You're gonna have to work twice as hard as everybody else."

"Why?" I asked innocently.

"Because you're a girl, Cindy."

I didn't know how to be a girl.

I didn't take that record deal, and I can't tell you why. Except that ever since I was a little kid I've been running away. From home. From what everyone thinks I'm supposed to do or be. From myself.

When I was as young as three or four, I remember going into my older brother's room and wondering why he had all the things I wanted—the toys, the clothes, the sneakers. Oh, those sneakers—Red Ball Jets. I wanted those high tops, not Mary Janes. I wanted shoes that a big boy would wear, with the thin red line that ran around the side of the sole. I wanted to pee standing up. I cried every time I had to wear a dress. When I played with my friends, I was always the father or the brother, the evil king, or the brave prince. Every night before I went to sleep, I prayed that I would wake up fixed, that God would make my body right.

One time, as that young kid, when I ran away, I ran a mile down the road and hid inside the piled-up tires in our neighbor's yard. When I was six, my family moved from the suburbs of Boston to "the country." West Newbury was a farming town where all our neighbors were mechanics or farmers. For some reason I was comforted by the junk in yards and the old rusting trucks and tractors in the fields. Sometimes I carried a long stick with a bandana tied on the end like a hobo. That was my fantasy. I wanted to be free. Free from my little world as it was. I already knew I wasn't like the other kids.

My parents drank. My father was a good man. He loved his five children. He was a proficient salesman but lost his job more than once. A decorated, wounded, and now partially disabled World War II vet, he was emotionally absent and held it all inside. My mother was outgoing, charismatic, and exhausted. She played bridge or bowled or golfed and imagined that one day, maybe, she'd be a socialite like her sister in the New York City suburbs.

I wasn't beaten. I wasn't abused. I was taught right from wrong and knew to put my napkin in my lap and to stand up for elders when they walked into the room. But they drank and fought and threw things at each other and sent the kids to Sunday school, so they could recover from their weekend hangovers.

This was the '60s, when no one thought about gender identity, much less talked about it. My mother tried in vain to get me to behave like a girl, but she also pronounced on occasion that I was different. "You've got more male hormones than female hormones," she'd say with a shrug. "You were born wrong."

I've sometimes wondered if maybe the doctors said something to her when I was born, although there is no evidence that I was intersexed.

One August afternoon, when I was twelve, I was playing outside at my friend Hendy Webb's house on Chebeague Island, Maine, shirtless like I always was. I absolutely never wore a shirt in the summer. I was lying on the warm, dry, prickly grass, laughing. A puff of ocean breeze made me turn onto my back, and my right hand brushed against my chest. I stopped breathing. I shivered in horror. I felt a pea-sized bump beneath my left nipple. *Oh no*, I thought, *now I'm going to have to pretend to be a girl for the rest of my life.*

Cindy at three years old. *Author's collection*

As a kid, my friends were equal parts boys and girls. But in high school, I fell in love with the girls. We had to wear skirts or dresses to school. I hid my T-shirt and jeans in the garage, so as soon as I got home, I could rip off my girl clothes and put on my *real* clothes, the uniform of me. I couldn't even wait to get up to my bedroom to change.

I ran away for real when I was fifteen with a girl from up the road. After helping get my little sisters their dinner, I told my mother I was going to the library. I left the house, stopped to fetch my friend's sixteen-year-old sister Jane, who was eager to tag along, and we walked to the bus stop at the gas station on Route 1. Jane and I rode into Boston's South Station where we got another bus to New York City.

We arrived at 2:00 AM into Port Authority with $22 in cash between us. (Jane had the twenty-dollar bill.) We had no idea where we were going to go. It was the middle of January, and there was a subway strike. Jane had the long brown hair of a beatnik, and I looked, well, like a teenage boy. It was 1965, and we were both wearing our peacoats. Jane's suitcase was packed with cans of soup and tuna fish, and it felt like it weighed seventy pounds. I'd brought my notebooks filled with lyrics to all my songs with me and then forgot them up on the luggage rack on the New York bus. The plan was to go to Greenwich Village. *My* plan was to get a job as a musician.

Cindy at fifteen years old. *Author's collection*

This is how I remind myself that there is a power greater than myself: I look back at moments like this in my life and think, *Something really is watching over me.* Sleazy guys were walking up to us and offering us places to crash. Thank God I already had enough street sense, from my days and nights hanging out in Boston with my friends, to know *that* wasn't happening. Then this big, tall African American man approached us and shook his head. "Do you need a place to stay? I'll take you to one."

I looked straight into his eyes. "Jane, we are going with this guy," I announced. I knew he wasn't going to hurt us. I can't tell you how I knew, but I did. He grabbed Jane's heavy suitcase, and we followed him out the door and onto 42nd Street. We marched behind him down Eighth Avenue in the frigid cold, in the wee hours of the morning, all the way to West 34th Street. We turned the corner, and there was the YMCA.

"You are staying here," he said. We followed him up to the front desk. The haggard old man on night watch looked at us suspiciously as the tall Black man turned and disappeared.

We paid two dollars each for the night's stay. The next day we got a room in a fleabag hotel off Washington Square Park in Greenwich Village. The room had an iron. I heated up our soup by placing the cans on top of the propped up, upside down iron on its highest setting. It worked. I read every issue of my brother's *Boys' Life* magazine. I coveted his Boy Scout handbook. The survival techniques would surely come in handy someday (though the iron trick probably wasn't in either one of them).

I immediately began knocking on the doors of all the folk clubs in the West Village—Café Wha, Folk City, The Gaslight. I pretended to be a boy. "I'm a musician. I play guitar and drums. Know of anything I can do?" I don't know what it was that gave me the audacity to go into these darkened basements and ask for a chance. I was fifteen years old. Courage? Anger? Maybe it was just sheer will, some inexplicable life force. I was going to be somebody. I had to be.

Jane was "cleaning needles" for a couple of guys we met in the hotel. At least that's what she told me. Her mother was a nurse, and she explained to me that she knew how to sterilize them with alcohol. These men seemed so old to us, but they were probably in their twenties, and while they hit on both of us, I never did anything with anyone. Addicts though they were, they were nice guys and watched out for us.

Ten days after we arrived, the New York City police barged into our room at the hotel. "I am *not* going home!" I screamed, as they pulled us through the grimy, dark hallway and down the three flights of stairs. The cops let us know in no uncertain terms that they had beaten up one of our protectors and forced him to tell them what room we were in. I was enraged.

My mother and her sister, the socialite with her bright red lipstick and white gloves, were standing in the lobby. As the police pushed me toward them, Jane behind me, I gave my mother a silent, spiteful look. I had planned not to ever go home.

Back at school I got suspended, but not for running away. I bragged about it, and *that* was a whole lot more dangerous. Who knew what kind of rebellion I might ignite? Jane got expelled. (My mother threatened the school board, with what I never knew, so that I would not get kicked out.)

I begrudgingly finished high school, after which my mother insisted, against my will, that I enroll in some kind of college. I wanted to be a rock star, now! But my mother continued to be a force to be reckoned with, and I went back to New York, this time to acting school—The American Academy of Dramatic Arts.

I was pretty good at acting. Only I didn't fit into many molds when it came to parts. I looked young, but I was too tall to play a kid. I almost never wore women's clothes, but even if I did, I definitely didn't fit the ingenue image. I made the most of the character roles to which I was relegated. My first part at the Academy was described as "a weird hermaphrodite."

After I graduated, I got four callbacks for the Cherry Lane Theatre production of *Godspell* and two for Broadway's *You're a Good Man, Charlie Brown,* but didn't land either one. I did end up on Broadway though, with three lines and in the band of the musical *Lysistrata* with Melina Mercouri, the Greek star of the film *Never on Sunday*—but only because I could play a guitar on stage "like a guy." The show closed after six weeks.

I got called back a few times for an Off-Off-Broadway improvisational group down in the Village called *Lemmings* featuring a couple of unknown comics, John Belushi and Christopher Guest. That one looked really promising. But I decided to run away again before I heard back, this time to L.A.

I was twenty-three years old, skinny, and wide-eyed. I had a hundred bucks in my pocket this time, a backpack, and my guitar. I had a reel-to-reel demo tape of my songs. What I had most of all were dreams.

2

HOLLYWOOD HOT

Hollywood hot
Hol-ly-wood hot
And they like it a lot
Foxy fever got you hot to trot
Glam and glitter get you hot

"Hollywood Hot" by Bob Crewe & Cindy Bullens
©1974 Tanny Boy, Stone Diamond Music/BMI

WHEN I FIRST GOT TO L.A., a friend of a friend introduced me to another friend who, sight unseen, let me sleep on her couch. Eventually she'd become a Hollywood bigwig, a producer for Johnny Carson and Jay Leno, but in those days, Helen Gorman was working at the *Hollywood Reporter* and apparently didn't mind taking in a stray.

I hitchhiked every morning from the Santa Monica side of West L.A. to Jerry's Phillips 66 on the corner of Little Santa Monica Boulevard and Manning Avenue near the Mormon Temple, where Jerry himself had given me a job. I refused to wear any kind of girl uniform, so a job like waitressing was out for me. I'd pumped gas all through high school and loved it, so why not now? There was no self-serve then. I liked checking the oil and putting the air in tires. I liked yakking with the guys who came in to chat with Jerry and seeing the quizzical looks of the women when I washed their windshields. Sometimes I thought that if I didn't make it big in the music business, I'd find a way to buy myself a gas station.

One day I came home in greasy jeans smelling like gasoline, and Helen met me at the door.

"You've got a demo tape, right?"

"Yup," I said with a mental question mark, wondering what was coming next.

"You're going to take the tape, tonight, to my friend Diane's. I told her all about you. I told her how talented I think you are."

"You did?"

"Well, yes! You've got to clean yourself up though. Do you have anything decent to wear?"

"Um . . ." Helen sighed. "Well, Diane is a columnist at the *Reporter*, and her husband Peter is Bob Crewe's attorney, and Bob is having dinner with them tonight."

"Bob Crewe?" I asked. "Who's he?"

"Honestly? Have you ever heard of the Four Seasons? 'Sherry'? 'Big Girls Don't Cry'? 'Walk Like a Man'? How about Mitch Ryder and the Detroit Wheels?"

Of course I knew who the Four Seasons were—I had an older brother and sister. I'd heard them on the radio growing up. That smooth, polished sound wasn't my music, but Mitch Ryder? Now you're talkin'! I won many a dance contest in high school winding and grinding to "Sock It to Me Baby."

"So, Bob Crewe wrote all those songs and produced them," Helen continued. "He's a genius. He's a hit maker. He could turn you into a star."

"And I'm going to meet him?" I was stunned. I'd only been in L.A. a couple of months.

"Absolutely not!" announced Helen. "Diane says you are to go the back door of their house and give the demo to whoever opens the door. They will bring it to her, and she will give it to Bob. Under *no* circumstances are you, for any reason, to go into that house. Do not attempt to go into that house. Do you understand? Do not go into that house."

"So why do I have to change?"

"Put on a clean T-shirt, OK?"

An hour later, in Helen's car, I was driving through rows of palm trees in Beverly Hills, past one gated mansion after another. I found the right gate. Pressed the button. Told them who I was. Drove in. My little three-inch reel-to-reel demo tape that I recorded in New York before I left was on the seat beside me.

I rang the doorbell at the servant's entrance and waited. It was dark. I rang again and heard footsteps. The door opened with a wide swing. A ruggedly handsome man stood before me, his silk shirt was open almost to his navel. He was wearing tight hip hugger bell bottoms and a wide leather belt. His blond hair flowed almost down to his shoulders. I couldn't take my eyes off him. It was a kind of a gravitational pull. For both of us. He grabbed my arm and pulled me into the kitchen. Helen's command, "Under NO circumstances are you to go into the house!" echoed in my head.

"I've got this demo tape for Bob Crewe," I stuttered.

"Well, I'm Bob Crewe," he laughed. "And who are you?"

Because I felt so uncomfortable in my body, it was often hard for me to own the effect my look had on other people. In the '70s a lot of male rock stars were androgynous—I was a girl, but it was hard for people to tell *what* I was. I questioned it myself. I attracted attention from all persuasions—men who liked women, women who liked men, women who liked women, and gay men like Bob. I guess I had something they wanted, call it qi, call it charisma, call it sex appeal. That fact would prove to be a blessing and a curse.

Bob insisted that I not only come in but also join his friends for dinner. He literally dragged me into the other room where these music business heavy hitters were having drinks and sitting down to eat. "Set another place!" Bob announced grandly. The butler handed me my very first ever glass of champagne.

A woman was glaring at me. It was Diane. Helen's voice echoed again: "Under NO circumstances are you to go into the house!" It was *her* house. I tentatively sat down at the dining room table next to an older balding man who looked strangely familiar. He smiled at me.

"Didn't we meet on a plane a few months ago?" he asked. It turned out I sat next to him when I'd flown from New York to L.A. The flight I was supposed to be on got cancelled, and for some inexplicable reason, the airline put me in first class on the next flight. Jimmy the Hook was the road manager of Sly and the Family Stone and Frank Sinatra. Now he wanted to introduce me to the head of MGM Records.

The whole night had that feeling of something between *The Beverly Hillbillies* and kismet. I was the hillbilly. But just maybe I was falling into this improbable situation that was going to take me somewhere. Everyone was leaning in, fascinated by the new kid and this remarkable coincidence. But Diane was clearly furious. After dinner, she got up from the table and returned a moment later with an old beat-up guitar with five rusty strings.

"Why don't you play something for us?" she said with an acidic smile.

And play I did, rusty strings and all, because the only times I felt truly all right was when I played and sang. That was my power source. Feeling emboldened by the reaction to my song, and at Bob Crewe's request, I sat down at the grand piano in the living room.

> *I got a Hallelujah chorus in the back of my mind*
> *Just waiting for the day when my stars are gonna shine*
> *If I can weather out the storm I think I'll be just fine*
> *For another day*
>
> "Rainy Sunday" by Cindy Bullens
> ©1972 Cindy Bullens

"That sounds like Aaron Copland," Bob gushed. And now everyone was applauding and giving me their phone numbers.

"Honey, you've got to call me. We've got to talk."

"If you need anything . . . " said Bob, handing me his phone number. And it turned out I did. Because by the time I drove Helen's car home to her apartment in West L.A., Diane had called her, fuming about how I had ruined her dinner party.

"Out!" Helen announced. "You are out."

Now it's true I hadn't been paying rent and I'd been eating her food and not even looking for another place to crash, but still, I was stunned. I had only been making a pittance at the gas station, and I was giving Jerry what little I made for a used VW Bug I wanted to buy in his lot. I had almost no money.

The next morning, I slung my backpack over my shoulder, grabbed my guitar, and left. I walked down Wilshire Boulevard with no idea where

I was going to go. I sat down at the counter at the House of Pies and ordered a cup of coffee, the only thing I could afford.

Two girls who were sitting close to me at the counter started chatting with me. They were runaways. Was I a runaway, again? I didn't know anymore. I only knew that at that moment, I was homeless.

I fingered a dime in my pocket, took a deep breath, excused myself, and went to a pay phone out on the street. I paced around in a circle for what felt like an hour with only one phone number in my pocket. At this point, what did I have to lose? Still, I was terrified. Finally, I dialed Bob Crewe's number.

"Hi, It's Cindy Bullens," I said. "From last night. Uh . . . I don't have a place to stay anymore. Do you think you could help? Do you know of anywhere I could stay?"

"Call me back in an hour." Bob replied quickly. I walked back to the House of Pies. The runaways were still there. They told me they were staying at a house on 14th Street while the three girls, who were roommates, were away.

"Come stay with us!" said the runaways. "I'm sure it'll be fine for a couple of nights." I called Bob Crewe back and told him I had found a place.

"Good!" he said. "Be at Sound Factory tomorrow morning at ten. I want you to sing backup on a record I'm producing."

If Helen Gorman hadn't kicked me out, I don't know if I would have ever had the guts to call Bob Crewe, ever. The three roommates came home, and the two runaways left. But I stayed with the roommates on their couch in the house on 14th Street in Santa Monica for a couple of months, until it became clear, after the one session became many, that I was now tethered to Bob Crewe.

After my time with the roommates, I ended up living for the next year and a half in Bob Crewe's storage unit in the basement of his Empire West penthouse apartment building on Alta Loma Road in West Hollywood. I became his protégé. I also became his gopher, his driver, his sidekick, and his nursemaid.

Bob was a genius. He was charming, talented, and impossible. I was twenty-three years old, wildly in love with who he was, ready to do anything for him, and I pretty much did. I answered the phones. I drove him around. I made his appointments with young men who did "massage" and left the room when they arrived. I picked up his drugs.

He went to bed drunk, woke up, did a few lines, and started swigging vodka straight out of the bottle. I cleaned up his messes. In return, Bob gave me an education in the making of pop music that I could not have gotten anywhere else. I learned how to sing backup, how to make a record, how to mingle with the music business elite. How to drink. How to snort cocaine.

Lyrics flew out of him like he was channeling them, or as though he were being possessed. "*Gitchi Gitchi Ya Ya Da Da,*" he sang as he and Kenny Nolan wrote the '70s hit, "Lady Marmalade." "*Voulez-vous coucher avec moi, ce soir?*" I was there, watching, as Kenny banged on the piano in the living room of the penthouse, churning out the chords as Bob stood grandly beside him, riffing. I was there when Patti LaBelle came to listen to the song for LaBelle that Allen Toussaint would produce.

Bob didn't play an instrument (he couldn't read music), but he knew just what rhythms and sounds would get inside your head and stay there, sound worms repeating themselves over and over. He didn't do any of this self-consciously or analytically. He just did it. He just knew. He was completely commercial. Only Bob Crewe didn't play to the market; he created it. He was the great innovator of pop music.

Still, Bob Crewe hadn't had a big hit since the late '60s, and when I met him, in 1973, he was trying really hard to get back to the top of the charts. Disco music, which was just starting to emerge, made that seem possible for Bob's unique pop talents.

But for someone who wrote such upbeat songs, Bob had a lot of darkness inside him. He drank most of the day and all night long and sometimes retreated to his bedroom, which he had painted black, and threatened to kill himself. He'd slash his own paintings with a knife, cursing at himself and the world. I watched, petrified, that he'd slash himself next. He could not be intimate. He paid for sex. He had no capacity for the truly personal. He scared the shit out of me.

Life got wild. Parties. Drugs. Everything was about alcohol and drugs. We went somewhere and did drugs. Someone came over, and we did drugs. We had drug dealer friends. I quickly forged an intimate relationship with cocaine but still managed to keep things together for Bob, which is what I had done when my parents drank as a kid. I was used to it.

At restaurants he would demand the best seat, special service, extra accommodations. He'd fly into a rage if everything wasn't just perfect and maybe throw a chair across the room.

"Don't you know who I am?!" he would shout, as if it would explain or forgive everything if they knew. In the '70s in Hollywood, it seemed everyone was coked-up and out of their minds. There were no consequences.

I was meeting everyone in L.A.—major recording artists, record company executives, producers, and top recording engineers. One night I'd be out to dinner with Jerry Wexler, who founded Atlantic Records and

Cindy and Bob Crewe 1974.
Photo by and courtesy of Todd Everett

produced Aretha Franklin and Ray Charles, and the next, playing a song in a room at the Sunset Marquis hotel with Paul Butterfield, Artie Traum, Steve Goodman, and Kinky Friedman among others, invited by Bobby Neuwirth. Bobby was known as Bob Dylan's best friend and was considered the purveyor of all things cool. Through Neuwirth, I met Bonnie Raitt, T Bone Burnett, Stephen Bruton, Fritz Richmond, and others in those early days in and around Laurel Canyon. I started doing session work—with Rod Stewart, Don Everly, and Gene Clark of the Byrds. I was getting around and meeting people. Now people were beginning to know who I was and what I could do. All directly or indirectly through Bob Crewe.

I got a call from New York one day. Some guy invited me to appear on this new show they were doing called *Saturday Night Live*—the second episode. Bob Crewe told me to turn it down. "Don't waste your time," he told me. "Where is that going?"

I didn't go.

Bob Crewe controlled my life. We spent every day and every night together, except when I went down to crash in the storage room filled with his paintings. He didn't pay me a salary. He just handed me $20 bills from time to time. One minute he was loving to me, the next cruel. He was impossible and remarkable. I was utterly in awe of him. I was devoted to him. I loved him. I survived.

———

No one talked about trauma when I was growing up. Something happened, you got over it. Or you pretended you did—you fought your way through life. I don't look back on my parents' drunken fights, or the fact that I was sexually assaulted by my high school English teacher or rejected as an athlete because I was a girl and say that was the experience that wrecked me. Because despite everything, all of it, I was not wrecked. Maybe it was my anger—my need to prove myself—that saved me.

When I was thirteen, I shot my friend Jimmy in the head. We were shooting cans off a fallen tree in the backyard with my father's .22 caliber rifle. Jimmy, who was eleven, handed me the gun butt first, and it went off without me even touching the trigger. The bullet went right through his skull, missing his brain by an eighth of an inch. By the grace of God, he didn't die.

When I saw the geyser of blood gushing six inches high out of the hole in his head, I raced inside, pushing past Mrs. Elwell, the old lady who was babysitting my little sisters and me, and called the West Newbury police chief, Shikey Willis.

"I shot Jimmy!" I shouted into the phone. "I shot Jimmy Vynorius."

Then I called Jimmy's house. "I shot Jimmy in the head!" I shouted. Jimmy's brother, Wayne, who was twelve, ran out, got in his grandmother's car, and drove over. His parents weren't home. Wayne arrived at the same moment that Shikey pulled up in his two-toned '55 Chevy Bel Air.

"He's over there!" I yelled. "He's down there in the field!" I pointed, almost throwing my arm out of its socket. I couldn't go. I thought he was dead. I thought I had killed my friend.

Shikey carried him up from the side field and laid Jimmy in the back seat of his car, the blood from his head smearing the shiny blue vinyl. I stood motionless at the edge of the driveway as they drove off.

Mrs. Elwell called my parents, who were visiting my older brother at his college in Pennsylvania. The minister from the Congregational Church and my mother's best friend, Mrs. Curtis, came by to comfort me. Soon after, the Massachusetts State Police arrived to question me. That's when I found out that Jimmy was going to make it. His skull was shattered, and he'd probably have to wear a protective helmet for the next year or so. But he would live.

The next day I went to school. When I got on the bus you could hear a pin drop. (Mr. Elwell, the brother of our babysitter, was the bus driver.) A kid at school made fun of me for shooting Jimmy, and without a thought I punched him, whack, right in the face. Later at lunch, he apologized to me. "Man, I thought it was all a joke!"

When I got off the school bus at the end of the day, my mother was standing on the lawn waiting for me. I was terrified that I'd be severely punished. She greeted me with a rare hug. Everyone knew it was an accident, but still. . . . My mother could be very unpredictable.

Then she sent me down the road by myself to stand before Mr. and Mrs. Vynorius, Jimmy's parents. Doris Vynorius was like my second mother; she was the mother I wished I had. She didn't drink. She didn't yell. There were no loud, late-night parties every weekend. I don't remember what I said. Or what she said. Though I know I was still and always welcome in their home. But that was it. Nobody sent me to therapy. Nobody asked me to talk about it, and I didn't. My parent's attitude was, you deal with what's in front of you, and you move on.

Bob Crewe didn't want to sleep with me (and I didn't with him), but I guess he was happy to pass me on to his friends. One day we drove to this big house in Malibu for a day at the beach.

"Why don't you stay a little longer?" Bob said to me, as he stood up to leave. We'd had a pleasant day in a beautiful home in a beautiful spot overlooking the ocean. The sun was sinking now, creating one of those gorgeous Pacific sunsets.

"You and Paul can talk about music." I thought it was weird that Bob thought I'd want to stay here without him. But I was naïve and oblivious.

"No thanks," I said politely. "I'll just go home with you." But when I came out of the bathroom, Bob was gone. The next thing I knew, there were hands around my waist and a mouth on mine. *Oh no. What do I do now? Where do I go? This is Bob's friend!* The sofa was a sickly green and hard. He forced me down and turned me over. I succumbed. An arrangement had been made—with me as the commodity.

I don't remember how I got out of there. I don't remember how I made it back to Bob's. But I never talked about it. I didn't confront Bob. Move on.

What possessed Bob Crewe to take me in in the first place? What was it about me (or about him) that compelled him to allow me all the way into his life? I don't know the answer. I never asked. But there I was, ripe for the picking. Was it my androgyny? Or maybe my naïveté was a lure in itself. I never caught on to what was going on behind my back.

The next time, it was a female publicist who Bob thought I could "spend some time with." Sue was doing some publicity for Bob's various projects. She was gay and a few years older than me. Bob would take me with him over to her house for strategy sessions. We would snort some coke and talk. I felt like I had a part in the plans. Bob always made me feel that way—in the studio and in his meetings with producers and record companies—like I had something to give to the situation. Something that mattered. No one had ever done that before—at least not professionally.

But then he'd leave Sue's house and tell me to stay. Sue didn't attack me. She was OK. I wasn't at all attracted to her. She had an air of roughness around her that at times repelled me, but I felt like maybe we could be friends. I had only one true friend in Los Angeles at that time; she was newly married, and I wasn't in touch with her. Every single ounce of my being was tied to Bob Crewe. There was no room for anyone else. But here was Sue, who Bob kept encouraging me to get to know. Was Bob tired of me? Trying to get rid of me? Very possible. I was his witness.

Sue was nice to me, but she was relentless. She wanted to sleep with me. She plied me with alcohol and drugs, tantalizing tales of the musicians she knew, and literally led me almost to my death. And she had a child—a beautiful four-year-old girl.

I was horrified when after several visits to her house, Sue introduced Mora to me. *What?! A child in this house? With who knows what kind of people traipsing in and out at all hours and all the illicit activity going on?* Mora looked like she could have walked out of a twentieth century Kentucky coal miner's kitchen—with straggly, wavy, dirty blond hair just past her shoulders, a stained tan T-shirt and worn Oshkosh overalls.

I had two younger sisters who I looked after when they were little. Debbie was born when I was seven and Suki when I was nine. My older sister Nancy was almost eight years older than me, and my brother Rick was five years older. Nancy and Rick were mostly gone when the girls were babies, and the responsibility of caring for them a lot of the time, at least in my mind, fell to me.

I immediately felt very protective of Mora. I stuck around. In the coming weeks, I bought groceries for them, healthy food for healthy meals. Some nights I read to Mora until she fell sleep. I took her for walks and whenever I was in the house, I paid close attention to where she was at all times.

While I tried to protect this child, I could not protect myself. One night, late, after a fair amount of tequila, Sue stood up from the couch, looked at me straight on, and in a deliberate but hushed voice said, "I'm going into the bathroom to shoot some coke."

I looked at her, stunned. "What?"

She repeated herself. "I'm going into the bathroom to shoot some coke." Her thin lips curled up on one side revealing her uneven and potholed teeth. Then she added, "Do you want to? It's good." Her eyes looked straight at mine, piercing through any vestige of the barricade I thought I had built between us.

My half-drunk mind tried to sort out what was just offered to me. *Shoot up? Like a junkie? There is no way on God's green earth I would ever put a needle in my arm.* That's what I would have said ten minutes earlier. *Where am I? WHO am I?*

Though I drank alcohol at the time, I almost never got really drunk. I didn't like it when I felt I was out of control. Drugs, stimulants exclusively, afforded me the illusion that my mind was fully functioning, and my feet were on the ground. But tequila was not a stimulant, and that illusion was not intact on this night. Sue picked the perfect moment to ask.

What the fuck, I thought.

Journal Entry—June 14, 1975, Boston, MA

I did it! I met the Rolling Stones! Went to the concert with Earl McGrath and Jerry Greenberg [President of Atlantic Records]. *After the concert I met Faye Dunaway (who was all over me) and Peter Wolf. Then we all rode in the limousine together back to the hotel and proceeded (Faye to me) to get friendly. After a while Faye, Peter, Earl, and me snuck away to the Stones suite and I met them all and hung out for a while. Faye practically begged me to go home with Peter and she* [sic]. *Earl, too, wanted me to stay. I figured best to go home.*

The "home" I was going to was my parents' house in Topsfield, Massachusetts.

I'd met Earl McGrath through Jerry Wexler. Earl, a sharp, irreverent, fun, and very sweet man, took a liking to me and became another guide through the wilds of the Hollywood and New York arts and music communities. He was working at Atlantic Records at the time (he later became president of Rolling Stones Records) and knew I was close to Boston visiting my folks.

As I was driving back to Topsfield from the Sheraton Hotel in Boston, I had to laugh at myself. I had just been hit on by Faye Dunaway in the Rolling Stones personal suite (they were all there), surrounded by a bunch of music business elites, and I was on my way to sleep in my old bed, in my old bedroom, next to my parents' room, that I ran away from ten years before at fifteen.

I wanted love, but I was terrified of sex. I was attracted to both men and women. Was I gay? Was I straight? I didn't know what I was. I was alone; that's all I knew. And, like my mother told me, different—"born wrong."

No one would ever understand that even though I didn't have guy parts, I was a guy. I didn't feel comfortable having any kind of sexual interaction with anyone. How was I to be myself, sexually? Forget about enjoying it! Lots of people seemed to find me sexually attractive—gay men, gay women, straight men, and straight women—but I loathed who I was. When I got out of the shower, I'd put my hands up to hide my breasts. If I didn't look at them, maybe they weren't really there.

In 1971, when I was an acting student in New York, I went to the New York Public Library to try to find out what I was, what was wrong with me. I found a book on gender. There was a term that described people who felt like they were in the wrong body: transsexual. That was me. There were procedures, protocol, a way to change your sex. *Really?* There was an address in the back of the book—Tulane University. I immediately sent away for all the information. *Where can I go in New York City to change my sex?*

When the package arrived, I tore open the large manila envelope and pored over every last word of every brochure and booklet. Go to this clinic for consultation. And here for hormone therapy. It was all there. *I can do this!* My head was swirling. Then I thought of my family. I had no money. *No. I can't do this. I* can't *do this.* There were a thousand reasons why. And there was not one soul on earth I could talk to about any of it. And I didn't talk about it. I was alone in my own hell. Move on.

Meanwhile, Bob Crewe was making deals, making records, and trying to produce a hit that would equal his success with the Four Seasons. We had seen this hairdresser on Johnny Carson, Monti Rock III. Bob had this crazy idea that Monti should sing the disco song that Bob and Kenny Nolan had just written, "Get Dancin'." We found out Monti was in L.A. and drove over to the Hollywood apartment where he was staying. It took about five seconds for Monti to agree to the project. The studio group Disco-Tex and the Sex-O-Lettes was born. And suddenly I was a Sex-O-Lette. We recorded the track at Cherokee Studios, and within weeks the single went Top Ten.

I was writing a few songs with Bob now. I'd come up with a guitar lick or a few chords, and Bob would just start singing along. *Hollywood Hot, Holl-y-wood Hot gets ya Hot to Trot, L.A. fever yeah, it's what cha got Hollywood Hot. . . .* That's how we wrote "Hollywood Hot," which, despite Bob's full-blown rages and the train wreck of the recording session, was catchy and of the times.

It instantly started climbing the Billboard Hot 100 Chart and the disco charts. We wrote "Street Talk" next—by B.C. Generation. Another disco hit. But I didn't want to be associated with any of this. I was grateful for the success, but disco wasn't exactly my cup of tea. I wanted to *say* something, *feel* something in the music I wrote. I wanted to play rock 'n' roll in an arena, not put together pretend groups for their good looks and create commercial music in a studio. Bob had me singing in a high falsetto-like voice akin to Frankie Valli. High voices have more energy, he would say. It wasn't my real voice, which was lower and more resonant. I felt restless and trapped. By this time, I too was doing a lot of drugs and drinking, which didn't help.

But I loved the L.A. scene, and I started having some success. I was part of a band now, Kemosabe, with musicians who'd played with everyone from Van Morrison to Blood, Sweat & Tears to Boz Scaggs. We were managed by one of Bob Dylan's former managers, Bennett Glotzer. We were writing our own songs. I was one of the lead singers. We were playing gigs here and there. I was part of something. There was hope for more. I felt like I belonged.

Journal Entry—July 11, 1975

I have a one-way ticket to NYC—leaving tomorrow. Supposedly to play a gig with Bobby, T Bone, possibly Dylan.

One day Bobby Neuwirth called me out of the blue. We had become good friends, and he included me in many of the spur-of-the-moment musician soirees where he held court all over town. I knew he was in New York City working on some art and hanging with his friends there.

"I'm sending you a plane ticket to come to New York. Next week. Don't say no. You have to be here."

I would be part of Bobby's band with T Bone Burnett and Steven Soles, who I already knew from L.A., at the venerable Greenwich club The Other End (formerly and now again The Bitter End). I was thrilled! Once again, I'd be playing and performing with people who spoke my musical language.

The bands billed for that week at the club were the local Jake and the Family Jewels and Austin singer-songwriter Rusty Wier. They were there, but whatever the arrangement was, Neuwirth was taking over.

Bobby's week at the club became the talk of the town. Bob Dylan was there hanging out every night. Whatever musicians who happened to be in town showed up to play, along with the locals—Mick Ronson, Patti Smith, Loudon Wainwright, Ramblin' Jack Elliott, Sandy Bull, Eric Kaz. I was onstage, backing up almost every one of them.

On the first night, as we all gathered in the small, funky green room in the back of the club, a small, skinny young guy with a head full of brown curls walked in, violin case in hand. He looked about fifteen.

"My girlfriend Jenny told me you were looking for a fiddle player," he said a with a very serious look on his face. He knew Bobby was the ringleader.

"Yuh? Maybe." Neuwirth replied warily, looking him up and down. "How old are you?

"Eighteen." He looked straight at Bobby, daring him silently to question him any further.

"Well, pull out the damn fiddle! Let's hear it." Neuwirth barked.

David Mansfield turned around and carefully laid his violin case down on a folding chair behind him. The rest of us watched, wondering what this kid had to offer. Unbothered by the crowd gathered in this tiny room, he opened up the case, carefully lifted out the fiddle, picked up the bow, nestled the fiddle into his shoulder, rested his chin, looked somewhere out into the distance, and proceeded to stun every single one of us in the green room.

Neuwirth laughed in a "well-looky-here" kind of way, obviously elated at this new discovery. "All right then, let's go play!" He shouted, waving everyone out the door and into the club.

David Mansfield would become not only a major player that week and beyond, but he would become one of my dearest friends.

Word spread fast, and every night was sold out. After the shows at the club, we would all sit in the bar next door; all the tables in the room filled with musicians, artists, poets, writers, and friends, till the wee hours of the morning. I would listen intently to all the stories bouncing around the room. One early morning, Dylan even sang some songs he had written for a new album, "Ballad of Joey Gallo" and "Hurricane." I soaked up every second. This was where I wanted to be. This was what I wanted to be doing. We got written up in *Rolling Stone* magazine, the *New York Times*, the *Village Voice*, and the *Soho Weekly News*. There was my name, in print, alongside icons of popular culture. The contrast of being in the same room with Bob Dylan and on stage with Patti Smith, John Belushi, and T Bone Burnett in NYC, and then coming home to the Sex-O-Lettes was almost unbearable.

Cindy and T Bone Burnett at The Other End, July 1975. *Photo by Michaelangelo Ferro*

Before I went to New York, Bob Crewe had enlisted me in a project. He had produced a studio album and created a group name called the Eleventh Hour. (The original recording of "Lady Marmalade" is on that album.) The single was Bob's and my song "Hollywood Hot." Now Bob wanted me to help him put an actual performing group together, which we had started to do. When I got back to Los Angeles, we began rehearsing for possible performances. Bob had chosen people primarily based on their looks. I got him to add some actual musicians. It wasn't going well. Bob was becoming unhinged.

One night, after imploring him many times, Bob finally relented, and I took him to his first AA meeting, I was desperate. I needed help. He was out of control.

I knew nothing about Alcoholics Anonymous. But I had a vague memory of somebody mentioning it somewhere, at some time in my life. I grabbed the Yellow Pages from a cabinet in Bob's kitchen one day when I was alone in his house. Now he was living on Appian Way on top of Laurel Canyon, two doors down from Carole King. I was down the Canyon in my little hovel on Honey Drive with the orange shag rug and no bathroom door. I called the AA Central Office.

Bob didn't get sober then. It got worse. And now I was pissed. During the Eleventh Hour rehearsals, he raged about every note, every chord, to every musician. Nothing was right. No one said a word—out loud. They didn't dare. But I knew what they all were thinking.

What in God's name did I get myself into? How does Cindy put up with his shit? But they stayed. They were getting paid.

But I was done. I'd already been offered a record deal (though I didn't take it). I'd been on stage with great artists in New York. I'd even been in *Rolling Stone* magazine! With Neuwirth and friends, I was starting to feel like I belonged somewhere. But now here I was in this lavish rehearsal studio trying to make a disco hit sound good with Bob Crewe and half a band. I was raging inside. The next time Bob snapped at me, I stormed out.

I knew where I was going: Cherokee. They were hosting a press party for Rocket Records who had just signed Neil Sedaka. The cofounder of Rocket Records was Elton John. I knew he was going to be there. Again, I wasn't invited.

I walked straight into the control room when I got to Cherokee, greeted by the owners, who were my friends, the Robbs. The control room was like being in a fishbowl, looking out through the thick glass windows at the party. Journalists, publicists, record company staff, friends of the company—a lot of people were roaming around. I didn't know a soul. I recognized Neil Sedaka, and there was Elton John himself, standing in the far corner of the studio talking with several guests.

"I'm going in." I announced without flare, moving toward the studio door.

"No, you are *not*," said Dee Robb, the oldest of the three brothers, sounding like the parent of an errant teenager. "You can't."

"Oh yes I can," I countered, without looking back. I opened that big, heavy studio door and headed straight to the food. I got a drink, strode a few feet into the room, and stood there like I belonged. A guy was standing alone close to me munching on some hors d'oeuvres. After a few minutes, I walked up to him and started a conversation, hoping we could find some connection.

"I work with Bob Crewe," I said, not giving any hint of my anger. There it was. Everyone knew Bob.

We started talking about music and I prayed that no one would come kick me out. I had on my blue Superman T-shirt and an embroidered purple velvet jacket that I had been told belonged to Andrew Loog Oldham, the manager of the Rolling Stones. It had been given to me by Bob Crewe's younger brother Dan. I was wearing bell-bottom jeans and my Frye boots. And I had the hair, that mane of '70s hair.

Suddenly, Elton caught my eye from across the room and started walking in my direction.

Uh-oh. He's going to kick me out, I thought.

"I don't believe we've met yet," he said when he was close. "My name is Elton." He stuck out his hand to shake mine.

My mind went blank. He was one of the most famous people in the whole world, and he was introducing himself to me, with an absolutely disarming innocence. His introduction was generous, friendly, and genuine.

"I'm Cindy," I said, blankly.

I had no idea what Elton's impetus for walking up to me was. But if it had anything to do with my androgyny, well, now he knew. If I'd said my name was Chris or Sandy, maybe the mystery of whether I was a man or a woman would have continued. He didn't flinch. I never said what I did.

He just wanted to see who, or maybe what, I was. After a few minutes of our casual chat (I don't remember one word after "My name is Elton"), someone pulled him away. But I guess I was in. Nobody kicked me out.

Not long after that, a young woman introduced herself to me. Connie Pappas.

"What do you do?" she asked. She was very nice, but I got a hint that she wanted information.

"I'm a singer," I said with a bit of an attitude.

Connie nodded. We chatted for a few more minutes, and I figured that was that. She smiled and walked away. After talking with another journalist or two, I was just about to leave when Connie came up from behind me and tapped me on the shoulder.

"What are you doing for the next two months?" she asked.

I had no idea who Connie was or where her question was heading. But for some reason, I kept my options open.

"I don't know," I shrugged, curious to hear what was coming next.

I did know that Bobby Neuwirth had asked me to be a part of Bob Dylan's Rolling Thunder Revue starting in late October, which, during that whole New York Other End week back in July, had become an idea and then a reality. With Dylan, I'd be on stage as part of his band with T Bone, Steven Soles, and David Mansfield, and I'd get to sing a song or two of my own.

Dylan was thought to be past his glory days. Rolling Thunder was supposed to be a kind of comeback tour. Putting together this revue with a wide range of hipsters like Allen Ginsberg, Joan Baez, Roger McGuinn, and Mick Ronson on board was the perfect way to create a buzz. I was all in until . . .

"Elton wants to know if you want to go on the road with him? Rehearsals start on Friday."

It was Wednesday, September 17, 1975.

Huh?! Elton John? Stadiums and huge arenas. Rock 'n' roll! *Holy crap! I have to make a decision between Bob Dylan and Elton John, right now?*

Journal Entry—September 17, 1975

So after a day of "screaming" and shaking my fist at the world and at Bob [Crewe]*—literally stating my hopes that this was the*

darkness before the dawn—I end up with a prospective gig with
Elton John! I mean who would dare to dream it!

Connie Pappas, it turns out, was part of Elton's management team under John Reid. I also didn't know that Connie had a sister, Renee, who was married to Jerry Wexler. Jerry and I had spent a lot of time together with Bob Crewe, and I had become friends with him and Renee. Maybe someone told Elton that now that he'd asked me to go on the road, he better find out if I really could sing! That question, through Jerry Wexler, I figured, was answered in short order.

On Thursday, the next day, a limo pulled into the cracked concrete parking area of my tiny, one-story, old stucco apartment complex on Honey Drive. I watched out the window as a man got out of the back seat and headed for my door. He held a stack of Elton John records. Already, in 1975, this guy had a *stack* of hit Elton John albums that I swear was a foot tall. I opened my door, and he handed them all to me. I had twenty-four hours to listen to them and to be ready for rehearsal *the next day*, Friday! The tour itself would start in one week.

The choice to tour with Elton and not Dylan was hard. You couldn't pick two more iconic artists. Why did they have to be touring at the same time? I loved playing with all those singers and songwriters and artists—my friends— at The Other End. It was loose, and easy, and fun. I loved Bobby Neuwirth. He always brought me into his circle, wherever he was and whatever he was doing. He made me feel special and a part of the whole. Bobby believed in me as an artist, not just a good-looking young kid with a guitar. I was incredibly grateful for that. But I could not resist this rare opportunity to perform with the number one rock 'n' roll artist in the world. I was a born rock 'n' roller, after all. It would be a challenge for sure. I would have to be the best I could be. Elton John was taking a chance on me, for whatever reason, I didn't know. This was the pinnacle, right now, at this moment in time. I better be good.

But there was something else that went beyond the music. Something about the way Elton had looked at me and introduced himself, something about how he had talked to me. He made me feel seen. He didn't look at me and see a man or a woman. I believe he saw me in all my complexity and contradiction. Elton made me feel like someday it might be safe to be who I really was.

3

FINALLY ROCKIN'

I was wonderin' what the hell was wrong
I've been holdin' back for far too long
I got so much inside me with my music to guide me
I know I'm gonna come on strong
I'm finally rockin'
Finally rockin', finally rockin'

  "Finally Rockin'" by Cindy Bullens
  ©1978 Gooserock Music/BMI

ON WEDNESDAY SEPTEMBER 29, 1975, another limo pulled up to my door on Honey Drive. Bell-bottoms on, my rock 'n' roll jacket on, I was whisked off to the Burbank airport. We drove onto the tarmac, and there was the private jet—ROCK OF THE WESTIES painted on the side. The Starship! There was Elton standing in front of the plane. I climbed the steps and walked into the plane. A young woman in a little outfit immediately offered me a drink. *THIS is rock 'n' roll, baby!*

"Come sit next to me." Mike Hewitson called out, pointing to me and then patting his hand on the space beside him. Mike was Elton's dear friend and personal assistant. He had become my grounding point. A handsome British gay man, always casually yet meticulously dressed. He sported a thick, blond pageboy haircut with not a hair out of place. Mike had a steady way about him, honest and direct.

Cindy on the *Starship*, September 1975.
Photo by and courtesy of Mike Hewitson

Where am I? Somehow, I had been transported from hiding in my childhood neighbor's stack of tires, from the dingy, cheap hotel room in Washington Square, from pumping gas at Jerry's Phillips 66 on Santa Monica Boulevard, and from Bob Crewe's Empire West penthouse, to where I now sat. I was on the *Starship*, surrounded by Elton John's band, management, and entourage, headed to San Diego in a private jet to do the first show of the *Rock of the Westies* tour.

The three young female flight attendants welcomed each person enthusiastically as they came aboard—Elton's lead guitar player Davey Johnstone, drummer Roger Pope, guitar player Caleb Quaye, bass player Kenny Passarelli, his keyboard player James Newton Howard, and Jon Joyce and Jay Haas, my fellow backing vocalists. I watched, safe beside Mike, as each one boarded. I was still unsure of how to *be* in this situation. By this time, I had met almost everyone in Elton's professional circle, his agent, management, publicist. John Reid and I clicked right off the bat. They were all here.

Everyone was upbeat and excited, greeting each other, laughing and talking. In the front cabin, the first-class seats remained, but almost all of the coach section was what is best described as a flying lounge. A long, red velvet sofa lined the full left side of the plane and another took up part of the right side. In the very back of the plane, there was a private bedroom into which Elton could disappear.

"Enjoy it all." Mike leaned into me, grabbing my leg and squeezing it, as if he were as excited for me as I was. "Everyone wants to be at the first show." He said gleefully, looking around the plane.

Elton was kind and funny and easy with me. A week before, on the second day of rehearsal, the head of Decca Records worldwide (soon to become EMI), Ken East and his wife, Dolly, walked into the large hangar-like space where we were rehearsing off Sunset Boulevard in Hollywood. They were in the States from the UK and were close friends of Elton's. Coincidentally, I had met them a few weeks before with Dan, Bob Crewe's brother, who knew them through his own music business dealings.

The moment Ken and Dolly entered the space, they shouted out, "Hey, Cindy!" and came straight toward me, arms outstretched, walking right past Elton and company. Elton had this confused look on his face.

I'm sure he was thinking, *How in the world does this young, unknown backup singer know the head of a major record company, my dear long-time friend from England?* I played the game.

"Ken! Dolly!" Big hugs all around like we had known each other for decades. They must have known through Dan that I had gotten the gig and decided to have some fun with Elton.

From that moment on, I felt that Elton saw me differently. He brought me quickly into his circle of friends and associates who were constantly around him. He was so kind, and I felt seen.

Today, Bernie Taupin was standing at the *Starship* bar, which took up the rest of the right side of the cabin. Elton, in his navy blue sweat suit, bounced from person to person, greeting each one with his acerbic humor, or a smile and a pat on the back, depending on how well he knew you.

"Blanche!" He leaned down and puts his hands on my shoulders.

"Watch out for that old queen!" He said in a thin, devious little voice, nodding and grinning at Mike.

Almost all the men in Elton's entourage had acquired women's names—Brenda, Betty, Vera, Dawn. I learned it all started with Long John Baldry christening Elton with the name Sharon way back when Elton was starting out playing in his band. Elton continued the tradition and named you appropriately depending on your looks and personality. Even though I was a woman, I got a woman's name.

Over the course of rehearsals, as I grew more comfortable, I allowed myself to show my own humorous side. I frequently fell into a character I created in high school, Blanche from Boston.

"Hi, I'm Blayanch, from Sawgus, Mayass. I'm on my way down ta Fenway Pahk to cheeah faw the Sawx!" For some reason, they thought my put-on extreme Boston accent was hysterical. Blanche sticks.

———————————

At the very same time I was starting with Elton John, I was sinking into the reality that I might be a drug addict. Bob Crewe was finally going to Alcoholics Anonymous meetings and on many a night, I went along for the ride. Bob and I had reconnected now that he was getting healthy. I liked going. The stories. The laughter. The spirit of redemption and recovery kept me coming back.

"Hi, my name is Harry, and I'm an alcoholic. I was beaten as a kid, got drunk and robbed a grocery store, spent three years in jail, got sober, and now I'm a successful screenwriter at Paramount."

I was not an alcoholic in my own mind. But I knew I was in trouble. The tracks in my arm had been visible for some time now. My shame, only a month before, of going home in the middle of summer, after The Other End week in New York City, to see my family in Maine and having to wear long sleeves, tore at my edges.

"Cindy, for heaven's sake! What's the matter with you? Aren't you eating?" Gasped my mother, horrified at my emaciated body as I entered our house on the beach.

My siblings stared at me suspiciously. My brother took me aside and grilled me.

"What the hell are you doing? What are you taking? What is *wrong* with you?"

I lied.

But when Elton John comes calling, it is time to take stock. This was, my second red light. Bobby Neuwirth and the invitation to join Bob Dylan's coming Rolling Thunder Revue was the first. I stopped shooting up. And truth be told, even though I was not yet clean and sober, I would not or could not have stopped without the help of the Twelve Steps.

After the Rodeo Drive meeting in Beverly Hills one Friday night, I confided in LuAnn Simms, a beloved sober friend of Bob and Dan Crewe. LuAnn was a teenage singing sensation and star on the Arthur Godfrey radio and TV show in the fifties. The story of her own alcoholism and meteoric downfall I found shocking. The fact that she was now here, sober for almost fifteen years and such a positive, loving person was amazing to me. Shooting up cocaine had been my dark secret for several months now.

One early morning having not yet been to sleep, I was sitting on my single bed on Honey Drive staring down onto the orange shag rug, stoned and afraid. I knew I was pushing my luck. *What am I doing to myself? I am on my way up in life, not on my way down!*

"Look, honey," LuAnn began earnestly in her gravelly ex-smoker voice. The way she said "honey" at that moment made me feel like there was no one on earth more important than me. "You have to pray for the strength to confront this head-on. There's no going back now. It's over. Pray for God to guide you. And after you tell Sue it's over, that you can't see her anymore, get up and walk out. She's going to try to convince you to stay."

I had been chained to Sue, the publicist, of my own volition for months now. I could only have a needle stuck into my vein if she did it for me. I didn't have the nerve to do it myself. I kept going back to her, against my own will, for that short but ecstatic high.

LuAnn turned and leaned across the front seat of my car as I pulled over in front of her apartment after driving her home from the meeting. She looked me straight in the eye.

"After you say your piece, don't engage with her. Do you hear me? Walk out. Keep asking God for help."

I was not sure who or what God was. Certainly not the Sunday school God that punished people for no good reason. But I was desperate, and I trusted LuAnn. I felt I could die on Sue's bathroom floor if I did not.

I did exactly what LuAnn told me to do. My cocaine-centered asso-ciation with Sue ended. I left her and, sadly, her little daughter Mora behind. Shooting up was the worst of it for me. That part was now over, but I didn't stop using.

The roar. It was deafening. I stood below and behind watching, listening with awe. San Diego Sports Arena, September 29, 1975. As the *Starship* came in for a landing in San Diego, a line of limousines was stretched out below. Seven of them, like black rectangular beads on a string. The plane taxied and parked right up next to them. The mobile stairway rolled up to the door, and the attendant pulled it open from the inside.

"BVs first!" The tour manager shouted.

"Jon, Jay, Cindy, let's go!" I quickly grabbed my jacket and exited the plane as charged, all the while feeling like I was in a dream. Jon Joyce, Jay Haas, and I climbed into the very first limo in the line. I stared out the back window watching as each limousine behind us received its designated passengers. Then on cue, with police escort, we started to move. I barely took my eyes off the line of black stretch sedans behind us for the entire trip, as we weaved from the airport through the city, police lights flashing in front of us and at the rear, all the way to the arena.

Showtime. The most famous person on earth ascended the ramp alone to the stage in the dark. The brightest, hot, white spotlight burst from the rafters of the arena and onto Elton sitting at his piano.

"It's a little bit funny. . . . " The crowd erupted. *"Your Song,"* solo. His voice echoed, sending thousands into rapture. The lights were beautifully blinding. Time was frozen. I stood below and behind, watching, listening in awe. *This is me. I am here.* He ended the song, and I walked up that ramp.

The show was four hours and thirty-one songs long. It was a marathon of music, stagecraft, and sweat. Elton commanded every square inch of air and space—the rest of us, on stage and off, were swept up in the frenzy of the moment and by his brilliance. How Elton did this night in and night out was a mystery to me. Everyone in the band gave every ounce of energy they had. That said, I was so hyped up by my new reality—being onstage with the biggest rock 'n' roll star at the time, not to mention the effect of his music itself—that I slowly abandoned all expected protocol. I was dancing, jumping, playing Pete Townsend air guitar, pumping my fists—getting more animated on each up-tempo song with each succeeding night.

No one that I could see did drugs on the plane to the gigs. Some people had a beer or two. I didn't. I couldn't screw up! I needed all my facilities to pull off these marathon concerts. I was still learning the songs. However, after hours, in the hotel rooms, cocaine was ever-present, and I had no problem finding my own. I found my people to do it with, too. On stage, even without the immediate effect of drugs, my sense of place was starting to recede back into a blur.

For the first nine days of the tour, we were based in Scottsdale, Arizona. We flew out and back to each city for each concert. The band was staying at the Camelback Inn. Elton and Mike and others were at John Gardiner's Tennis Ranch just up the mountain.

On the first day off, I decided to walk the mile or so in the midday sun and soaring temperature, up to the house Elton was occupying. I wasn't invited. Halfway up the hill, I was questioning my decision. This was a kind of hot I had never in my life experienced.

What am I doing? Am I crazy? Yes, I am crazy, I decided. Crazy for being outside at noon in the desert. Crazy for thinking I could just appear at Elton John's door without an invitation. Crazy for feeling like I belonged. There was no going back. I kept walking. Flushed, parched, and exhausted, I was greeted at the door by Elton and Mike.

"What in the world, Blanche!? Come in here and get out of that heat!" Elton grabbed my arm and pulled me into the kitchen.

They were both in disbelief that I trekked all the way up the mountain from the hotel. I was in even more disbelief that I had the chutzpah to come at all.

Mike thrust a glass of water into my hand. I drank. He led me into the living room.

"Sit down." He said sternly pointing to the couch. "My God, Blanche, you could have *died* out there!"

They didn't kick me out. I spent the afternoon lounging and laughing and listening to their stories, feeling lucky to be alive.

Later, after it cooled down a bit, Elton announced that he was going to play tennis on the house's private court—with Billie Jean King.

"She should be here any minute." He said with enthusiasm. "You'll love her!"

Billie Jean King arrived at the door dressed ready to play. Honestly, Billie Jean—I could tell just by looking at her—seemed to be prepared to be ready for anything. I was once again struck with awe. Almost immediately, before we even sat down on the couch together, Billie Jean started asking me all kinds of questions. Straightforward questions, like an interview. She wanted to know about *me*!

Billie Jean King was the fireplug the world knew her to be. Just a year before, she became an icon with the Battle of the Sexes, winning the globally publicized match between her and Bobby Riggs. She was the spark that was leading women in sports (and in culture) into competing for equal pay, and equality period. I was now in the same room with *both* Billie Jean King and Elton John. It was electric. That said, they were both just plain folk, chatting away, and walking around in shorts and tennis sneakers.

"Where are you from? What do your parents do? Do you have brothers and sisters? What do they think of you being a singer? When did you know you wanted to sing?"

I could barely think between each question. She sat straight up, turned sideways to look straight at me as she asked, through those gold wire-rimmed glasses, with her thick curly brown hair framing her face. I realized she really wanted to know the answers.

"Um . . . uh . . . Boston—yes—good—four."

I felt flattered, but I was taken aback by her directness. As much as I loved attention, there was a lot I didn't want anyone to know. And did I really deserve *this much* attention? Why did she want to know? There were parts of the answers to some questions that I could not tell. I grew uncomfortable and squirmy, wishing I could shrink into the fabric of the sofa. I had little reference for this. And I had zero foundation for anything close to deep, intimate human interaction. I was being squeezed into a space between Billie Jean's authenticity and Elton's inclusiveness—two present-day cultural icons, here and now, with me. I was at once pulled in and blown apart.

Billie Jean King and Cindy backstage, 1976. *Photo by and courtesy of Mike Hewitson*

It was clear that Elton and Billie Jean had a close friendship. He made her laugh, and she kept him honest. Even through my naïveté and self-consciousness, I could feel the recognition and respect they had for each other and their unique place in the world. Finally, Billie and Elton went off to the tennis court. I was still reeling from the collision of questions and being in the presence of not one but two of my idols, but I stuck around the house and hung with Mike. Thank God for Mike.

—

My use of cocaine did not waver much. It only shifted back from arm to nose. In fact, I was in constant search of more. I kept my ever-growing need as hidden as I could, while also making it known to the band and crew that I was among those who liked to indulge. The focus before the shows was on doing the best show I could. After the show, the focus was:

where is the good stuff and how do I get it? Most nights now turned into mornings, and the high life was in full gear.

The first time I ever snorted cocaine, a few years before with some high school friends back East, I didn't like it at all. It made my heart race and my throat numb. And that was it, I thought, I would never do it again. But that changed in L.A. when I was living with Bob Crewe. I did it because he did it. I started to drink more alcohol because he drank. It didn't take me long to be a full-on user.

Cocaine did not mix well with my lack of self-esteem and my ego-split. My highs became higher while my lows became lower. The disparity within my being became larger. It was getting harder to control which part would show up at any given moment. I couldn't seem to land anywhere in the middle. And it was getting more difficult to hide.

I didn't let on to Elton how much I used. My time with him was sacred. Some days, during the tour, he let me into his private world. Just me and him in his hotel suite. We shared simple things, like twelve-year-old kids who were becoming friends.

"What's your favorite thing to eat?" He asked me as room service delivered coffee, English Breakfast tea, and a wide assortment of pastries.

"Ice cream," I announced as I longingly eyed the chocolate croissants.

"Risotto!" He countered as he poured his tea and handed me a croissant. Mike came in and out taking care of various tasks, while joining in on the conversation when he could. We talked favorite movie stars, films, politics. At some point, the conversation came round to sex. I knew, by this time, that Elton was gay.

"I don't know if I am gay or not," I admitted. "I'm attracted to women, but I like some men too." I immediately flashed back to the New York Public Library—to that word I discovered in a book there—transsexual. *Forget which gender I am attracted to*, I thought, *I don't even know what gender I am!*

In his San Francisco suite (on top of the Hyatt), we watched the 1975 World Series together—the Red Sox and Cincinnati Reds. Who knew he was a sports nut? I am a dyed-in-the-wool Boston fan. Elton rooted with me for the Sox. We shared life stories and listened to the new music of the day. His unpretentiousness was disarming. He was gracious and attentive to me. But the more I was let in, the more I saw. I started to notice the complexities of true stardom. I began to witness the constraints of being *really* famous.

One day in Portland, Oregon, I was invited to join Elton, Mike, and Elton's bodyguard to go to a local record store. Elton loved to buy the albums of the new artists and bands he had heard or read about. They closed the entire store during regular business hours, at a designated time before we arrived, keeping all regular customers at bay. We drove up to the back entrance in an unassuming station wagon; Elton, in his sweat suit and ball cap, tried to appear as anonymous as possible.

"Come on. Quick. Everybody out!" commanded the bodyguard scoping out the scene. We literally ran into the store. If anyone caught sight of Elton, it would be all over. Word would spread like wildfire, and a crowd would gather quickly. He could go nowhere in public. He couldn't be seen riding in a car, walking down the street, or even peeking his head out of his hotel window. His registered name at the hotel was fictitious. He was trapped by his own fame. At least that's how I saw it. My bubble about fame started to burst.

I always wanted to be famous. I wanted fame more than I wanted the money that came along with it. I wanted the praise, the validation. I wanted to be known as *somebody*! I was never enough in my own mind. My vision of what that amount of fame was like quickly hit a wall of reality. The dazzling, majestic grandeur of Elton John on stage at night stood in stark contrast to the confines of his hotel suite during the day. Oh, he had every "need" taken care of. Every request fulfilled. But there was something else I started to see—his need to be normal, to be seen and loved for being *himself*. Mike saw it. I'm sure there were other friends who saw it. I started to see it too. I started to feel it. My heart cracked open. Now I saw *him* differently.

Even with my realization that fame was not all it was cracked up to be, I still wanted the recognition that came with it. I was desperate to *feel* a sense of worthiness. These people around me now saw something in me. Why couldn't I see it? *I belong with them, right? Now that I'm here? Don't I?*

Elton was engaging with me more each night. He yanked me from my mic in the middle of Jon and Jay and pulled me toward his piano, which was placed on the background vocalists' side, stage right. There were pieces of clothing on the floor all around him that fans tossed up during his performance. He picked up each piece, one at a time, a shirt, a bra (lots of bras), a hat, a skirt, and dressed me with each one. I stood there, his model. Throwing me off stage (into the arms of security guards) became a nightly routine. He even had me sit down on his piano bench with him during a song or two.

I never saw myself as a backup singer. That was never on my dance card. I saw myself as a rock 'n' roll *star!* Nothing less. Even after Bob Ezrin told me it was going to be twice as hard for me to make it because I was a woman, I didn't buy it. When I was singing backup vocals on records—that was OK. That felt cool and good. It was a huge learning experience—how to sing on mic, how things worked in the studio, how record producers like Bob Crewe molded the songs and sounds of an artist. I was fascinated by it all. I didn't feel out of place as an observer or as a small piece of the whole. That stuff was just a stepping stone. On stage with Elton, it wasn't so much that I wanted to replace *him*—I didn't, and no one could—I sincerely wanted to be the best I could be *for* him. But being under the bright lights in front of thousands of his adoring fans every night set my psyche on fire.

At the same time, Mike and I were becoming closer and started spending a lot of time together. We explored the various cities together on tour, sometimes just the two of us, sometimes with another member or two of the entourage. We frequently dined and hung out together after the show or on days off. He, with his sweet, funny, but straightforward demeanor, kept me at least somewhat grounded. I felt safe. Mike at times was a bridge between me and Elton. But Mike was his own person, and we had our own relationship.

When I got back home to Los Angeles and Honey Drive, between the tour and two upcoming shows at Dodger Stadium on October 25 and 26, I fell apart. The juxtaposition between Elton's hotel suite and his sold-out, screaming (or steaming) arenas and my orange-shag-rugged little hovel with no bathroom door grew wider with every breath I took. I sank. I lost my keys and address book somewhere. My old Saab was in the shop. I had no car, and I had no drugs. I called LuAnn. I made a little mental note to myself, surprised that I was calling LuAnn and not one of my friends with drugs.

"Honey, Bob and I are going to Ohio Street. Do you want us to pick you up?"

She and Bob Crewe were going to an AA meeting. I needed the camaraderie. I needed the laughter. I didn't want to be alone. But knowing I
had two shows ahead at Dodger Stadium, that thought made me happy.
I was still with Elton.

"Don't let the sun go down on me. . . ." Elton sang these words as
though he were being lifted into the heavens in the great arms of love, as
the sun literally sank behind center field. At the same moment, the flames
of tens of thousands of lighters flared to light up the dimming of the
sky. I was singing, too. Looking out onto a sea of human beings, I stood
between my fellow background vocalists in awe, witnessing this moment
in time. A wave of what I can only describe as Spirit ran through my
body. We all knew we were a part of something that night much bigger
than the sum of its parts.

The Dodger Stadium shows were beyond description. The whole week
before the shows was crazy. Elton got his star on Hollywood Boulevard. His
new album *Rock of the Westies* debuted at number one on October 24, the
day before. The shows were historic—the largest concert events ever done

Cindy at Dodger Stadium rehearsing with Elton and singers
from the James Cleveland Choir, 1975. *Photo by and courtesy of
Terry O'Neill*

by a single artist at that time. Tens of thousands of people each day jammed into the stadium, all absolutely enthralled by Elton John and ecstatic to be there. Emmylou Harris, the James Gang, and Joe Walsh opened up for us. Billie Jean King came out to sing "The Bitch Is Back" with us BVs on both days. The James Cleveland Choir backed Elton on several songs at the end of the second set, sending us all even further into rapture. Both performances by Elton were truly otherworldly. There seemed to be no space between any person within miles. We were all one. No kidding. We were.

Journal Entry—October 26, 1975

Well, it's over—all of it. Hardly seems possible—all seems so distant right now. Dodger Stadium—yesterday and today. Magic!! Elton was magic! 60,000 people each day! It's hard to describe feelings at this time—I'm totally mixed with happiness, sadness, peacefulness, anxiety—it's a wash of sentiments. Elton cried after it was all over. And I loved him for it.

Elton, the BVs, and Billie Jean King at Dodger Stadium, October 25, 1975. *Photo by and courtesy of Mike Hewitson*

4

POWERLESS

It's serious
Beginning to think I'm delirious
My head signals no
But my lips say yes
I'm powerless over your love baby
Powerless over you
I'm powerless over everything
I can't get through

> "Powerless" by Cindy Bullens
> ©1979 Gooserock Music/BMI

AFTER THE *LOUDER THAN CONCORDE* US TOUR, my last tour with Elton, I was a mess. It was early fall in 1976. I felt broken and rudderless. My body was depleted. I had this intention and that intention, this goal and that aim. I couldn't seem to get it together enough to do anything productive. Whatever glue was holding me together had disintegrated over the summer.

July 4, 1976, was one of the greatest days of my life. Schaefer Stadium, Foxborough, Massachusetts—Massachusetts, where America began—*I*, a Boston native, was playing on the *BICENTENNIAL* of our country with Elton John! My entire family was there: parents, siblings, cousins, high school friends, and my local drug dealer. Elton, entourage, and the band helicoptered in from the airport. Billie Jean King flew in with us. The pilot made several intentional flyovers of the stadium, circling the perimeter. We all stared down at the thundering crowd of eighty thousand. We could actually hear the people cheering through the chuff of the propeller blades. The spectacle was beyond anything of which I could ever have believed I would be a part.

Backstage, I was coming apart—excited, nervous, and nearly unhinged. I made the mistake of doing a few lines of cocaine. I had too many people there. I had too many emotions and mixed-up feelings.

"Mom! Dad! Everybody over here please! Try to stay out of the way."

My heart was racing wildly. My brain was overloaded. I corralled all these pieces of my life in a small space backstage, waiting, like everybody else, to introduce them to Elton. Thankfully, all were gracious.

"It's so nice to meet you, Elton! Thank you for taking such good care of my daughter."

I took a deep breath. My mother apparently decided not to embarrass me. I was terrified that there would be a long diatribe about how up to date she was on his social life, or whether he would consider me good marriage material. I ushered them out with their tickets, and the show started.

The show was utterly amazing. Elton in his shiny, red, white, and blue silk shorts, suspenders, and T-shirt was clearly inspired and on. His hands flew across the keyboard, improvising and alternating sophisticated jazz licks with Jerry Lee Lewis rock 'n' roll chops with a sudden recognizable classical phrase. He did this *every* night of course, but on some shows it was as if he were tapping into some other dimension. This was one of those nights. Elton featured me any way that he could throughout the show. On this tour, we had been singing a duet together, Leslie Duncan's "Love Song." Finally, at the end of the set before the encore, he started introducing the band. One by one, he made his introductions, Jon Joyce, Ken Gold (our new third vocalist), Roger Pope, Kenny Passerelli, Caleb Quaye, James Newton Howard, and Davey Johnstone, who was usually last. He finally turned and looked at me.

"And from Boston, Massachusetts. . . ." No name was needed at that moment. The crowd erupted. "Cindy Bullens!" He grabbed me and pulled me to the front of the stage. We wrestled for a minute, and then he picked me up and threw me into the crowd. Usually, that act was planned with security in waiting. Not so that night. Somewhere in midair I wondered if I would hit the ground, just as I felt several arms and hands and bodies catch me. They held me high, bouncing me up and down. I felt electrified by the energy running in, around, and through me. The crowd was wild by then. Finally, I was placed safely, without harm, back onto the stage. We exited, the crowd still at maximum decibels. For the encore, Elton returned to the stage dressed as the Statue of Liberty, torch held high, regally standing on his piano. As the daylight faded, the spotlight burned bright on him alone as this Bicentennial night became history itself.

Elton John and Cindy onstage July 4, 1976.
Photo by Ron Pownall

In just over a week, on July 13, I blew it all to hell. Greensboro, North Carolina. Among other things, we were all warned that there would be specific law enforcement present to do drug surveillance. We brought nothing with us on the plane or into the arena. Everyone was already tired and tense. I had a terrible, lingering cold. We had been on the road for the most part since late March. Feeling like our every move was being scrutinized by some unknown person lurking around backstage did not contribute to a relaxed atmosphere.

After my heady experience in Foxborough, aided by deep fatigue, a bad cold, and my crushing cocaine habit, my sense of place in our bubble dissolved completely. Elton had been nothing but loving and giving to me since the end of the *Rock of the Westies* tour in the fall of 1975, through the UK segment of the *Louder Than Concorde: Not Quite as Pretty* tour to now. He invited me into his home in Los Angeles. I saw him in New York. On occasion I went to dinner with him and a few friends. He often surprised me with gifts.

Before the beginning of the UK tour, Elton flew me first class, just the two of us, to England. I stayed at his Windsor home. I met his mother Sheila and stepfather Fred. His generosity humbled me. And when I was with him, I felt I could just be me. I adored him. Mike and I had become even closer as well, and I felt almost a part of a family within Elton's inner circle.

Back in December, when everyone was in Toronto recording Elton's *Blue Moves* album, I was invited to come to the studio there. It just so happened that the timing coincided with Bob Dylan's Rolling Thunder Revue's two shows in town. I called Bobby Neuwirth and asked him if I could sit in and play a song. It was after all a revue, a core group of touring musicians with ever-changing pieces wherever they went. I told him that Elton would come to the show.

On December 1, 1975, I went with Elton and Mike to the Maple Leaf Gardens on the first of the *Revue*'s two nights there. They wanted to support me, as well as enjoy a Bob Dylan show. Backstage was chaos. Joni Mitchell was joining them for these shows.

Joni Mitchell was probably the single reason I taught myself the piano and learned to play guitar in different tunings, not to mention her completely changing and expanding my sense of lyrics. I stayed up many a night into the wee hours in my late teens and early twenties listening to *Clouds* and *Blue* and *For the Roses*. I was standing beside her now as Neuwirth was trying to figure out where to put her in the lineup. Dylan, Roger McGuinn, Joan Baez, Mick Ronson, Ronee Blakley, Ramblin' Jack Elliott, Gordon Lightfoot, and multiple other notables wandered in and out. The original band from our week at The Other End, T Bone, Soles, Mansfield, plus bassist Rob Stoner, drummer Howie Wyeth, violinist Scarlet Rivera were also there. It was a madhouse. I felt completely out of place and started to regret that I even asked to play. Clearly, they had too many people. I felt like I was forcing something that should not have been happening. I mean, *Joni Mitchell is here tonight!*

Cindy and Bobby Neuwirth at The Other End, July 1975.
Photo by Ruth Bernal, Soho Daily News

"OK, Cindy, you'll come out with me and play in between a couple of my songs. Joni will come on after me," Neuwirth said, clearly stressed. He knew Elton was in the audience and expected to see me.

I sang my song, nervously, in front of the packed house. I stayed on stage for a few more songs with Bobby and the band, which I fully enjoyed. I then found my way up to Elton and Mike's box seats to watch the rest of the show. I loved being with my good friends in the Revue who were there on this night. I was extremely grateful that Bobby Neuwirth introduced me to all these people and gave me so many opportunities to shine. But I was happy I made the decision I made to go with Elton. I wanted to be a rock 'n' roll star, not a folk singer. I wanted to play in front of sixty thousand people, not a just few thousand. These were heady times for me. And my head clearly did not know how to handle it.

Journal Entry—July 12, 1976, Atlanta

Arrived 4 AM here in Atlanta after a long day from NYC to Pontiac Stadium [Michigan]*—big, huge, hot gig. Nice hotel—Hilton—28th floor. I've been feeling just plain shitty—awful cold—the worst I've had in years. Today was off. In bed till 3 PM then sun, rest, dinner—then went out at 1 AM with EJ & JR to a nice club. Now in bed. Just feel blah!*

In Greensboro, the bulk of the show went well enough. No one in the audience would ever be able to tell when it was not the best night ever. Elton brought his usual brilliance every night, as did this incredible band of musicians. They were all masters of their instruments.

We backing vocalists were pretty good too. Jon Joyce was a sought-after session singer in Los Angeles, known for his exceptional work on recordings and commercials. Ken Gold had the same reputation in England. I was the exception in terms of prior reputation, but I knew how to blend with the best of them. I got to test out that aspect of my voice when I sang on Gene Clark's *No Other* album in 1974. Singing vocal parts for Gene's beautifully written and recorded songs with Poco's Timothy B. Schmit and vocalist extraordinaire Claudia Lennear was a highlight of my early career. So was singing on Don Everly's solo album *Sunset Towers* that same year. I remember spinning my older sister Nancy's 45s of all the Everly Brothers hits on our RCA record player back in the early '60s—"Bye Bye Love," "All I Have to Do Is Dream," "Claudette." Those harmonies became part of my inner musical fabric. Jon, Ken, and I were all on stage on this night doing what we did best.

In the middle of "We All Fall in Love Sometimes," toward the end of the set, something wasn't right. The song felt directionless, like somebody made a mistake. The band hung on a chord. There was a moment of confusion. The BVs had a choice to make, come in on time, when we were supposed to come in, or hang back and let the song come back around. Meaning, let Elton take charge. For some reason, we come in and sing. No one in the audience suspected a thing. The song continued, and the band fell in. But Elton, clearly agitated, suddenly turned around on his piano bench, away from the audience, shot us a hard, piercing glare, and gave us the finger. We had made the wrong choice.

Immediately, out of nowhere, a burning sensation started in my toes and began crawling slowly up my body, spreading through me like some dark, vengeful alien being. The song played on, and I was being consumed by a deep, searing, unabashed rage. By the time it hit my head, I was literally seeing red. *What is this? Where is this coming from? Who am I?* When the set ended, I walked off stage and straight back into Elton's dressing room, by now completely outside of my own body and unable to stop myself. I watched myself, horrified and completely split, as I stuck my finger in his face.

"Don't you *ever* do that to me again!" I yelled. I felt something breaking apart inside of me. I had absolutely no control over my own actions. And I was oblivious to the mass of people around us.

"What?" Elton stiffened, startled and momentarily frozen, clearly caught off guard with my aggression. Several people around us immediately grabbed me, yanked me away from Elton, and whisked me quickly out of the dressing room. I was escorted down a long hallway, bodyguards on both sides of me, and put into a restroom shower stall in some other part of the arena. It was all a blur. *Is this a dream?*

"Don't move!" commanded Elton's agent, who had followed us to this faraway place. "Someone will come and get you."

Slunk down on the cold black-and-white tiled shower stall floor, withering in my absolute shame, I heard the band playing the encore in the distance, the music echoing off the cold concrete backstage.

"What have I done?" I muttered to myself over and over as my anger turned to tears and then terror. "What the fuck was I doing? What is *wrong* with me?" I didn't have an answer.

Journal Entry—July 15, 1976, Atlanta, 6 AM

Emotional drain. Dawn erupts. Learned my lesson well.

I knew that I had hurt Elton deeply. He trusted me. He felt safe with me. He brought me into his inner sanctum. And I had turned on him. I had betrayed him. *Who do I think I am?* My shame grew ever deeper. I honestly loved this man. Not because he was Elton John. Because he just was. I had been with him now in many more settings where he didn't have to be on. We spent a lot of time together just being. Was he complex? Sure. How could you not be complex being that famous? But he had a heart of gold, and he had done nothing in our time together but treat me with kindness and respect. He was loving and funny and real. I felt that he saw me for who I was in a way few ever had. Elton didn't fire me, but he avoided me for the most part for rest of the tour. I didn't blame him one bit, but I was devastated.

On the last date after the seven shows at Madison Square Garden, at the gathering to celebrate another successful tour, we finally spoke.

"It's your turn now." Elton whispered in my ear. He kissed me and hugged me tightly. "The world is there waiting for you. Go and do it."

I felt a little better after we spoke, but the shame of my actions that night in Greensboro clung to me like a cold, wet rain. I could never undo what I did. Not only had I broken a bond of friendship (I thought forever), but I had broken some hinge in the core of my own being that I wasn't sure I could ever reattach.

I didn't care whether I would tour with him again. (I wouldn't.) I only wished I could erase what I had done. I didn't know it yet, but my actions on that night in Greensboro, North Carolina, were the neon sign that would lead me shortly to a life-changing reckoning.

Elton and Cindy on the front page of *London Daily Mail,* March 1976. *Photo by David Parker for* London Daily Mail

Back in Los Angeles, I moved into a new apartment on Glen Green in Beachwood Canyon below the Hollywood sign. Finally, I had a really nice place, sunny and bright and big. It too had orange carpets, but at least they weren't shag. My good friend, guitarist, and Kemosabe bandmate Trevor Veitch and his wife Evan, lived below me in this stucco four-unit building. Trevor let me know when this unit was available, and I grabbed it, leaving Honey Drive in the dust. It felt like a fresh beginning. Our band's drummer Rick Shlosser soon moved into the building. Trevor and Rick were like brothers to me, and I knew I would be safe and welcomed there. But I was still uncomfortable in my own skin.

I bought a baby grand piano from Cherokee Studios. The piano, an old leather couch given to me by Bob Crewe, a bed, and my guitars were all the possessions I had. I tried to form another band with Trevor, Rick, and some other musician friends. I tried to write songs. I tried to stop drinking and using. But I couldn't seem to make anything work. I had little will and no willpower. At twenty-six years old, I felt I was failing at life.

"It's your self-will run riot, honey," LuAnn said. That's a term I would come to know intimately. "Stay close."

I kept going to recovery meetings. Now Dan Crewe was sober along with Bob. LuAnn was becoming like a second mother to me.

I was meeting sober people my own age as well—Bob, Dan, and LuAnn were all older. I encountered young people with a shine in their eyes and a lightness about them. These kids were not losers. In fact, I couldn't pick out a loser among any of the hundreds of folks, of any age, I met in "the rooms." To me, they were all heroes. Still, I was reluctant to commit. Was I really an alcoholic? I still asked myself the question. But in my gut, I knew the answer: yes, I had a problem with alcohol.

But I didn't drink like my mother and father. My drinking didn't look like theirs. There was no scotch and water, whiskey and soda, or vodka gimlets in my vocabulary. There was red wine and an occasional beer. That's it. But how *much* red wine? And what did it do for me? These were among the questions and concepts I heard over and over in the meetings. There was no doubt in my mind, however, that I was as much of a drug addict as I had ever been. I may not have been putting a needle in my arm, but I was damn sure I would do whatever it took to get the cocaine I needed for my nose.

I thought back to one point in our two-week stay in Chicago earlier in the US leg of the *Louder Than Concorde* tour, when I found myself in the basement of a club buying a big bag of cocaine from some serious dealers. This was to be distributed among others on the road with me. There were guns on the table as I shelled out the cash. Me, alone. I was 115 pounds soaking wet—a white, blonde, androgynous female trying to look and sound tough, like I knew what I was doing. I was praying they thought I was a guy. I didn't give my name.

I walked out without incident and with the drugs.

On Friday, November 12, 1976, I was hanging out at my dealer's house in Van Nuys, California. A few of us were sitting around snorting coke and drinking beer, whiling away the warm autumn afternoon. Earlier in the day, feeling the weight of my past actions and future apprehensions, I decided that the next time I saw my friend Marlin, with whom I had done copious amounts of cocaine, I was going to ask him if he would score me some heroin. He had confided in me one late night at my Honey Drive apartment that he liked to shoot an occasional speedball.

"Really?" I remarked. "What's it like?" I really wanted to know.

"It's heaven," he said with a little smirk on his face. "You just have to be very careful. Don't tell anybody, OK? Nobody knows."

"I could never do it," I said definitively, snorting another line. But his smirk stuck in my mind.

Never, ever before did I have a desire to use heroin. I knew I would die from an overdose. I knew it like I knew I would die if I was bitten by a rattlesnake alone in the desert. It had been over a year since I had shot up cocaine. But the last time I was at Marlin's house in West Hollywood, a couple of weeks before, I stole a discarded needle and syringe that was in his bathroom wastebasket. I wasn't sure why I did that at the time—again, I had no control over my actions. I was just hedging my bets, I guessed, as I hid it the back of my own bathroom cabinet. It would be there—just in case.

As I was considering another beer in Van Nuys, I realized that I had forgotten I made a date with Dan Crewe to have dinner that night in Beverly Hills. It was five o'clock, and the traffic going over the hill would be horrific. Dan had recently offered to manage my career, though I wasn't sure I wanted to get involved that deeply again with either of the Crewe brothers. But for some strange reason, keeping this date with Dan seemed imperative.

In the summer of 1974, during my time living with Bob Crewe, Dan Crewe arrived at Bob's Empire West penthouse apartment door from the East Coast. When the doorbell rang, I ran to greet this person. I was excited to meet Dan, having heard so many wonderful things about him from Bob. Dan was the savior, the fixer. When Bob was in trouble and needed help, Dan came to the rescue. If Bob was the Golden Boy, with natural talent oozing out of every pore and success at every early turn, Dan was the self-made man, a US Naval Academy graduate and a brilliant entrepreneur.

I opened the door flashing my toothy grin. "Hi! I'm Cindy."

He stood stone-faced on the other side of the doorway, shooting a split-second glare in my direction. Then he walked straight past me without a word. I was perplexed but shrugged it off, figuring he was tired from his long flight from New York. Dan was handsome in a Kirk Douglas kind of way. He had an air about him that reeked of competence and confidence. He ignored me the entire evening. I went to bed in the storage room wondering what was up with this guy. When I walked into the penthouse the next morning, Dan was in Bob's bed ailing, and Bob was gone.

"Hello," I peeked into the bedroom. "What's wrong? Are you sick?" I asked tentatively.

"Just a flare up of something I have. Nothing too serious."

"Can I get you something? Water? Ginger ale?"

"That would be great, thank you."

I cared for him all day, without a thought to the night before. I didn't recognize the name of the condition he claimed to have, but nevertheless, I did everything I could to make him comfortable.

Upon Dan's arrival the night before, it turned out that he was picked up at the airport by none other than Diane, Mrs. Bob Crewe's attorney. Remember the Beverly Hills dinner party? Diane, who, along with Bob's current songwriting partner, Kenny, fed Dan their theory: I was a manipulative, conniving young girl who was trying scam Bob into giving me money, a place to live, and a career. Not only that, I was plying him with drugs and alcohol, causing *him* to be an alcoholic!

Really? Was I given a place to live? Yup. Was Bob helping my career? Definitely. Was I plying him with drugs and alcohol? More like the other way around—though I was happily complicit.

Dan figured out in short order that I was not the evil child of the corn I had been made out to be by my detractors. He recovered from his malady quickly, and we suddenly found ourselves in Bob's living room alone, dancing and singing to Elton John's new *Goodbye Yellow Brick Road* album over and over again.

He enthusiastically cooked gourmet meals for Bob and me and any friends who happened by over the next few days. We found some commonality and a shared sensibility. I felt happy that he was around. Plus, I was free from the responsibility of watching after his brother Bob. By the fourth night, we found ourselves together in the loft bed of the storage room.

"Have you ever been with a woman before?" I asked shyly, as we climbed up the wooden ladder onto the thin, single mattress.

"Not really. I dated a girl in high school for a short time. I knew I was gay when I was young."

"Well, I don't *feel* like a woman, but I am one. I've always been more attracted to women myself." We both laughed at the irony of us in the here and now. I was attracted to women, but I loved men too. But what I really loved was what men had. I was attracted to their bodies, not because I wanted them sexually—but because I literally wanted a man's body! I didn't plan to sleep with Dan. But I did.

Dan was about to turn forty, and I was twenty-four. He had been in several long-term relationships; I had been in none. Dan had as much qi as his brother; it was just completely different. He was no-nonsense, down-to-earth, and seemingly in command at all times.

I was feeling mostly powerless over anything in those days—my instincts and street smarts had not been engaged since I moved in with Bob. Dan was puzzling and mysterious. I was naïve and wore my heart on my sleeve. I found what he had sexy. And a huge relief! Again, I didn't have to be always on full guard with Bob. Dan was here, and Bob was his ballgame now.

As we drifted through our (occasional) sex, (lots of) drugs, and rock 'n' roll haze in the summer of 1974, Dan and I tried to make some sense of this strange attraction we had toward each other. Dan moved that fall to Los Angeles from Connecticut, got Bob out of his business troubles, became president of a brand-new record company, and bought a house in Malibu overlooking the Pacific. We moved in together.

I tried to be what Dan wanted me to be without understanding what that was. I had no reference for relationships. I only wanted to be loved. I felt like a fish out of water. I was flopping around on dry sand catching an occasional glimpse of the sea, knowing that the water was where I was supposed to be. The sand I was on at that moment was suffocating. There was little physical relationship and no intimacy. But I tried, hard. And I believe Dan tried. But clearly, he was unhappy. The whole affair lasted about eight months.

One afternoon he told me that we needed to talk. "I have to be on my own." His voice was nearly monotone but not unkind. "I think we need to take a break. Do you have a place where you can stay?"

I knew it was coming. Hurt, but resigned, I nodded my head. "I can probably stay with Tommy Kaye in Topanga," I said, knowing there was no discussion on the subject. Thomas Jefferson Kaye was a songwriter and record producer who was also in my band Kemosabe.

"Good. Can you call him?"

The next morning, in Topanga Canyon, after I got up from my mattress on the floor of Tommy's house, I drove back to Dan's on Rambla Vista in Malibu to pick up some things I had left behind. Maybe there was a chance he'd let me come back. *Maybe if we just talk,* I thought. Dan opened the door in his white terrycloth bathrobe. There was a stairway to the left. The master bedroom was at the top. The door was open. Out of the corner of my eye I saw movement. I looked up.

"Oh" Dan said flatly, "That's Michael."

It was a solid forty-five minutes from Van Nuys to where Dan lived in the Beverly Hills flats, even in light L.A. traffic. I didn't want to be late for this dinner date we had made days before. I wasn't sure why I felt so anxious about it. It was like my body was directing my brain rather than the other way around. I waved a hasty goodbye to my friends and rushed to get to Coldwater Canyon, hoping that because I was going toward the city, it would be quicker. I was wired from the cocaine, but I also had a feeling that I was being pulled by some strange force toward this meeting with Dan.

I didn't have to go. Any excuse would have worked. Dan knew I was not in the best of mental states these days. Even though I was "visiting" recovery meetings, I tried to avoid giving any pertinent information about my doings to my sober friends. I pulled up to his apartment building, and he buzzed me in.

"You're stoned," he said, sharply looking at me like a parent.

"No, I am not!" I lied.

"Come on. We are going to dinner," he stated firmly. "I'll drive."

We had dinner at a local Italian restaurant and talked about the music business and what was new with Bob Crewe. Then we got into his car. Dan drove a short distance from the restaurant across Santa Monica Boulevard and parked right in front of the church where the Friday night Rodeo Drive meeting was held. It was the same meeting where LuAnn helped me plan my escape from Sue and my needle-tracked arm.

"What are you doing?" I asked incredulously. I had decided that day in Van Nuys that I was never going to another twelve-step meeting again. I had my plan B in the back of the medicine cabinet, which seemed more and more like the better option in my mind.

"If you don't want to go in," he said, "you can walk home." He turned and walked into the church vestibule without looking back, and then into the meeting room.

It was a trap! My mind raced. I couldn't walk back to his apartment to get my own car. It was too far. *But if I go in that door*, I thought, *into that meeting—it's over for me*. I knew this as well as I knew my own name.

For some reason, in that moment, on that night, it was clear the moment had come: get clean or die. Images of my actions over the last couple of years lit up my brain like fireworks on the Fourth of July—shooting up in Sue's bathroom, the guns of Chicago, my lips constantly stained with red wine, and a thousand tiny uncontrollable acts of an addict. Elton.

I walked in.

Nearly hyperventilating, I sat in the front row of the large room in between Dan and Bob, with several hundred people sitting behind us. When they asked for newcomers with thirty days or less, I lowered my head, and I raised my hand. I didn't have to say a word out loud, but my arm up and pointing toward the high ceiling said, "Hi, my name is Cindy, and I'm an alcoholic and a drug addict."

LuAnn, who was sitting directly behind me, put her hand on my shoulder and whispered in my ear.

"It's about time, honey."

5

SURVIVOR

You're a survivor
You'll work it out
And you'll carry on
You're a survivor, baby, yeah
Your light will shine
As the shades are drawn

> *"Survivor" by Cindy Bullens*
> *©1978 Gooserock Music/BMI*

I STRAPPED ON MY BRIGHT RED CUMMERBUND and attached it around my waist. I looked in the full-length mirror in Dan's and my master bathroom in our newly built, ultra-modern, multilevel home on Appian Way, across from Bob Crewe, on top of Laurel Canyon, overlooking all of Los Angeles. The morning layer of fog that spread over the flatlands to the south and west was dropping now just below the tops of the palms in the foothills beneath us. My all-white rented tuxedo—short jacket with tails, bell-bottom pants, white high-collar shirt, red bowtie, and red Capezio shoes—stared back at me. I was on my way to the Grammy Awards, nominated for the second year in a row.

The year before, I was nominated with the cast of 1978's *Grease* for the *Grease* movie soundtrack album. Early that year, 1977, out of the blue, my phone rang.

"You're gonna get a call from my friend Louis St. Louis later today," Bob Crewe said matter-of-factly. "He's producing some songs for a movie soundtrack. They want a girl who can sing in a young teenage voice. I suggested you."

"Wow. Great! Thank you!" I assumed it was for background vocals. *Ninety bucks!* I thought. That's what singers were paid for one three-hour recording session.

One year later, at the Twenty-First Annual Grammy Awards, I was sitting in the third row of the Shrine Auditorium with the entire cast of the movie (sans Olivia Newton-John and John Travolta, who were up front and part of the show). I had sung three lead vocals on the *Grease* movie soundtrack: "Freddy My Love," "Raining on Prom Night," and "Mooning." It was nominated for Album of the Year.

My new beautiful shiny, black baby grand piano that I bought from Cherokee Studios with the money I made from the Elton tours was now my prized possession. Over the two years since the end of those three tours, I found myself sitting at the keyboard looking out my apartment windows on Glen Green, through the open top, toward the Beachwood Canyon mountainside, flushed with bursts of creativity.

At the end of a cul-de-sac, the hillside out the back provided the perfect muse. The smell of sage and monkey flower and dust, the silhouette of the crest against the bright blue California sky inspired me. I was in my place, clean and sober, clear, and unencumbered. One hot, dry early summer day in 1977, I wrote a song on that piano that would become the theme of my life, "Survivor." I knew this song was good. I knew it was special. I knew it was the beginning of a new era for me. Then I wrote another, "Desire Wire." Trevor Veitch, who I lived above, and I then wrote a song together: "Anxious Heart."

"Trev, we've got to record these songs right now. I really think they will get me a deal."

Trevor agreed to produce a demo, and we went into the studio. A few days later it was done. I had no management at the time, so I decided to hire an attorney to help me pitch it to record labels.

Journal Entry—July 16, 1977

[They] *won't say yes, won't say no. They are just afraid of me—in terms of knowing what to do!*

Over the next few months, I got a meeting with just about every label in Los Angeles and received real interest from several of them. Chrysalis, Epic, Portrait, RCA, Warner Brothers, 20th Century—multiple meetings over time. I even played a few songs live in Arista Records star-making President Clive Davis's office on a short trip to New York. (I walked into his office and crawled under his desk, with him sitting at it, to plug in my little amplifier that I had brought with me so I could play my electric guitar. It's an image of myself I still laugh at today.) A vice-president at Arista kept me on the hook for over a month, but finally Clive turned me down. No one, at that point, was willing to give me a deal.

I knew I didn't look the part. I knew I didn't fit into the typical "girl" artist category. I wrote all my own songs. I played *electric* guitar!

"We already have a woman on the label," I heard more than once, as if one woman on any label was the absolute limit. Nicolette Larson, Linda Ronstadt, Stevie Nicks in Fleetwood Mac, Blondie. They were all great, but none of them were like me. *Why didn't I take that deal with Al Teller at United Artists when he offered it to me at the Dr. John party three years ago?* That opportunity was gone. I was angry with the business and angry with myself, but I still believed something would happen.

I kept writing and plugging away. I did more sessions.

In October, I got a call from T Bone Burnett. "Hey, Cindy, we're going on the road for a month and want you to come with us."

He, along with Steven Soles and David Mansfield, my friends from the Rolling Thunder Revue, formed the Alpha Band and signed with Clive Davis at Arista Records. I was just coming up on one year of living a clean and sober life and settling into the idea that sobriety was indeed a long-term commitment. I was not sure this was a good idea, but my AA sponsor Jack told me to go: "What are you waiting for? Get out there!"

Plus, I wanted to play, and I wanted to get out of my own head.

In just a few days, I flew off to New Mexico and then Oklahoma and Texas. I played guitar, piano, percussion, and sang. I was part of the

"B-band" with bassist David Miner and drummer Scott Sansby. I had been so busy trying to be a solo artist, I had forgotten how much fun it was to be part of a band—a great band. I "celebrated" my first sober anniversary, on November 13, 1977, on a day off in Dallas, Texas. A friend of a friend took me to a local meeting. I had a lot to be grateful for.

Back home in Los Angeles, at the end of November, the phone rang. Bobby Neuwirth was on the other end. He was very excited, almost frantic.

"I have this great idea! I think you and Mick Ronson need to get together and start a band. I've already talked to Tony Defries; he's working with Mick, and he wants to be involved." Tony Defries was David Bowie's ex-manager.

I loved Bobby. He was crazy and impulsive, but his brain never stopped working, and his ideas were at times visionary. He was the great connector. *Really? Mick and me? A record? A band?*

Mick Ronson added a distinct element to the Rolling Thunder Revue. He remained a part of Dylan's band for the whole tour. He was a brilliant producer, musician, and, in my mind, a true rock icon, having worked with David Bowie and Lou Reed. Not to mention, he was a sweet guy.

Tony Defries called me. There was a plan in the works for Mick to fly to L.A. to meet with me. I was excited. Mick never came. That plan seemed to fizzle out. I never knew why.

But Tony continued to call. "What do you want to do? How do you see yourself? Where do you want to be a few years from now?"

He kept asking me about my own vision for my career. This intrigued me. He listened to me. He seemed to *hear* me. I mentioned his name to friends and found out that Tony was a controversial figure in the music business. But I also discovered that he was the one who paved the way for David Bowie to become a star. The wholly androgynous, out-as-bisexual David Bowie.

Finally, before Christmas, I flew to New York to meet Tony. I told myself that I would just show up and see what happens. I saw myself as a rock star, but so far the powers that be didn't share my vision. I felt I needed to take some chances now.

"Come in, come in, come in!" Jamie Andrews, Tony's associate from MainMan, Ltd., enthusiastically greeted me at the door of Tony's high-rise apartment on the Upper East Side. Thirty-something Jamie's prematurely gray curly hair jutted out of his head in every direction. He wore clear aviator lenses, and his infectious smile made me take a small, relaxing breath. The view of the city and of Central Park out of the floor-to-ceiling windows was the first thing I noticed as I entered the living room. It was breathtaking. The furniture was sleek and modern—leather and metal. There were mirrors and fine art on the walls.

Tony Defries was in his mid-thirties and very well groomed—British. With piercing green eyes and short brown hair, he sported a mustache, a close-cropped beard, and an ever-present cigar. He was dressed in a suit and tie and had a formal way about him. I remember thinking that he presented himself more as a sixty-five-year-old parliamentarian, not a thirty-five-year-old rock 'n' roll manager.

I met his young, beautiful, waif-like wife Melanie and his baby daughter Fleur. His assistant Marilyn was also there. Everyone was upbeat, friendly, and attentive toward me. Tony seemed to have a permanent grin on his face, even as he swirled his cigar around in his mouth as he spoke to me. I felt vulnerable and unsure of what I was doing. I awkwardly played a few songs as requested. I went back the next evening, and the next, for more of the same, feeling just a bit more at ease with each visit.

"Don't work with this guy. He'll screw you." My lawyer strongly discouraged me from working with Tony Defries, citing his troubles with Bowie, John Mellencamp, and others.

"He'll screw you" stayed in my head. It was Jamie who told me about Defries insisting that Mellencamp change his name. Tony didn't think anyone would buy an album with a last name like Mellencamp. Defries landed on Johnny Cougar. Mellencamp hated the name but went with it anyway just for the chance to release an album (*Chestnut Street Incident*, 1976). But Tony now was the only one who I was beginning to think truly believed in me. Every single record label I approached had rejected me.

As we spent more time with each other, Tony told me more about how he saw me moving forward and being successful. It sounded real and *possible*. He also believed that my androgyny was a plus not a minus. That alone to me was worth what might be a high price of working with him. I prayed—a lot.

Journal Entry—March 4, 1978

I went to a meeting and then to Tony's where I promptly got involved in a high blood pressure conversation about my masculine/feminine hang ups. God, it's hard to deal with. Does this mean I'm nearing a turning point with this? Am I going to have to face this issue so soon (with him)?

"I think you see yourself as a man," Tony said to me one day alone, face-to-face, in his apartment. I stopped breathing. My chest contracted. I felt caught in the moment. My heart started beating through my chest. I said nothing.

I had tried very hard not to categorize or label myself as anything. I rejected every label anyone tried to put on me. *Why can't I just be who I am?* Still, I thought Tony believed in me.

Scared out of my wits, I finally agreed to move forward. The deal between MainMan and me was steep. My lawyer implored me not to sign it. Dan did too. But I felt I had no other options. I felt I may never have another chance. Defries agreed to front the money, and from February to May 1978, I recorded my first album, *Desire Wire*, on "spec" in New York City.

MainMan, Ltd., made a licensing deal for the completed *Desire Wire* with United Artists Records, ironically. Al Teller was no longer there. Jerry Rubinstein and Artie Mogull were now in charge. My single "Survivor" was released at the end of 1978. I signed with CMA as my booking agency.

My first tour would be starting in the South opening for Styx. (It was a group I couldn't stand; their music sounded pompous to me. It turned out that most of the band was too, though Tommy Shaw was nice.) We tacked on some dates in the Northeast and Midwest for me and my band—guitarist Mark Doyle, keyboardist Trantham Whitley, drummer Frosty, and bass player David Miner. It was all coming at me fast—radio interviews, press, TV appearances, store appearances, record warehouse handshakes, gigs. I could barely sleep at all on the tour bus (insomnia has been a lifelong issue for me), and every minute off stage it seemed I had to be somewhere or talk to someone. I was exhausted. But all of it was what I wanted. I was being me—the crazy, wild rock 'n' roller, down on my knees with my guitar, jumping off pianos and sound speakers, singing and playing my heart out. I was not Mick Jagger. But maybe he would have approved.

———————

"Cindy, Mick Jagger was here tonight," Mark Doyle, my guitar player, blurted out sheepishly. We were backstage at the Whisky a Go Go, now back in L.A. I was sweating and panting and close to vomiting after a particularly inspired night by my band. And an even more than usual energetic performance by me. It was just after we returned from the East Coast and Midwest tour. Many of my live show reviews by this time had referred to me as the "female Mick Jagger."

"What?!" I looked around at all the guys in the dressing room. Everyone in the band knew except me.

"Why didn't you tell me?" I was incredulous.

"We didn't want you to be nervous." Mark squeaked.

Nervous?! Now I was angry. I idolized Mick Jagger as a kid. No, I *was* him at fifteen years old! I was not him now. I was me. But man, I would have loved to have known he was there. I would have played right to him. It turned out Earl McGrath brought him to see me. Apparently, Mick wanted to see me for himself.

A short time later, with "Survivor" at number fifty-six with a bullet on the Billboard Hot 100 Chart only three weeks after its release, United Artists was absorbed into (its parent company) EMI and was, in effect, no more. If a single wasn't aggressively promoted by the record company to radio, it went nowhere. So, what was a promising start for the single, and for me as an artist, suddenly came to a crushing halt. Even though I was technically still under contract, I was unwanted by EMI, and soon I was gone.

Within a few months, negotiations with the notorious Casablanca Records started for the licensing of my second album, *Steal the Night*. Dan had a good friend at the label who helped get the ball rolling.

Neil Bogart was the cofounder and president of the label. He was used to signing acts that were a bit outside of the mainstream, and he liked me. Casablanca's first signing was Kiss in 1973. Neil Bogart had found and brought this bar band from Queens, New York, out to Los Angeles. According to accounts, Bogart added some "magic effects" to their act.

Cindy at Whisky a Go Go, 1979.
Photo by Donna Santisi

Bob Crewe was invited to their very first showcase for record companies, that year, in Los Angeles. I was living with Bob Crewe at the time and went along with him for the ride. I was not impressed. Kiss was loud and ostentatious and, to me, obnoxious. (What did I know?) Casablanca also had the funk band Parliament and Donna Summer. With Donna Summer's hit "Love to Love You, Baby" (the long 12″ vinyl club version), Casablanca became known for its disco hits, later including "Y.M.C.A." and "Macho Man" by the Village People. In 1974 Bogart released "My Happy Birthday, Baby" as a single by the Bob Crewe Generation. It was a syrupy, saccharine, bubblegum song written by Bob and Kenny Nolan.

> *Blow out the candles*
> *Whisper three wishes*
> *This is that day dedicated to you . . .*

> © *1974 Stone Diamond Music, Tanny Boy Music (BMI),*
> *Kenny Nolan Publishing, ASCAP*

But it was *my* first single! It was a duet. I was the girl. When I heard the song, I felt completely split. Here I had been asked to sing a lead vocal on a Bob Crewe song—holy crap! But it was *so* out of my sense of what I wanted to do with music. It was so shallow, absolutely the opposite of anything I wanted associated with my name. But here I was. There was no way I was not going to do it.

It was in this session that Bob told me I had to sing in a high voice. "Cindy, you're going to have to hit these notes!"

"I don't think I can. Honestly, I don't. I can't sing like that," I said, shaking my head.

"You must!" he said emphatically. "Think high. *Think* it! Pull your voice up into your throat." He placed his large hands, palms up, below his waist like a ballet dancer about to do a plié. He pulled them up past his chest as he breathed in what seemed to be all the air in the room. He exhaled loudly, arms exploding out to the sides. "High notes have more energy!"

I had a naturally alto voice. Of course, with my masculine tendencies, I always wanted to make it as low as I could. Singing high was an anathema to me. But Bob insisted.

"Think high! Think it!" He repeated.

Think Frankie Valli, I thought. OK, it worked for the Four Seasons. In 1974, Bob Crewe produced the hit singles "Swearin' to God" and "My Eyes Adored You" in New York with Frankie Valli. I sang backup vocals. I watched as Bob sang literally every note with every inflection that he wanted Frankie to sing on the track before Frankie ever got to the microphone. It was amazing to witness.

But I wasn't Frankie Valli. I couldn't use a falsetto voice on this track we were recording right now. I was a girl and needed a girl voice. So, I found a notch above where I had ever sung before. I *became* a girl. When it was released as a single, "My Happy Birthday, Baby" was my proudest moment—for a minute. Then I never spoke of it again.

Journal Entry—November 13, 1978

Two years [of sobriety] *today. What a difference! I'm not the same person. Really. I even very recently considered the possibility that I might be able to stand being a woman.*

"I think we should get married," Dan casually announced over the phone one day as we were making plans to go to dinner and an AA meeting. I held the phone away from my ear and looked at it. I felt like I was in a scene from a movie.

"Um . . . I don't know about that, Dan." Dan and I had gotten to be close friends since we both got sober. We had been spending a lot of time together both in and out of AA. He had become softer in sobriety, more open. I knew he cared for me. I cared for him. But what was he talking about? What was happening? I was in the middle of launching my career. Yes, we were friends, but a committed relationship, let alone marriage, was the furthest thing from my mind. Not only that, I had also not forgotten what happened the last time we got involved. Dan was still gay.

"No, really Cindy, I think we should be together now. We are great friends. We have the same values." He persisted. The word *love* was not mentioned.

There was not a shred of my being that was looking for a life partner of either gender.* I wanted to be focused on one thing, my career. Even with all the uncertainty surrounding me artistically, I was still determined to "make it" in music.

But now my mind started running away with me. I did have feelings for Dan. What were these feelings? Was it love? Why did I want to be with him so much? Why would I drop everything when he called? I was confused. He was a physically attractive man. And the same things that drew me to him when we first met—his seeming command of life and his take-charge attitude—still attracted me now. I panicked. I suddenly

---

* In the 1970s, the identifier of *nonbinary* was not widely known or used in popular culture. But it has been around for as long as civilization has. In fact, nonbinary gender has been recorded as far back as 400 BC to AD 200, when Hijras—people in India who identified as beyond male or female—were referenced in ancient Hindu texts. Psychiatrist John F. Oliven of Columbia University coined the term *transgender* in his 1965 reference work *Sexual Hygiene and Pathology.*

felt very insecure in my own body and mind, like I was being taken over by a force unknown.

Steal the Night was released on December 1, 1979, on Casablanca Records. I produced it with my guitar player and friend, Mark Doyle. Like on my first album *Desire Wire,* I sang with my high "girl voice," still believing what Bob Crewe had told me. Plus, now I was kind of trying to fit into the emerging New Wave genre. I knew I physically could not play the game with my looks, so why not try musically.

Steal the Night got less-than-stellar reviews, and the promotion was minimal. Granted, it wasn't my best effort. Soon after, Neil Bogart left the label. I was already contemplating my third album when the new president called me into his office.

"I want you to be more like Pat Benatar," said Bruce Bird, a large, imposing man, as he leaned back in his black leather office chair and peered at me. Pat Benatar had just burst into the Top Forty as a new artist with her single "Heartbreaker." She was now the template for all female rockers to come apparently. I came before her, but that didn't matter.

"Try to be more like Pat Benatar," he stated again firmly, straight out, with no apologies. "Start wearing tank tops and some dangly earrings," he continued. "Oh, and for this new album, find some other songs and a good producer." Meaning, don't write your own songs, Cindy. And don't even think about producing.

I left Bruce Bird's office resolved. I was resolved *not* to do one thing that he suggested. Hadn't *I* already received a Grammy nomination for Female Best Rock Vocal Performance for *my* song? I did go into the studio to record some tracks, just for spite. I wrote them and produced them. (I also recorded a cover version of the Yardbirds' "Heart Full of Soul.") I took the tracks to Bruce, stating that these songs were not written or produced by me. (I made up the names.) He loved them.

I acquiesced to record the album with a producer (who did nothing but talk on the phone—I fired him shortly after we started). But the pressure continued from the top—be more like a girl . . . and there was a silent *or else*, I knew.

At the same time, Tony Defries and I were becoming more disengaged with each other. He was very unhappy with my developing relationship with Dan. He was afraid, I think rightly, that Dan would steer the focus away from my career. I was struggling to find my own footing among all these powerful men in my life.

I finally walked out on my contract with Casablanca, knowing they would not put any effort behind the album. My third album *Reckless* was never released.

In June 1979, Dan and I moved in together on Appian Way. Months had gone by since the first time he shocked me with his initial proposal. We spent more and more time together. We talked a lot about *being* together. I was slowly coming to terms with what seemed to me like the inevitability of our relationship. The chutzpa that had led me to run away from home at fifteen, to go to Los Angeles with no money or place to live, and to crash a party where I knew Elton John would be, had by this time already started seeping out of the ever-accumulating cracks in my psyche. The record business was making sure of that.

Bob Crewe had seen me for who I was and could be. Bobby Neuwirth had seen me and my potential as an artist. Elton John definitely saw me. Maybe Dan Crewe was seeing me too, but in a different way. Maybe, just maybe, my dream of being a rock star was not meant to be. The idea of living a "normal" life started to weigh in. I was twenty-eight years old. Way in the back of my mind was a thought about having kids. The third time Dan asked, I said yes.

I didn't care so much about sex, necessarily. I had avoided intimate contact as much as possible, though in my drug days that self-consciousness about what body parts I did and did not have subsided somewhat. What I craved was touch and intimacy. Dan and I had made love clumsily in our first attempts years before. Dan was attracted to men. I felt I was a man, but I definitely had a woman's body.

There was no word or term that described my aversion to my breasts and my sense that I should have had a penis instead of a vagina. It was not easy to put that aside. We made love now again, but as nice as it was to physically connect, I still had to disengage from my female body. I never felt right. I knew it wasn't natural to Dan, either. Could we make it work for the long term? I didn't know.

As the weeks and months went on, I was hanging on to my dream of being a rock star by a very thin thread. My recording career was failing to make headway, and the demands on me to be someone other than who

I was were getting too hard to fight. I was tired. I'd be safe with Dan, I thought. I would be secure. I loved him, I thought. Maybe just maybe, I too would be loved.

Somewhere in all this, I parted ways with Tony Defries. There was too much conflict between what Tony wanted from me (a career without a relationship), what Dan wanted (a relationship likely without a career), and what I was mentally and emotionally capable of handling myself. What I truly wanted I didn't know anymore.

On October 6, 1979, on a warm, gorgeous fall day, I married Dan Crewe. I was twenty-nine, and Dan was about to turn forty-five. We had a traditional New England family wedding in the Congregational Church in the middle of the quintessential Topsfield, Massachusetts, town green. Nancy, Debbie, and Suki, my three sisters, along with Helen Love, my good friend from high school, and Santi Meunier, my roommate and best friend from the American Academy, were bridesmaids.

I wore a cream-colored antique Japanese kimono in lieu of a wedding dress. It was soft and elegant with rose and green floral images along the edges. Dan and I had found it in Beverly Hills on a frantic search just days before leaving for the East Coast. My made-to-order white satin pantsuit from Bonwit Teller in New York was an absolute disaster. A traditional wedding dress was out of the question for me. I felt I had to compromise somehow for my parents, who were putting on the wedding, and not wear the man's three-piece suit that I had envisioned. Up on the altar, we recited the vows that we had so carefully written.

As we got into our Peugeot, waved to our families and friends after the reception at my parents' home, with the cool autumn air brushing up against my new tweed men's Polo blazer, I felt happy and hopeful. We arrived at our hotel in Boston and collapsed into bed. We didn't make love. It was our wedding night, and we didn't make love. My heart sank. That was not the way the story was supposed to go. We were supposed to connect physically—touch each other, hold each other, breathe into each other—at least emotionally consummate this union.

We went to Nantucket on our honeymoon, where Dan promptly got sick with the flu, and it snowed. I wondered to myself if these events were an omen of things to come in our marriage.

A couple weeks later, Bob Crewe hosted an extravaganza in Los Angeles where Dan and I announced our vows again to three hundred of our recovery and music business friends. As Dan and I danced alone in the great hall of the Ebell of Los Angeles event center with all the guests looking on, I suddenly felt completely empty. No joy, no love, no nothing. *What have I done? Who am I now?* What *am I now?* Pressed up against him, his arms now holding me, I was alone.

We were only days into the marriage, and there was little intimacy. I had let go of my career, piece by piece, and felt my dream of being a rock star slip further and further away. I didn't know how not to strive to *be* something. Dan was my white knight, wasn't he? He would save me from my desperate need to be wanted, right? At that moment, I knew he could not.

The music began fading into a hollow echo. I felt like my cells were shape shifting as we danced, morphing me into someone I would eventually come to not recognize.

The stretch limo pulled up to our house on top of Appian Way, high above the city. It was February 1980. Dan and I got in and settled back for the drive down the mountain to the Shrine Auditorium for the second time in two years. This year I was nominated for Best Rock Vocal Performance–Female for my single "Survivor." Having been dismissed from United Artists (now EMI), the single's label, it was a complete shock.

No sooner did I walk down the red carpet and into the lobby of the auditorium than a woman ran up to me waving her program in my face and almost screamed.

"Andy Gibb! Aren't you Andy Gibb?"

"No ma'am, I'm sorry. I'm not," I said almost apologetically. I didn't want *her* to feel embarrassed. "I'm Cindy Bullens."

The woman looked befuddled and then clearly disappointed that I was not who she thought I was.

"Oh! Well. You look just like Andy Gibb." She turned away with a whoosh and disappeared into the now gathering crowd of the rock 'n' roll elite.

6

MOCKINGBIRD HILL

I drove past our house up on Mockingbird Hill
The ghost of our love must be living there still
There's a bike in the driveway and a dog in the yard
And no indication that life can be hard
On Mockingbird Hill yeah yeah
And the mockingbird steals a song from the air
And he don't care

    "Mockingbird Hill" by Cindy Bullens
    ©2005 Mommy's Geetar Music/BMI

"I HATE L.A.!" Dan yelled out to no one in particular in our kitchen one day in early June 1980. In the miasma of my music business trials and his own failed attempts at finding a working place or position that satisfied him, he had had it with living in Los Angeles. He had begrudgingly moved there to help Bob Crewe rebuild his career, which he did, but he never truly felt comfortable. Now we were living in our beautiful, *Architectural Digest*-worthy modern spaceship of a house on top of Laurel Canyon, but Dan and I were both adrift. I was feeling defeated and beaten down, unsure of my future. He was looking for something meaningful to put his time and energy into.

"Let's move to New York." The words came out of Dan's mouth one day in our kitchen as easily as they would have if he were telling me what he wanted for dinner. We sold the house in six days. That's how he worked. There was little discussion. I was tired of making decisions. I was all for it. I'll run away again, one more time. Maybe it'll be better somewhere else. And I knew New York. Move on.

We bought a co-op on the corner of West End Avenue and West 76th Street in Manhattan. The minute we moved in Dan started renovating our first-floor, two-bedroom apartment, and I started to reconstruct myself. Drywall dust, splintered wood, and bits of my psyche were all parts of the scattered debris. *What do I do now? Who am I?* The scene had shifted, but now what? This was becoming the recurring theme of me and my life—thinking I was going with the flow, doing the "next right thing," only to find that the void within—no, the *split* within me—was still there. I constantly questioned myself. Maybe being married was enough. Maybe just dabbling in music, writing a few songs, producing a New York band here and there, would be enough. I was thirty years old now, and in my mind, time was slipping away all too fast. The feeling of being adrift didn't abate with the move. At the same time as buying the co-op, we bought ninety acres of farmland, with a barn, in the western Connecticut foothills of the Berkshires.

Dan and I had been married for almost a year at that point. I was acquiescing more and more to his wants and whims and paying less attention to my own. Let me rephrase that: I had less and less energy to resist Dan's will. He was in charge, and I was OK with that—at least on the outside. On the inside, I was shrinking. I knew that he was trying to make what he thought were the best lifestyle decisions for us, but I wanted some intimacy to go with it. There wasn't any. Somewhere in the middle of the following year, I started feeling that same sense of emptiness I had felt on the dance floor of our wedding reception.

I did what I could to keep myself busy in the city. I reconnected with old friends, made some new ones through them and through twelve-step meetings. I took a creative writing course at the New School. I produced a few demos for New York artists and bands. Though my desire was still high, my inspiration was low, and I recognized more and more that, at my age, and as a woman, I may not have much of a future in the music business.

Journal Entry—June 5, 1981

I'm a little lost right now. I can't see anything in my future. I have no idea of how it should be for the first time, really. A clean slate. I'm open. Onto other things.

Despite all indications against the idea, around nine months after our move, Dan and I found ourselves seriously discussing having a baby.

I hadn't been able or willing to address my feelings of inadequacy or the lack of touch in our marriage. I tried to find release and meaning in my bits of creativity and in "working" my AA program. During this time, I mostly blamed myself for Dan not being into sex.

"But I have to talk to you about something else," Dan said as we sat on the couch in our den on the first Tuesday night in June 1981. "What if I went out and had an affair with a man?"

I stared at him, startled. I said nothing.

"I've been fantasizing about it. A lot. I'm sorry." He had obviously been in a great deal of pain, and he was feeling guilty. I was truly stunned by his honesty. He was, after all, talking to his wife. But I also saw his vulnerability for the first time in a very long time. I felt empathy for him. I was having sexual fantasies of my own about women, and I told him so. It was a strangely welcome relief to be speaking out loud to each other about who we actually were—two non-straight people.

"Do we want to bring a baby into this world if there's any chance we are not going to be monogamous?" The question hung in the air. We sat silent for several minutes. There was a kind of strange, but deep trust we had in each other. We acknowledged it out loud. We talked long into the night. Fear, we finally decided, was not a good enough reason *not* to have a baby. What was it that would keep us from venturing out into our fantasies? And more to the point, what was it in each of us that dictated that we should be a married couple in the first place? I didn't know.

But I knew I wanted kids. The thought of having my own child was as natural to me as breath itself. It was an odd thought, though, for someone like me. Someone who felt more masculine than feminine, who also happened to have dreams of being on the road as a rock star. But there it was. I remembered one night on the road with Elton, when my backup singer cohort Jon Joyce and his wife Connie were talking about having kids. In the back of my mind a vision of three little boys appeared. I made a note to myself in that moment—*Oh! I want children.*

———————————

My sister Debbie was born when I was seven. I was not exactly thrilled. I was in full little boy bloom running free in the wilds of West Newbury, Massachusetts—flying around the bases on my homemade ball field or building forts with found objects in the woods or exploring the vast terrain surrounding our house. I knew nearly every inch of our own ten acres, and most of the surrounding farmland. I was almost never in the house.

When Debbie came, things changed. Though we now lived outside what was considered the suburbs at that time, my parents had a very active social life. (Most of their good friends followed them out of the immediate Boston area and into "the country.") My sister Nancy, seven and a half years my senior, was off most of the time doing what high school girls did. She was pretty, gregarious, and extremely popular. I almost never saw her. My brother Ricky was twelve. Though not excused from domestic duties (my mother made sure all her kids fulfilled their designated chores), he tried his best to avoid them whenever possible. Even when one of them was tapped to babysit, inevitably, when my parents left the house, I would be coerced, and at times bribed, to take over. Therefore, much of Debbie's non-critical care fell to me. It didn't help that we slept in the same room. Granted, it was a big room and kind of the Grand Central Station of the upstairs of our 1776 Colonial. The staircase entrance from downstairs was at the foot of my bed. The kids' communal bathroom was just to the left of the staircase. My parents' and both Nancy and Ricky's rooms fed into mine. There was no privacy. An old six-foot-tall blue wooden bookshelf, standing perpendicular to my bed wall, served as the only partition between my bed and Debbie's crib.

After the first few months, when the baby would wake up crying in the middle of the night, I would be the first and sometimes the only one to respond. My mother's belief was to let the baby "cry it out." I absolutely hated that. I couldn't understand it. It was an anathema to me. The baby's changing table was just to the left of the kids' bathroom door. I learned early on how to change diapers. In those days the diapers were cloth, and you had to fit and fasten them on the baby with actual safety pins. *Don't stick the baby!* It was a skill. My absolute freedom from care and worry had vanished literally overnight.

Sister Suki arrived two and a half years after Debbie, in mid-December 1959, at Boston Lying-In. By this time my mother had given up all maternal pretense, and at the hospital door handed off my newborn baby sister to now seventeen-year-old Nancy. My parents had a Christmas party to go to. Nancy drove the baby the hour up US Route 1 home from Boston to West Newbury. I, at nine, was Suki's restraint, holding her in my arms in the back seat of our 1956 red and white Ford station wagon, with little Debbie on the seat next to me.

Though I sometimes resented it, my little sisters elicited a sense of responsibility in me that I took very seriously. I watched out for them in precarious times, like a surrogate parent.

While my parents' daily drinking was always stressful for their children, at times it became dangerous. When I was around eleven or twelve, we were at a large family pool party of my parents' friends a few towns away. As night fell, I guess my mother thought it best to bring me and my little sisters home, so I could put them to bed. The problem was, my mother was so intoxicated, there was no way she could drive safely.

"Get the kids into the car." She shouted as she herded us down the driveway. My stomach was in knots.

"Mom, let's not go now. The kids will be all right," I pleaded, on the edge of begging. I wasn't sure exactly *when* we could go home. Neither Nancy nor Rick—who now had his own license—was with us. I surely didn't want us to be in a moving vehicle with her now.

"Get in!" she demanded, and in behind the wheel she went. There was no going against my mother. I'm sure Debbie and Suki could sense my panic, but they did as they were told and climbed into the back with me. There were no children's car seats back then, and I don't remember ever wearing a seatbelt. I knew now that it would be up to me to get us home without incident. I positioned myself in the middle of the back seat area, between my sisters, pressed up against the front bench seat of the Ford wagon. Standing hunched over and straddling the transmission tunnel for the half-hour drive home, I was my mother's eyes. I kept her between the lane lines on I-95 as the car would veer off one way or the other. On the dark, narrow back roads, which filled much of the trip, I guided her turn by turn, desperate to keep us and the car on the road. When we finally pulled into our own driveway, she told us to get out of the car, turned around, and drove herself back to the party.

There were countless other occurrences with my parents and their drinking over the years that all my siblings and I endured. None of them pretty. After Nancy and Rick had moved out of the house, there were frequent fierce and furious drunken battles that forced me out of bed in the wee hours of the night and into my younger sisters' bedroom. I would hold Debbie as she cried, while little Suki stared blankly into space.

"It's all right. Everything's gonna be fine," I whispered assuredly. But as time went on, I knew my words were empty. I had said them too many times before. Still, I was their protector. I could not leave them alone with their terror.

I knew early on how children should be treated, taken care of, and loved. (Some of that sense I believe is in my nature, but I suspect some came from trauma.) I became overly sensitive to conflict and hyper-responsible. I was extremely aware of whatever was going on around me at all times. Now, in 1981, as an adult, I was sober. My husband was sober. I believed I could be a better parent than my own.

In the flurry of starting his new venture of owning and running two Sedutto's high-end retail ice cream stores in New York City, Dan was worn out. I succumbed to the seeming lack of music in my life, donned a maroon-colored apron, and started scooping mocha almond fudge and vanilla caramel swirl into cones and cups in our Lincoln Center store. Somewhere in the first weeks after opening, both exhausted, we dedicated four nights in a row to the mission of making a baby. I could set my watch to my menstrual cycle. My next period date came and went. The weeks went by. Nothing. And then there was something.

Journal Entry—September 30, 1981

I awoke in the middle of the night (as usual), put my hand on my stomach, and there was this mound—hard as a rock—really round, distinctive. I was shaken out of a half sleep because of its realness, and I realized profoundly that there was something inside of me, other than myself!

"Breathe, breathe, push, push!" Lennox Hill Hospital, New York City. I could hear the nurse's voice, but it did not matter what she was saying. My body was engaging in exactly what it was supposed to do—breathe and push.

On April 2, 1982, at 2:30 PM, Reid was born. The bright sun reflected off the building across East 76th Street, through our windows and into the labor room, where I insisted on staying for the birth. Though it took twelve hours from the first contraction to her crowning, I was resolute about being awake and aware for every single second of the experience. It wasn't every day that my inner man would bear a child!

My tiny daughter was seven and a quarter pounds and a perfect ten on the Apgar score. I was absolutely in love with her from the moment she met the air. When the doctor laid her on my chest, Reid looked me straight in the eye. Her bright blue eyes I knew were those of a very old soul. Dan cut the umbilical cord.

My pregnancy had been the happiest time in Dan's and my marriage. We had a unified purpose. We felt together in all our planning. We were as prepared as we could be. We attended each of our Bradley Method birthing classes together with great intent. Beside ourselves with joy about our coming progeny, we were resolute in our desire to give our baby the best life possible.

At the moment of her birth, there was no doubt in my mind of some Higher Power. This baby, Reid Elizabeth Bullens-Crewe, was something from nothing. And she was mine. I lifted my red, wet, and beautiful daughter to my breast. The breast that I hated so much. My milk from my breast. *This,* I thought, *is the miracle of my life.*

Nine days after Reid was born, we left New York City for our ninety acres in Sherman, Connecticut. Dan had just finished turning the barn that we bought with the land into a rustic but beautiful three-bedroom, loft-like living space. New York City was no place for a baby, we decided,

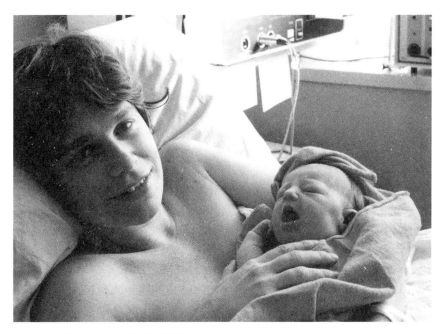

Reid at birth, April 2, 1982. *Author's collection*

and we were gone. Move on. For several months, Dan commuted into the city every few days to take care of business with the ice cream stores before he finally sold them. I loved every second of being a mother, but I was not prepared for how small my life would become.

———————

Wasn't I just in Los Angeles, down on my knees playing big, fat, crunchy chords on my Les Paul, sweating and heaving with the rhythm of the drums and the buzz of the crowd? Wasn't I just there? Now I'm sitting in front of the picture window, in this barn, looking out on the cow fields in the misty dawn. It's so quiet.*

"You've become a shadow of yourself," Billy Mernit blurted out as I was clipping coupons from the Sunday paper at the dining table in the barn. I hadn't seen him in a year or more, since we moved out of New

———————

* Excerpted from Cid's one-person show *Somewhere Between: Not an Ordinary Life.*

York. He was visiting Dan and me in Sherman for the weekend. Billy was an old friend who knew me well.

I didn't respond. I *couldn't* respond. As I took in a deep breath, I knew he was right. I had been laser focused on Reid, as a mother rightly should be, but I had also been shutting down every creative part of my being, cell by cell. I could not have created a greater divide between my rock star life and dream in Los Angeles and where I was at that moment if I tried. Did I try? If I did, it worked.

Suddenly, I wanted to take my baby, leave Dan, and get out of there. I didn't. But I did try everything I could to find some kind of middle ground. I started writing new songs, making demos, reaching out to music business friends. I felt desperate to feel some semblance of creative purpose. No, to feel some semblance of *self*.

But that was not to happen. Dan was now fully ensconced in rural Connecticut living, having started a construction company and now building houses in the area on "spec." When he wasn't on site, he was on his tractor somewhere in our fields. Again, intimacy was not coming easily to us. At one point, we saw a Catholic priest in Waterbury as our counselor. (We weren't Catholic.) He told us to hold hands more. We hired one of Dan's many aunts to be our nanny for a few months, to give me time to run my sacrosanct daily five miles, and to ostensibly work on my music. While I appreciated the opportunity for more time for myself, the chasm within me deepened. Was it selfish to want more from this life than what I had? Was I asking for too much, wanting to be creative while being a mother? *Look at what I have—I should be happy!*

———————————

"Hey, Cin! You wanna do a gig with Meatloaf?" Mark Doyle called me out of the blue one day in mid-January 1983 as I was getting ready to put little Reid down for a nap in the barn. He was on the road with Meatloaf as his lead guitar player. I was not a Meatloaf fan and Mark knew that, but *What?! Wow!* I thought. This could not have come at a better time. It would be a one-off—a charity event for the Wolf Trap National Park for the Performing Arts in Virginia. I would play rhythm guitar.

"One thing." He hesitated. "He wants you to wear lingerie."

I knew Mark was being the good friend that he was by making this opportunity to perform and get out of my cloistered existence a possibility for me. For me to be playing guitar and not just singing made it all the more enticing. Plus, Mark and I had a synchronistic stage presence together, which we had discovered right from the start when he joined my band in L.A. I loved playing with him. This was to be a star-studded event—Bob Hope, Sammy Davis Jr., Elizabeth Taylor (whom I had met twice before with Elton), multi-hit songwriter Paul Williams, and other notables across the entertainment spectrum. And Meatloaf.

"No." I said breathing in and not immediately out. "I can't do that." Still holding my breath, I felt the oh-so-familiar knot in my stomach accompanied by the constriction in the middle of my chest. It started to overtake me. *They don't get it. Nobody gets it.* Breathe, I urged myself, just breathe.

"OK. I know. I just had to ask. Let me see what he says. I'll call you back."

Meatloaf almost always had "a girl" on stage and on his records—great singers like Ellen Foley and Karla Devito. He liked a female foil. It was great theater; I'd give him that. But no, I could not wear lingerie for him, or for anybody.

"How about a dress?" I could see Mark's sheepishness through the phone asking this next question. Silence. "Never mind. I'll call you back."

I arrived in Vienna, Virginia, ready to play. I had been working out the rhythm guitar parts, blasting Meatloaf hits for two weeks in a small extra bedroom in the barn I had set up as my studio. The band gathered the day before the event to rehearse. With great musicians, and my good friend Mark beside me, I was in heaven. I didn't care that I never liked Meatloaf's songs or records. They were too bombastic and stylized for me. But I did appreciate his dynamism as an entertainer—he was a master on stage. Here, at that moment, with the band, I didn't care what songs I was rehearsing. I was *playing*! And, after all, these were *hits* I would be performing with the artist himself. And not for nothing—I was having fun! The band graciously made me feel like one of them the whole time.

Before the show, I corralled Bob Hope for a photo, reintroduced myself to Elizabeth Taylor (who at least pretended to remember me), said hello to Paul Williams, and just stared wide-eyed at the rest of the showbiz royalty as they wandered, mingled, laughed, drank, and consorted like they were at their twentieth high school reunion.

It was February 7, 1983. As the lights went up, I was standing stage right, with my cherry-red 1965 Gibson SG Jr. slung over my shoulder, my usual mop of blonde wavy hair ready to fly, and my rock 'n' roll attitude firmly in place. My black nylon "flight suit" with my red Capezio dance shoes, which had been one of my last stage outfits B.C. (before children), glistened in the rainbow of lights that danced across the stage. The spot came up white and bright on Meatloaf as he belted out the first lines of "Bat Out of Hell":

> *The sirens are screaming, and the fires are howling*
> *Way down in the valley tonight*
> *There's a man in the shadows with a gun in his eye*
> *And a blade shining oh so bright**

Meatloaf bellowed and blustered and sweat. Mark tore up his guitar. I played, looked, and felt for all the world like a rock star, and there was not a shred of lingerie anywhere in sight. Meatloaf didn't hire me again.

In the summer of 1984, I was pregnant again. It wasn't planned, and it didn't take four tries. One random night and boom. I was not as happy about it this time. Reid was two years old now, I was thirty-four, and despite the odds, I still couldn't shake the idea of maybe performing again at some point. Another baby meant realistically another two years *after* the birth before I could even think about that again. Time was ticking away. Nonetheless, I had absolutely no desire *not* to want this child. I was pregnant. Another human being would come through me, and I had to be the best vehicle for *this* little miracle I could possibly be.

"I cannot live here in the middle of nowhere! I am losing myself! I want to go back to L.A.," I blurted out one morning after a nearly sleepless night.

---

* By Jim Steinman ©Carlin America/Round Hill Music

Sherman, Connecticut, was too far from anything and everything that I needed in my life. I grew up in a rural town surrounded by acres and acres of farmland and forest. I loved land and green and gardening and running on hills. But I also needed company. I needed human interaction, some of it creative, and at least a bit of intellectual stimulation. *Sesame Street* reruns on VHS only went so far. Hell, if there were only a decent mall that wasn't an hour away! Bottom line: I needed to feel connected.

"No way!" said Dan emphatically. "I will *never* live in Los Angeles again!" So that was that.

"Well, we have to move *somewhere!*" I rarely stood my ground with Dan. But this time I did. He had hired an architect months earlier, and the plans had already been drawn up to build our Victorian, shingle-architecture dream house, high on the hill above the barn overlooking Candlewood Lake. The view might as well have been in Sweden or Norway rather than southwestern Connecticut. It was truly spectacular, as was to be the house. Dan was a gifted designer, and almost anything he touched turned to gold. But everything had changed now.

That house would not be built. We moved. Westport, Connecticut, was only an hour south down State Route 7, but it was worlds away from the isolation I had been feeling in Sherman. In 1984, it was the tony suburb in Fairfield County that it was known to be, but it still had some of its quiet New England charm, with local mom-and-pop stores lining the main street. Granted, Paul Newman and his wife Joanne Woodward lived there, as did Marlo Thomas and Phil Donahue. It was also Martha Stewart's home base. It had a yacht club and spawned one of the first Ann Taylor stores. But there was also the tiny (and award-winning) Westport Pizza and Gold's Deli, and the landmark hot pink Remarkable Book Store. The YMCA was in the center of town, and that alone made my world a better place. I could work out *and* take Reid to swimming or ballet lessons several times a week. Human beings were everywhere.

We bought a house on Minute Man Hill. It was two-story and gray-shingled with two large old growth trees in the front yard. The huge wide-open backyard stretched across the lot, with a vegetable garden in the back left corner and rows of blooming rose bushes on the eastern border. On a dead-end street above the main road, you could see Compo Beach and Long Island Sound from its perch on top of the hill. Dan and I had driven aimlessly around Westport one day exploring, just to see if there was a property for sale that might pique our interest. We found ourselves turning up a side street by a statue of a minuteman, and as we approached the last few houses, there it was.

"I want *that* house!" I exclaimed. "That's the house I want!" There was no sign on the lawn. There was no indication that it was for sale. But I knew it was mine. On a whim, we stopped at the closest realtor's office and asked what was available in town.

"There's a wonderful house for sale just up on Minute Man Hill. It's a lovely street!" she declared. Dan and I looked at each other without saying a word. And as we rounded the turn at the top, where Dan and I had just been an hour before, my heart suddenly skipped a beat. "This one," she said, pointing toward the gray house as it was fading in the waning light. "It just went on the market today."

February 24, 1985, Norwalk, Connecticut. Jessie was a big baby at just shy of nine pounds. And she came out quick! She had been so active in the womb; I was shocked when the doctor told me she was a girl. (I guess the deep binary myths and projections of gender carry over into everything.) But now here she was. While Reid came out looking like the Ivory Soap commercial, Jessie came out big, blue, bloody, and smushed. Her lips were mine—wide and thick across her face. Her tiny nose was shaped like mine too. Wisps of red hair, darkened with the fluid of birth, streaked across her head. Another miracle, grace personified. After her first flurry of checks and tests, her first feeding at my breast, and after Dan brought Reid in to meet her new little sister and left for home, I lay alone holding Jessie.

"Hi, Jessie, my baby doll. Welcome to our family." I said the words out loud with intention. "I am so grateful that you came through me. May you live a very long life and may all your dreams come true. I know you are going to make this world a better place. Mommy loves you so much!"

————————

Cindy Bullens, almost rock star, man in a woman's body, mother of two, married to a gay man, living in Westport, Connecticut, right smack in the middle of the Gold Coast, driving a minivan!*

Dan and I plunged even further into our new community and parenthood, now with two kids. Reid started preschool at a Montessori school in Wilton, Connecticut, that eventually became the center of our little world. Dan, once again, ensconced himself in renovating our home. The workmen were in the house so much that Reid thought they were part of our family and questioned us when they weren't around. Dan joined the school board and quickly became its president. Jessie was a growing ball of red-headed energy and even as a baby made us laugh out loud. It was as though a spell of domesticity fell upon us on Minute Man Hill.

Yet again, there were flashes of the various splits and fissures and disparities in me that always seemed to linger behind the curtain of appearances.

I loved being a mother; I had loved being pregnant and breastfeeding. But I couldn't relate to the other mothers at the school or in the neighborhood. I did everything they did—I shopped for Pampers and non-slip socks at Kmart and for OshKosh overalls at the local outlet. We went to every classmate's birthday party—Dan baked the cookies—and we carpooled. I attended every preschool performance, art show, or singalong. (I was asked to play guitar for the kids on occasion, and I did.) We had people over for cookouts and couples for dinners. There was always a playdate on the calendar. I even pierced my ears and donned a casual dress and Italian leather flats every so often to try to fit in.

But not far underneath the surface of this spell lay the reality of Dan and me. I was still a man in a woman's body. Dan was still gay. Not a soul around us knew our true stories. And the funny thing was, Dan and I were not intentionally trying to hide anything about ourselves. We were just us: married with two kids in Connecticut. But spell or not, like any force of nature, something had to give.

————————

* Excerpted from Cid's one-person show *Somewhere Between: Not an Ordinary Life*

Journal Entry—June 9, 1985

I feel lost sometimes. From myself. It's easy to cover everything over and just drift through every day. Of course, I feel joy and hurt and stuff about my kids. Them, I do experience. But not me. Dan—well right now it's fine. But we don't have a FULL relationship. We just have children together. We have a house together. We have a friendship together. (Is there more?) There's no passion. (Is there supposed to be?) Barely any touching. Same old stuff. I just cope with it better.

Dan has the mental constitution of a naval battleship. Whatever he deems is so at a particular time, is. Period. Everything else is moved down into the orlop deck, below the waterline, where no one can access the contents, not even him. I am not built that way. In fact, I am the exact opposite. No matter how hard I try, if whatever it is isn't in the realm of my own truth, it simply won't work.

The strands of the situation started to unravel. *I* started to unravel. All the different and various aspects of myself flew around inside my head, my heart, and my body like a swarm of locusts that would eventually end up splattered all over my windshield as I drove through the desert.

Within the year after Jessie was born, I rallied myself again and started to seriously work toward making music. I bought the newest home recording equipment. I wrote a few songs. I practiced my guitar. We had the luxury of having a young live-in nanny in those days (which I at once appreciated and hated), which afforded me some extra time for all of it. In the spring of 1986, I reached out to a few local professional musicians and put a band together—a good band.

There I was, a thirty-six-year-old, two-time Grammy nominee and mother of two, rehearsing during school hours down in my garage with five ragtag (but excellent) musicians, looking to snag a gig at the local Red Rock Café. It was a beginning. At the same time, I was becoming infatuated with a woman who lived in a nearby town who I met through a mutual musician friend. She was cute and sassy and energetic. And she was unavailable. Not only was she married with a child, but also, while she really liked me, she had no desire to have an affair with another woman. Nothing ever happened between us, and we remained friends, but the mere fact that I had a strong *desire* to be with her created the perfect conditions for the oncoming locusts.

"Mom, can you see the air?" Reid asked out of the blue. She and I were on our way back home after attending the Westport Fair. We had just driven past the full moon rising over Long Island Sound and had both remarked at how beautiful it was. Reid loved the moon. We were now turning the corner onto Minute Man Hill.

"No. Not really. I mean if it's foggy. . ." My voice drifted off into said air as she continued.

"I can." Her four-year-old voice said matter-of-factly.

"Oh, really? What does it look like?"

"Jesus."

"Jesus?" Luckily, I didn't repeat it as a swear word and I kept my surprise to myself. I tried hard to be that parent who just listened to my kids no matter what. She had my attention.

"Yeah. He's standing right over there." She pointed out toward the front of the car and to her right. "He's right there." No exclamation point necessary. She was calm, as if she were pointing out a tree she hadn't noticed before.

"What does he look like?" I was puzzled. Where was this coming from?

"He looks like Spirit."

Again, I was trying to be low-key. There was no discussion of Jesus in our home. We participated in no actual religious practices outside of the obligatory Christmas and Easter gatherings, and it was now June. "Oh. Does he talk to you?"

"No." She growled and giggled as if I were being silly. I told her I thought it was beautiful that she saw him. I was trying to be nonchalant.

"Did he die?" she then asked.

Channeling my good Christian White Anglo-Saxon Protestant ancestry I said, "Yes, but he lives inside each of us as Spirit, just like you said." There was silence now until we were entering the front door on Minute Man Hill.

Suddenly Reid sighed and said, "Oh, the wonderful Spirit of God!" We walked into the house, and that was the end of it.

I had never had a vision like Reid's, and I envied her. In fact, I didn't seem to have any hard and fast beliefs. While I had an overwhelming sense of *something* at her birth, and in other fleeting moments in my life, at my core I was haunted by a constant feeling of hollowness.

Now in my mid-thirties, I felt compelled to address the void. I started studying *A Course in Miracles*. I had sessions with numerous astrologers, psychics, channelers, and various other types of healers. On several occasions I would travel up to Kripalu Center for Yoga & Health in Western Massachusetts, or the Siddha Ashram with Swami Muktananda in New York State for weekend intensives on kundalini meditation or intimacy or breaking spiritual blocks. I dove into my inner child and my shame with John Bradshaw and learned about my codependency from Melodie Beattie. I started psychotherapy for the first time ever. Along with all of that, I sponsored a multitude of women in recovery.

I had been sober for ten years plus, and I was ripe for the picking. I wanted to experience anything and everything that would help me not feel like a failure and a fraud. I wanted so desperately to be . . . well, to just *be*, still and quiet. I genuinely wanted to experience God. Some God, *any* God. Or even any *part* of any God. The Twelve Steps were all about finding a Higher Power. That could be anything. I wanted a real God. Organized religion just didn't ring true, despite my statement to Reid regarding the Spirit of Jesus, so I knew I had to find It some other way.

I earnestly tried throughout my sobriety to achieve a sense of trust in my own ever-shifting sense of a Power Greater Than Myself. I simply could not hold on to it. I now knew what true and real and profound *love* was. I found that in my children. But I could not find love or God in myself. I loved my children's innocence and their interest and awe in everything around them. I coveted watching them move through this strange world in both big and little ways, discovering for themselves their own power and their own limitations. I studied them as they experienced the magnificence of beauty in one thing and the subtlety of it in another. They were my teachers from the moment they arrived, and as flawed as I could be as a parent, inexperienced and impatient, I never wanted them to be anything other than who they were. I reveled in their uniqueness, and I would love them no matter what.

Still, with all my searching outside and in, with my deep and boundless longing for something to bind the disparate strands of me, there was no center.

I was a wife with a gay husband, a mother who didn't understand women, a man inside of a women's body, someone who craved intimacy married to someone who could not give it, a homebody who couldn't stay home, and a rock star without an audience. There was no more room on my windshield for another splat.

Jessie, Dan, and Cindy Westport, Connecticut, 1985.
Author's collection

7

ROCK 'N' ROLL GIRL

Look into the light
Stand still for the flash
Someone whispers hold your temper
Pick up your guitar
Get ready to play
Girls with guitars are quite the fashion
Look at these pictures of my children
They are the only things that mean anything
Rock 'n' roll girl
What are you doing, girl?
Gotta get to a phone
Call my babies tonight
My little girl is having a birthday
Here comes the applause
Oh they love me tonight
But my little girl is blowing out her candles

> *"Rock 'n' Roll Girl" by Cindy Bullens*
> *©1987 Mommy's Geetar Music/BMI*

THE WOODEN SAWHORSES STOOD AS BARRICADES, supposedly to hold us back from being too close to the front of the stage. It was June 24, 1966, in Lynn, Massachusetts. The Rolling Stones were playing their first concert of their first American tour.

An outdoor venue, the undistinguished Manning Bowl, was filling up with every kid in New England. There wasn't an adult to be seen, except for a few scattered security people around the edges of the gathering crowd. As people filled in the grass and dirt below our feet, the Mods, a local band who won an opening spot in a Battle of the Bands, were playing. Then came the McCoys ("Hang on Sloopy"), and then Boston's own Standells ("Muddy Water") came on. Finally, Arnie "Woo Woo" Ginsburg, of Boston's great rock 'n' roll station WMEX, introduced the Rolling Stones. The crowd erupted.

My lower abdomen was being jammed up against the sawhorse I was standing behind, having slowly worked my way to the front during the opening acts. The Stones ran onto the stage. *"Not Fade Away."* More and more people were filling in all the space around me. As the music blared and the crowd grew louder, I figured I would take a chance.

"Sir, I'm getting crushed here. I promise I won't pull anything. Can I please stand with you?" I looked the police officer straight in the eye, innocently. I could pass for twelve even as a teen—a blonde, blue-eyed, skinny kid. This man, one of the few officers guarding the stage, apparently took pity on me and with a promise that I would behave myself, let me scoot under the barrier and into the forbidden zone.

There I was, only a few feet from Mick Jagger, directly down in front of him, with nothing in between us. *"Get Off My Cloud."* I stared up at him, watching him, studying him, as he strutted and preened and gyrated in his plain white T-shirt and tight beige bell-bottoms on that flimsy stage daring you *not* to want him. I was daring *him* to look at *me*. *"19th Nervous Breakdown."*

I glanced over every so often to Brian Jones and then to Keith Richards, watching how their fingers moved across the fretboards of their respective guitars—Keith on his 1958 Gibson Les Paul Custom and Brian with his Harmony Stratotone. Brian was cool. Keith was on fire. *"Paint It Black."* Charlie Watts barely moved his body while playing his drums. Even his arms rose and fell only slightly to the steady beat until the right one had to rise a bit higher to hit a cymbal. *"Mother's Little Helper."* Bill Wyman stood there like a statue. On occasion he would turn his head and look at Charlie or tilt it upward toward the sky. *"The Spider and the Fly."* But you could *see* the rhythm inside of Bill and Charlie. Neither one of them had to move to show it. They *were* it. *"(I Can't Get No) Satisfaction."* Mick's tambourine, held high, slashed the sky.

With every minute, the crowd was growing more restless and even louder. The air was thick and electric. The sky overhead grew dark and ominous. Would lightning strike us? It felt like it. You just knew the night was about to explode. The cops started yelling nervously at the crowd and at each other, sensing the oncoming deluge. They were outnumbered, big time.

"Get back! Get back! Stop! Move back!" But it was too late. I turned around to see eight thousand people suddenly push down the sawhorses and rush the stage. I immediately looked up at Mick Jagger who was almost within my reach. For a moment he seemed stunned. Then a look of fear came over his face, and, with the rest of the Rolling Stones, he quickly fled the stage.

It began to rain, hard. Seeing the band run off, the pack turned from pushing toward the front of the stage and suddenly surged to the left where the limos were lined up in back. I was swept up into them, tear gas now exploding around us.

Within seconds I found myself smashed up against one of the limousine's windows looking straight into the eyes of . . . yup, Mick Jagger. The tear gas had infiltrated itself into my eyes and lungs, painfully causing a gush of tears to stream down my face already wet in the downpour. The limousine drivers were desperately trying to avoid running people over as they tried to make their way from the now muddy field into the street. They finally sped off, with people diving left and right—like the rain, pummeling the ground—to get out of the way.

I was lucky not to have been hurt. I blindly stumbled and coughed my way out to the road with the rest of the wet and bedraggled and awaited my older brother to pick me up where he had left me off earlier in the day. Even with all the chaos and the near miss of disaster, soaked and burned, I was elated. This concert had sealed my fate. I knew, now more than ever, I was going to be just like Mick Jagger.

"Well, you have a record deal." Dan's voice was calm as he walked into Bob Crewe's house in Los Angeles, where we were all staying for a visit.

There was an undertone of self-satisfaction and pride that came through his words. It was August of 1988.

"What?! Really?" I was literally jumping up and down. "Tell me everything!"

For eight years now, Dan, as a happy side gig, had been managing Bob Clearmountain, the engineer of my first album, *Desire Wire*. Bob was by now becoming one of the top and most sought-after record producers and mixers in the world, having worked with Bryan Adams, the Pretenders, the Rolling Stones, and Bruce Springsteen, among many others. MCA Records offered Clearmountain a production deal, which Dan negotiated. I was to be one of the artists produced. I couldn't believe it! It was another chance.

It was ironic that the president of MCA Records in 1988 was Al Teller. The same Al Teller who had offered me a deal out of the blue in 1974 at the Dr. John live recording at Cherokee Studios, an offer to which I never responded. Eight years after I left Casablanca Records and Los Angeles, I finally had another chance—a big chance. This time with a record company president who I believed understood me and believed in me as a whole artist. I was thrilled.

With all our other issues, Dan knew that my role as a "Connecticut housewife" would not and could not fulfill me on any level.

"Why would anyone be interested in signing a Connecticut housewife?" asked a record company A&R guy a few months earlier over the phone after I had sent him a demo of my new songs. There wasn't a hint of humor or irony in his voice. I was stunned for only a moment. Then without response, I slammed down the phone and ran into the kitchen in a rage.

"Dan, you will not believe what this *asshole* just said to me!" Dan was cooking. I was screaming. Dan was furious. I was beside myself. The blatant disrespect and outright misogyny were more than I could take at that moment. We had just returned that June from Nelson Mandela's 70th Birthday Tribute Concert in London; Bob Clearmountain had mixed the whole live show. Dan was invited as Bob's manager. Backstage, during soundcheck, we were heading into the artist's tent. The security guy looked down the list for Dan's name so we could enter, found it but didn't see mine, or a plus one. He called over another man with an all-access pass.

"Oh, she's OK. That's Bob Clearmountain's manager's wife." I would never forget that moment. Now there was nothing wrong with being someone's manager's wife, or a Connecticut housewife for that matter. I assumed there were many. But I still had in my mind—who I thought I was—that image of me at four years old shaking my little body to the beat of Little Richard's "Tutti Frutti" all by myself in the kitchen, at fifteen sucking in my cheeks and practicing windmills on my air guitar in the mirror. And of course I could still remember where I was and who I *really was on stage with* on July 4, 1976—Elton John! Now I could see Annie Lennox, George Michael, and a few members of Dire Straits wandering around inside the tent. The legendary Harry Belafonte was greeting someone with his hand outstretched and his soulful smile. And wasn't that Eric Clapton in the corner by the bar? Being down at the third level of an introduction—somebody's somebody's somebody—felt like a bottom for me. After the phone call from the A&R guy that one night a few weeks later, in our kitchen with a boning knife in hand, Dan vowed that he would damn well get me on a new label.

The deal was signed in mid-September 1988. We were to begin recording in December at famous Hit Factory on West 48th Street, just off Ninth Avenue, in New York. Clearmountain, David Mansfield, and I were to coproduce. David and I had reconnected when I moved back to New York and eventually started working and writing songs together in his studio. Most of our cowrites would be on this new album, and he would play lead guitar. I enlisted members of my Connecticut band to fill out the musicians. I would also film my first music video! This was *real*.

As the reality of what was about to happen sunk in, I realized I was going to have to be away from my kids—a lot—at least in the short term. My joy in at last being creative and getting a new start in the music business, along with my eagerness to reconstruct my image and be relevant again, weighed heavily against that possibility. Yet another split in me was beginning to form. I could feel the edges of my psychic skin pulling in opposite directions. I knew this feeling all too well. Sooner or later a tear would appear. I had little kids for God's sake. Yes, I had been away for a few weekends here and there over their lives, and yes, I had *thought* of leaving Dan more than a few times (with the kids) when I felt I was living his life not mine, or even more recently during my infatuation with my woman friend. But I could not bear the thought of being apart from my precious children for any length of time. Yet, you could say now, *I* could say, that music—no, rock 'n' roll—won out.

Very quickly, the pace of my life sped up exponentially. I was back and forth between the East Coast and Los Angeles for meetings. I commuted to New York to record nearly every day, staying at David's and various friends' apartments if our time in the studio went into the wee hours. It was chaotic, exhilarating, challenging, and a whole lot of fun. I had never had as enjoyable of a studio experience as I did with this album. I felt like I was finally making the record that I wanted to make *for me.* I knew what *I* wanted the tracks to sound like. No high voice vocals, no self-inflicted pressure of trying to fit into the musical milieu of the moment, no mentors or ego-inflated, self-serving music biz types breathing down my neck. Just two friends, Bob Clearmountain and David Mansfield, offering up their respective genius as producers and a number of great musicians playing what I thought were some of my best songs to date. I was older and wiser too. I could relax knowing I was in the best of hands. I could not have been happier.

Journal Entry—February 24, 1989

Jessie's 4th birthday—my little baby! No more. What child is this? Brilliant, joyous, funny—totally charismatic. And sensitive to boot. Not to mention obstinate, defiant, stubborn, and bull-headed. I'm grateful for her—what a teacher! Reid too! All of the above. More sensitive maybe or in a different way. How fortunate I am to have been given these kids. Jessie says, tonight as we are eating her cake, "Thanks for the celebration." A four-year-old! Cracked me up.

"Mommy, do you have to leave again?" The kids were only tolerating me being away most of the time now. They did not like it one bit.

"Just for a couple more days, my baby doll," I leaned down to kiss Jessie's forever-red, luscious puffy cheek. "Then I will be home, and I'm not going *anywhere* for two full weeks." To a four-year-old, it was like hearing the parents talk in a Charlie Brown cartoon, "Wha, wha, wha, wha, wha . . . " She only saw me in that moment with my bag packed and my coat on. I knew Jessie would cry when I left. Dan would tell me so.

Reid held my leaving in her own way. She acted out in school, stealing kids' lunches, refusing to take part in certain activities, and being "mean" to the others. Reid had always reacted outwardly to anything she could not understand or resolve inwardly.

As a baby, Reid could not tolerate loud noises or more than a few people in a room or bright lights. We had to navigate through any situation that might have included those things. As a toddler, she might bite another child in her playgroup. I had to watch her like a hawk. She would have a meltdown in a large supermarket if it had too much fluorescent lighting. We couldn't go to parades or firework displays for years. I had to call ahead to schoolmates' birthday parties to see if there was a clown involved. No go.

Reid was scarily smart. She didn't miss a trick. And she had an amazing sense of humor. She had natural rhythm and could sing on key from the time she was two. She was fluid and graceful and loved to dance. I thought maybe she held some kind of ancient wisdom or insight deep within her (like her Jesus vision) that at times lifted her into the other worlds and sometimes weighed her down like an old rusty anchor. Just the year past, at six, when I was in what was termed a "clinical" depression, Reid threatened to cut herself up into "tiny little pieces." I was horrified. The prominent child psychiatrist Dan and I brought her to in Greenwich, Connecticut, diagnosed her as "*ultra*-sensitive" and told us that she absorbed what others were feeling. Clearly, I was not helping her now. The first layer of my psychic skin was cracked and open. I could hear the door click, Jessie's cry, and Reid's silence echo behind me as I left.

The album was mixed and mastered in early April 1989 and set for release on July 25. Al Teller and his team seemed to be very pleased with the record. There was no hint of anything otherwise. I spent the month of May rehearsing the band, and we played a few little practice gigs in Connecticut and New York. The video was set to be shot in New York in June, with fiery, young, and upcoming filmmaker Victor Ginzburg. Dan was for all intents and purposes managing me now, and July was full of meetings with MCA in L.A. and New York.

There were photo shoots and prepublicity strategies.

I had reconnected the summer before with my friend, agent Bobby Brooks at CAA in Los Angeles. He now came on board and would be

Jessie and Reid with Mac in Weston, Connecticut, 1989. *Author's collection*

booking me for any touring. In August, after the release, I went on the road for a three-week promotion tour for my first single "Breakin' the Chain." Hartford, Philadelphia, Baltimore, Charlotte, and Cleveland were only a few of the cities. It was grueling. Early mornings through late evenings, every day, I did multiple on-air radio interviews—breakfasts, lunches, and dinners with radio DJs, music and program directors, and other "reporting" radio station notables. I drove, flew, bussed, and trained up and down the East Coast and into the South and Midwest. I drank a lot of coffee.

Each region had its own label promotion guy (yes, all men). With every stop, I felt more and more uncomfortable. *Am I just out of practice?* Only a couple of them seemed at all enthusiastic about me or my record. *Is my music really so bad?* I tried really hard to make a connection with these guys. It didn't take me too long to get the feeling that my efforts to get radio to play the single were going to go for naught. Then there was radio itself. Radio had its own modus operandi.

"I love the single!" the music director at the great WMMR in Philadelphia exclaimed. "But I can't add it. That's just the way of the world right now."

Milli Vanilli, New Kids on the Block, and Richard Marx were among the male artists and bands that were on the Top Forty charts at that time. Gloria Estefan, Paula Abdul, Janet Jackson, Madonna, and Cher were the top women. Not much room I suppose for a Les Paul–slinging, "is that a guy?" female rocker, who made one small splash a decade before. The "wining and dining" was perfunctory. They would take what they could get out of the record company and my promotional budget. I had gone into this with such high hopes. I was so proud of the album we made. *Cindy Bullens* (the eponymous album) was the culmination of my dreams at the time. But those high hopes were waning with every rejection.

Still, I worked hard, unable to let go easily. Even Al Teller encouraged me to keep on. He would talk to his promotion team. They would get on board, he assured me. But it became more and more evident as I pressed on that everyone other than Al Teller and a very few others at the MCA were not going to work the record.

"Breakin' the Chain" got added to a few straggling stations. The kids and I heard it on the car radio one day driving home from the Wilton Montessori School. We cranked it. But in short order, "Breakin' the Chain" was done.

In the meantime, Bobby Brooks booked me for two weeks as the opening act for Joe Cocker starting September 28 in Auburn, Michigan. Joe Cocker! Again, it had come full circle from that night with Dr. John at Cherokee Studios in 1974. Joe Cocker, whose mic was thrown to me as he was falling off the stage where I made up some nonsensical "blues" lyrics and sang them like I was on fire.

It was all crazy, and I jumped at the chance to tour with the legend. At least I was going to get the chance to perform again, really perform—in front of a large audience who loved rock 'n' roll. I never asked him, but maybe Al Teller knew that this would be my last hurrah, and he wanted me to go out in style.

"STOP THE SONG! STOP. THE. SONG!" I was screaming off mic at Tom Devino, my drummer, at the top of my lungs. He didn't hear me. He looked at me strangely not knowing what I was asking or why. We were in the middle of the long, pounding instrumental break of my hard rocking, R&B-ish anthem "Where Did I Hide My Heart?" at the Sunrise Musical Theater in Sunrise, Florida, at the end of our tour with Joe Cocker.

At one point after David Mansfield's blistering guitar solo, there was a break before I would come back in with the last chorus where the whole band would stop. I would jump up as high as I could and do a split in the air—the band would come in at the precise moment I landed back on the floor.

For years, I never wore underwear. Just nothing between me and my jeans. It was simply more comfortable for me, and I never thought a thing about it. This night, as on every recent performance night, I was wearing my coveted pair of tight, black, cotton skinny jeans. They were thin and shiny and from the audience they looked like leather. (I had given up wearing leather pants on stage. They were too hot and restrictive.) I had owned this pair of pants since my *Desire Wire* days, but since I also wore several other outfits on tour back then, and the pants still fit, I saw no reason not to drag them out again.

Mid-split, as my legs were as wide apart in the air as I could spread them, I felt the rip. But not just a rip— it was the total disintegration of the backside of my pants, from my butt all the way down to the back of my right knee. My naked ass was literally hanging out in the wind.

"STOP THE SONG!" I yelled again. Nothing. The cue to stop the song was me going back to my microphone—but of course my mic was center stage and up front. I could not go there! Luckily, I was standing relatively close to my backing vocalist Holly Sherwood, who was happily swaying with the beat, fingering the sampled horn parts on her keyboard, smiling away. I always moved back to give David the spotlight for his solo. I backed up even more.

"GIVE ME MY JACKET!" I screamed at her. During the second song each night, I would take off my jacket at some point and fling it to the back of the stage with a flair. It was all part of my performance. Holly hadn't yet noticed my shredded pant situation.

"What?!" She yelled back.

"GIVE ME MY JACKET!!" We were all still playing away. I looked at her sternly and pointed my head down toward my pants. By this time, I noticed Joe Cocker's crew all gathering at the side of the stage to witness the unfolding spectacle. Holly saw. Sporting her widest, most infectious, toothy smile, she danced out from behind her keyboard, picked up my hand-painted jean jacket, walked calmly over to me—with the beat—and wrapped the jacket around my waist. We were all still vamping.

"GET BEHIND ME," I yelled. Holly, who was 4'11", pressed up against my backside, holding the jacket in place between us. We sauntered together, in step—and still to the beat!—up to my microphone, like it was all planned, and I started singing.

Where did I hide my heart?
Now that I need it
I just can't find it, no
Where did I hide my heart?
Maybe tonight I will remember
With you holding me tight . . .

With its usual flourish, the song finally ended. "Thank you! Thank you!" I waved to the crowd. Only four songs in, we exited the stage—Holly hugging me tight from behind all the way to the dressing room.

Everything went downhill from there. Al Teller suddenly moved on from president of MCA Records to head of all Universal, leaving me without a champion anywhere in the company. Radio was not responding. The album, though getting some good reviews, was not selling. Bobby Brooks was feverishly scouring the upcoming tours for a possible opening slot for me. (I got a very short and very unpleasant stint opening for Jack Bruce in the Northeast.) There was a second single release, but of course, no promotion.

By Christmas it was all over. I was devastated. And I was exhausted. Maybe it was the times. Maybe it was the music. Maybe it was me. Or maybe it was just not meant to be. I had worked so hard. I had done absolutely everything MCA had asked, subjecting myself at times to side glances, put-downs, and belittling brush-offs, some subtle and some not so much.

For over a year, Dan had devoted much of his time and energy to me and this project. Moreover, I had subjected my two young children to this relentless quest of mine. And now with my fortieth birthday in

clear view, I knew that my ever-elusive dream of having a career in rock
'n' roll was finally, really, and truly, dead. I would never be the rock star
that I believed, on that day so long ago—while caught up in the white-hot
rain and riot in Lynn, Massachusetts—was my absolute destiny. What in
God's name would I do now?

Cindy publicity shot, NYC, 1989.
Photo by and courtesy of Carol Friedman

8

SEND ME AN ANGEL

Send me an angel
As fast as you can
I been runnin' down this dead-end street
And crawlin' back again
I know I'm in trouble
'Cause I can't see no light
Someone told me if I talk to you
You might help me out tonight

> *"Send Me an Angel" by Cindy Bullens*
> *©1990 Mommy's Geetar Music/BMI*

DON WAS CALLED ME. It was mid-February 1990. I was in Los Angeles once again, this time trying to figure out what I was going to do from now on about my so-called career after my failed MCA ordeal. My friend and former publicist Sarah McMullen had called me earlier that morning to ask if I had yet spoken to T Bone Burnett.

"No, I don't know anything about anything," I said, squinting my eyes in anticipation—of what, I didn't know.

"OK. I'm going to talk to Don Was, and I'll get back to you."

The upcoming Roy Orbison Tribute to Benefit the Homeless at the Universal Amphitheatre was being put together and produced by Roy's widow Barbara Orbison. Roy had died suddenly of a heart attack a couple of years before at the height of his comeback. I had never met him.

Barbara enlisted T Bone Burnett and Don Was to be the Tribute's music supervisors. T Bone, my good friend from the early L.A. days, had been instrumental in Roy's recent rise, having produced the 1988 Cinemax special *Roy Orbison & Friends: A Black & White Night*.

I met Sarah McMullen years before when she was Elton's publicist, and she was a gem. She had always treated me, a lowly backup singer at the time, with respect and kindness. When Connie Pappas from Elton's management (now Connie Hillman) became my manager in 1979, Sarah worked with me.

Somehow between Sarah, T Bone, and Bob Clearmountain, who was going to be mixing the live show, I got a spot in the "all-girl" band that was to perform Roy's hit "Pretty Woman" in the Tribute. The band consisted of Bonnie Raitt, k.d. lang, Emmylou Harris, Debbi Peterson of the Bangles, Tina Weymouth of Talking Heads, Lisa Coleman and Wendy Melvoin of Prince and Wendy & Lisa, Carla Azar on drums, and me.

Within an hour, the phone rang. "Is there a song you'd like to sing yourself for the Tribute?" Don Was asked. "It doesn't have to be a Roy Orbison song, just something that might tie in."

This whole thing just happened upon me. Being a part of the "Pretty Woman" band was amazing on its own, but this development was almost beyond belief!

"Yes, I think I have a song that might be good," I replied. "It's new."

"Bring me over a tape at 1:30 today," Don said without a shred of concern that that might not be possible on my end. It was 11:30 AM.

"Um. OK. I'll see you then." I didn't have a tape of the song. I hadn't made one yet. I had just written it at home in Connecticut a few weeks before.

I scrambled. I was staying at David Mansfield's in West Los Angeles. David was by now a highly successful, bi-coastal musician and film composer. He generously let me stay in his apartment on Little Santa Monica Boulevard whenever I was in L.A. and when he was back in New York. He had a rudimentary recording setup in his spartan, one-bedroom place, but I'd be damned if I could make it work. Even my little Walkman cassette recorder didn't seem to want to record without a warble at that moment.

Shit! The clock was ticking. If I was anything in this world, I was on time! I hurriedly threw down a guitar/vocal on the Walkman, warble and all. Just in case, I grabbed my guitar, threw it into the back seat of David's old, gray BMW 318i and headed over to Don's house.

"Come on in! Great to meet you. Would you like something to drink?" Don smiled and was pleasantly welcoming as I entered his quintessential California-style home. He graciously signaled for me to sit down. To my surprise, I was not being rushed in and then out.

"I'd love a glass of water, thank you," I replied, dry-mouthed. I sheepishly explained to him that I did indeed have a cassette of the song, but that I was not happy with the quality. I told him I could play it for him now, live, if he preferred. I was never a fan of presenting a song one-on-one. I hated auditioning when I was in acting school in New York. Please, just give me ten thousand sets of eyes and ears over two or three. Now it was one. There would be no buffer between me and judgment. But I had no choice, and I was ready.

"Get your guitar!" Don exclaimed, pointing his finger outside. "Play it for me!" The Southern California sunshine that flowed through the front windows into his living room seemed to brighten as I opened the case and pulled out my guitar. I sang.

> *And if I let go*
> *Tell me will I fall apart*
> *Can you change this heart*
> *Or have I gone too far*
> *And if I surrender*
> *Will I cry tonight*
> *You know I could die tonight*
> *But maybe I'll fly tonight*
> *Send me an angel . . .*

"That's a great song," said Don, nodding his head. "Really nice. I'd love it if you would perform it for the Tribute." I couldn't believe it. *What have I done to deserve this?* I didn't know. But I was now in the lineup.

I told Don that I'd like David Mansfield to come out and play dobro on the song with me. The two of us had done it live once, just before I left for Los Angeles at the Bottom Line in New York, where a show had been booked long before the record deal ended. It sounded so good! David was on everyone's A-list now, and he had worked with Dylan and several other artists already on the Tribute's roster. This made it even more appealing, I think, to Don Was. And for me, if there were any magic to be made, David would seal the deal.

Writing my song "Send Me an Angel" would turn out to be a turning point in my career and indeed in my life. I had been so dispirited over the past month or so. Crushed after the year and a half of promise with MCA leading up to the album release, only to have my hopes dashed once again. The failure of the *Cindy Bullens* album felt almost like a death to me at the time. And it was a death of sorts. I was grieving the end of a lifelong dream. For my entire professional career up to this point, I had written songs that were intended to be records—rock records. Even if the song was slow, or simple, it was going to have a beat and a band behind it.

One day right after New Year's, I sat down on the chair in my home studio in Weston, Connecticut. (Dan had finally convinced me that we had to sell Minute Man Hill to take advantage of the high real estate market. We built a house in the more rural town nearby.) I picked up my precious 1969 Martin D-35 that I had proudly bought new at Manny's Music store that year in New York and prayed. I prayed to be open. I prayed for something different. And it came—*Send Me an Angel.*

I vowed never again to write a song that I couldn't play *by myself* with either a guitar or a piano. I no longer wanted to be a slave to the record business. I just wanted to write and sing songs. I would now sing that song on this very special night.

It was Jessie's fifth birthday, February 24, 1990. This was the date of the Roy Orbison Tribute. I was tortured by the fact that I was not home in Connecticut with my birthday baby and Reid and Dan. That tear in my psychic skin had been ever widening over the months with each kiss goodbye on my children's cheeks. I knew my internal compulsion to do what I thought I was meant to do was affecting them. And not in a good way. My ever-present splits were swallowing me up, my kids were acting up, and none of us were happy. I hated myself for always leaving them. But here I was.

After my run-through of "Send Me an Angel" with David that afternoon, Emmylou Harris stopped me in the hallway backstage as I was walking into the green room. We had already been on stage together rehearsing "Pretty Woman" and had acknowledged each other but had not yet spoken.

"You must come to Nashville," she said in her sweet but serious, I mean it, sort of way. "Songwriters there would welcome you. Here's my number. Let me know when you're there."

I had already been corralled by Radney Foster and Bill Lloyd of Foster & Lloyd, the Nashville alt-Country duo on the Tribute roster that was making waves on the Country charts. They too, strongly suggested that I go to Nashville. They were both interested in cowriting songs with me. They gave me their phone numbers. I was intrigued, my interest piqued.

The last time I had been in Nashville was in December 1979 when I was touring to support my *Desire Wire* album. I played at the venerable rock club on Elliston Place, the Exit Inn. My memory of that trip was threefold: 1) My tour bus pulling up to the old Ryman Auditorium at around 6 AM, our bus driver excitedly pointing out the window and exclaiming loudly to whoever was awake (me) that this was the home of the Grand Ole Opry, 2) that it was a packed, sweaty, sold-out show, and 3) that I slipped and fell off the stage doing one of my plyometric stage moves. Nashville past for me, in a nutshell.

Later, backstage at the Universal Amphitheatre, I was waiting along with everyone else for the evening to begin. The rehearsals had been fantastic—Bob Dylan, Emmylou Harris, k.d. lang, Levon Helm, John Fogerty, David Crosby, B.B. King, John Lee Hooker, Chris Hillman, John Hiatt, Chris Isaak, Dwight Yoakam, and others were all dutifully doing their part to make sure the show went smoothly. This included my old friend Bonnie Raitt, who had just won Album of the Year for her *Nick of Time* album two nights before at the Grammy Awards. I got to watch, live and in person, having been invited to the show by another friend.

"*Nick of Time!*" declared Ella Fitzgerald. Everyone in the Shrine Auditorium erupted and jumped to their feet cheering as Bonnie, clearly shocked, slowly made her way to the stage. She accepted the Grammy from Ms. Fitzgerald and Natalie Cole, with Don Was, who produced the album, beside her. We were all still on our feet, still cheering. We all knew that finally, after years of being the underdog—on the road month after month, year after year—playing every small club and medium-sized venue she could find, making great records while battling her personal demons and the business of being a woman in a man's world, she got her due. I was so happy for her. Now here at the Universal Amphitheatre, two days later, she was among all these artists. And so was I. David Mansfield had flown in from New York, and we were set to play. This was the day! I kept pinching myself. I didn't exactly know how I got there.

"Is Cindy Bullens in here?" I was sitting backstage on the orange woven-fabric couch in the green room with David and Steven Soles, who had been brought on by T Bone to fill out the house band. Holly Sherwood, from my Westport band days, who happened to be in town, was standing over us. I had a phone call.

"Are you sitting down?" Dan's voice was on the other end of the line. I wasn't sure what was coming next. "We're here—in L.A. I flew out with the Reid and Jessie this morning to surprise you. We arrived a couple hours ago. I'm at Holly's sister's house dropping the kids for the evening. We'll pick them up after the show. I'll be on my way to the Amphitheatre in a few minutes." I spun around and looked at Holly. She gave me her biggest grin. I wanted to cry. Dan and I had a lot of personal issues, too many shortcomings on parenting to count, and a ton of trouble being married, but loving our children, and knowing that the other loved our children, was not one of them. I was infinitely grateful. It was Jessie's birthday, and I would indeed be able to be with my kids.

The Roy Orbison Tribute to Benefit the Homeless could not have gone any better. It was truly an extraordinary night for a very worthy cause— a singularly special one in my life. "Pretty Woman" performed by our all-woman band was a killer. Later in the show, David and I performed "Send Me an Angel" to perfection. We got a long, warm ovation. I was humbled by the outpouring from not only the audience, but also from other artists as well. Did I use the word "magic" earlier? If there was such a thing, it happened on this night.

After the Tribute, aglow from my moment in the sun, and a few days in L.A. celebrating Jessie's fifth birthday, I flew home to Connecticut for a couple of weeks. But I quickly found the need to get myself back to Los Angeles. Somewhere inside, I hoped there was still something there in L.A. for me. I figured that my recording artist days were most likely over, but I wasn't quite ready to throw in the entire towel.

Nashville was now on my mind, but I was unsure about going to a place with which I was so unfamiliar. The music business in L.A. hadn't exactly been kind to me, but at least I thought I knew how it worked. I still felt, at this point, that if I had any future opportunity at all in the business, it was there. I had friends. I knew people. I had connections. I had my deep recovery roots in L.A.

Being onstage that one night in February with all those musical icons and artists was a blessing and a curse. On one side, that experience showed me that I was still viable. I could still move an audience as a singer and a performer. In shedding my rock star skin that night, I *got it*. It wasn't so much about my stage swagger—how I moved my hips or curled my lips—it was about singing the song itself *for* itself. Maybe, just maybe, I too was becoming an artist.

"Cindy, come over here!" Rod Stewart waved me over and patted his hand on his knee for me to sit down on his lap. It must have been three in the morning. It was March 24, 1990—Elton John's birthday. Richard Perry, the illustrious record producer, had scooped up a small group of people from Elton's star-studded birthday gathering at the chic Le Dome restaurant, and here I was, somehow among them.

I had sung backing vocals on Rod's album *Atlantic Crossing* and a couple of other projects, way back in 1975. We had seen each other here and there over the years, mostly when I was with Elton, but we weren't exactly friends.

Richard Perry was, at the time, one of the top record producers in the business. He had produced Carly Simon's "You're So Vain," the Pointer Sisters, Barbra Streisand, Diana Ross, Ringo Starr, and Rod among many others. Back in 1978, Richard had wanted to be the first to produce me after seeing me perform a live showcase at the Starwood in Hollywood. I can remember talking on the phone with him as I sat on my bed in my Glen Green apartment under the Hollywood sign.

"I think you are the next big thing." I heard him say. The words pinged around in my brain like a pinball. The lights were going off, but the slope of this pinball machine, I knew, was steep. I wasn't sure I could play the game.

I had already recorded *Desire Wire* for Tony Defries and MainMan. The album was slated to be released on United Artists. The choice I had to make was agonizing: remake the entire album with Richard and wait another year for it to come out, not to mention deal with Tony Defries, or release it imminently as it was with MainMan and UA. After a week of sleepless nights, I passed on Richard Perry. I'll never know what might have been. Anyway, I was among those few at his home now.

Rod was calling me to the piano bench where he was sitting, snuggled next to Elton, who was playing oldies but goodies on Richard Perry's grand piano. Richard's living room was warm with soft white furnishings and wonderful splashes of modern art on the walls. It all felt very intimate. There were only perhaps a dozen people gathered around, looking on. I wasn't quite sure what to do as I looked at Rod waving me forward. I was standing, almost frozen, beside my trusted old friend Mike Hewitson, who had come with Elton. He gave me a silent nudge.

"Cindy, c'mon!" I slowly walked over to the piano and sat on Rod Stewart's lap. I was in Richard Perry's Hollywood Hills home, sitting on Rod Stewart's lap on the piano bench next to Elton John, who was playing the piano, singing old '60s hits in harmony with them both. No one was taking pictures. No one was asking for autographs. Everyone present was simply appreciating the rare and beautiful moment of us all casually singing along, with a couple of guys, in the very wee hours of the morning, celebrating a birthday. I may not have become the rock star I thought I would, but I have had many moments like this to cherish, both onstage and off.

Journal Entry—June 3, 1990

One step forward, two steps back about sums it up. I've been retreating into my negativity, slowly but surely. At least it seems that way. I can feel that I'm just barely keeping my head above water. The "almosts" were almost too hard to bear in this last month. Almost made a video with [film director] Michael Cimino, almost wrote a song with Elton, almost got (another) gig with Joe Cocker. None of these things did I initiate. They were all "offered." Why, then, didn't they happen? Who knows why.

I flew back and forth from Connecticut to Los Angeles for the next six months, working every connection I had, trying to find songwriting partners, music supervisors who might get my music on TV or in film, or a music publishing deal—something, anything, to keep my toe in music. David Mansfield and I were working on a new demo, knowing that it was extremely unlikely that I would get another label deal.

Thank God for David, I thought. He was helping to keep me moving. But I was just firing shot after shot in the dark that were going nowhere.

"Hello, Radney? This is Cindy Bullens. We met at . . . Yes. Yes. How are you? I'm planning on coming to Nashville. Are you going to be around?"

In October 1990, I took a leap of faith and called both Radney Foster and Bill Lloyd in Nashville. My longtime friend Doreen Ringer Ross from BMI Los Angeles hooked me up with Roger Sovine, the head of Nashville BMI, my music rights organization, and I scheduled a meeting with him. I booked a room at the Shoney's hotel near I-40 and Music Row, piled my bicycle and my guitar in the back of my Jeep Cherokee Sport, and drove south.

Roger Sovine took me around town and under his wing. He introduced me to the powers that be at BMI Nashville. He told them to pay attention to me. He drove me from studio to studio and hosted lunches with a couple of songwriting icons and a few young unknowns. He encouraged me to keep coming to town, assuring me that I could become a part of the new hot crop of songwriters that was starting to emerge. Country music was growing and changing.

"You're a good writer. You've already got a name. Try it. It might be a good fit." For some reason, I believed him.

That first week, I wrote with Radney Foster. I wrote with Bill Lloyd. They in turn each introduced me to other songwriters and musicians. Nobody cared that I was a rock 'n' roll "almost was." In fact, they were interested and impressed with what I had done in my career. Nobody cared that I didn't have a current hit on the Top Forty. They were happy to have some outsider energy and maybe some fresh ideas. Sure, everybody wanted one of their songs recorded by a big Country artist, but underneath that desire was an elemental understanding. This was a cowriting town. It was all about partnership and community, sharing, and the *love* of music— the opposite of L.A. They didn't care that I had written only a handful of songs with other people (I was, for the most part, a solo writer), or that I didn't know the first thing about writing lyrics for Country music (a very different approach). Those first exhilarating encounters compelled me to make new plans to go again.

Over the next few visits, I was passed from songwriter to songwriter, each one endorsing me to the next with admiration and appreciation— writer after writer, day after day. It was like a human chain roped around a demolished building salvaging broken bits of me from being forever lost. It felt so organic. I listened, I learned, I brought what I had to the experience. I felt alive.

Each songwriter had a slightly different way of approaching a new song. Some came in with a lyric or a guitar lick, and some just showed up. Some writers only wrote lyrics, and some were better at music and melody. I could do both, or I could fill in the spaces. I felt good when I arrived at a session with *something*. I love titles. I get inspired by a good song title. So, I'd at least try to think of one before meeting a new cowriter. But I could adjust and flow with whoever I was with, and I did that in those first few sessions.

The welcome mat was laid out for me at the back door of Music Row. I would never be a Country artist; that was the front door. But that wasn't why I was there. I was a songwriter now.

Nashville gave me something else as well—relief. Slowly, something deep within me shifted. I was no longer searching for that ever-elusive ring of a record deal or for anything that even hinted at recognition or stardom. I didn't have an image to project or protect. I just wanted to work.

Songwriting, cowriting songs, is work. It is a process. You schedule a writing session at a certain time and place. You show up. Somebody else is in the room with you and you write. Those somebodies change, sometimes every few hours, sometimes by the day. The rooms change—tiny eight- by ten-foot writing rooms in music publishing houses—two chairs and maybe a small upright piano. Hotel rooms, living rooms, garage studios, backyards, and bedrooms. You come up with a song or you don't, but you are writing. You are also laughing and talking and thinking and drinking lots of coffee. You are *creating*. I was a middle-distance runner for decades, and I never felt as tired as I did after a day of cowriting.

Nashville gave me more stability. I was more productive and left home less often. I was no longer looking for the *chance* to do something; I was doing it. That "new crop" of songwriters that Roger Sovine talked about included some incredibly talented people, of whom a good number became close friends. On top of all of that, I became a much better songwriter myself.

My L.A. hopes faded in the mists of memory, and over the next five years I enjoyed some success as a songwriter, and I had one hell of a good time. My little kid dream was dead, and at forty years old there was no chance of resurrection, but *I* wasn't dead yet. I had plenty more to give. Nashville not only became my second home—Nashville saved my musical soul.

9

BOXING WITH GOD

She's boxing with God
She's showing all her stuff
But it wasn't quite enough
But she's a fighter
She's boxing with God
And it's all in the plan
I'll never understand
But it don't matter

> "Boxing with God" by Cindy Bullens
> ©1997 Mommy's Geetar Music

"I AM NOT LEAVING THIS OFFICE until you tell me what is wrong with my child!" Our pediatrician stood motionless. Dan had taken our ten-year-old Jessie to see her once again after months of reassurances that what she had was just a lingering flu, or maybe a parasite. Every symptom or body ache had been explained away by this doctor since the summer. "Kids get the darndest things" was always what we walked away with. It was now just after Thanksgiving in November 1995.

Only a week earlier, I had taken Jessie in for the umpteenth time. The doctor ordered a blood test and called us with a diagnosis of anemia. That was it.

No, I knew in my gut it wasn't. This was *not* just anemia. She was now coughing; she had a fever; she was exhausted and had lost weight. This time Dan was not having any of it and demanded more be done.

Dan and I were separated now. We had moved to Portland, Maine, in the summer of 1991 on a whim, after spending the summer on the idyllic and sparsely inhabited island of North Haven, twelve miles off the coast, in Penobscot Bay. We had grown tired of the growing air and importance of status in Fairfield County, Connecticut, and realized in our time on the island that we wanted a more modest, relaxed, and unaffected place for our kids to grow up.

I had ancestral roots in Maine and had spent almost every summer of my life until adulthood in the house my grandparents built on Goose Rocks Beach in Kennebunkport. Dan loved Maine as well, and once we moved back east from California, we spent as much time there as we could in the summer and on winter school vacations.

Now, after moving out of our house in the spring of 1994, I was living in an apartment in Portland and Dan in an old farmhouse he renovated twelve miles up the road in the rural town of Cumberland.

Our pediatrician ordered another blood test for Jessie, and when the results came in finding a high white blood cell count, she immediately prescribed a chest X-ray. The next day, Jessie and I went to Maine Medical Center for her X-ray and then drove back up to Dan's in Cumberland to await the results. He was standing in the doorway as we walked up the stone path to the back door of his house.

"The doctor called. Jessie has to go right back to the hospital. She's going to be checked in," he said as he stood motionless in the frame of the door. There was a look of panic on Dan's face that only I could see. I knew he didn't want to say out loud what they thought it even *might* be. Parents, no matter where our imaginations may go when our kids get sick, never *really* imagine the worst. Maybe with ourselves, but not with our children. Any thought of existential illness is quickly dismissed along with the flash of horror that comes with it.

We packed a small bag for our younger daughter and headed back to the hospital.

Journal Entry—December 5, 1995, 11:55 PM

What happened!? What hole in the Universe did we just fall through? Every page before now seems filled with trivial nothingness. I am in Maine Medical Center with Jessie asleep in the bed beside me. We've just gone through nine hours of tests and examinations—every one making her predicament sound worse. She is very sick—with what they aren't sure, but it's either a massive infection or—dare I even utter it—cancer. I am numb. My mind races and then slams shut. My baby. Right now there is no way I can even connect with the possibility.

Jessie's lungs and stomach were filled with tumors. That's the way I heard it. The doctors used all sorts of technical words to describe what tests they did, what they found, what they thought, what they didn't yet know. I just knew that everything that went before now was irrelevant—dust. My baby was in pain and critically ill.

Journal Entry—December 7, 1995, 4:18 PM

Jessie has been poked, prodded, and even drilled into today. She had a bone marrow biopsy, which came back clear, but they have to operate tomorrow to remove tissue and lymph node from either her lung or stomach. She has been a trooper as usual! She is sleeping now. I sit here alone barely able to think. I couldn't sleep last night naturally. Reid and Dan just walked in.

A few days later we were told that it was definitively cancer—stage four Hodgkin's disease. The oncologists at the Maine Medical Center's Children's Cancer Program, where Jessie would be treated, were wonderful. Our two doctors, along with the social workers who were assigned to our family, the nurses, and everyone else who worked in pediatric oncology, became lifelines, not only literally for our child, but emotionally for us as well.

Dr. Gary Allegretta sat us down in a tiny glass enclave off the hospital visitation room after the final test results came in. Dan and I sat on the little leather bench across from him in anticipation of we didn't know what. The doctor sat across from us in a pale blue plastic chair.

"Hodgkin's disease is very treatable," he assured us. "There is a ninety-five percent cure rate." We took a breath, hanging on every word.

"But Hodgkin's is very rare in ten-year-olds. Only one-tenth of one percent of patients are ten and under."

I didn't at all like the "but," and both Dan and I knew what he wasn't saying: that it was already stage four, and there were great risks.

"Everybody reacts differently to cancer," he said. "Some things we just don't know."

Still, my mind was stuck on the 95 percent cure part. He told us what chemotherapy protocol Jessie would be doing—one in coordination with Dana-Farber Cancer Institute in Boston, St. Jude's Children's Hospital in Memphis, and a place in Seattle. I couldn't keep up. But we left the conversation feeling hopeful.

Jessie came home from the hospital a week before Christmas. She now had a "central line"—an implanted port and intravenous (IV) line that went all the way up to just inside her heart—where her chemo and medications would go. It had to be cleaned and tended to frequently. It scared the bejesus out of me.

She would start her chemo protocol after New Year's, but she had now been given prednisone to help her appetite. It made her puffy, and she would laugh about it.

Jessie knew she would lose her hair. And Jessie's hair was not just ordinary hair. It was a texture and color that would make old women stop on the street and exclaim that they had been trying "all their life" to find that color and "Oh! What I would give to have hair like that!" It was red and thick and wavy, and she never went unnoticed by anyone.

"Jessie, you should get a Mohawk before you lose all your hair," Reid stated emphatically at dinner one night.

"Yeah!" Jessie yelled out loud with her usual exuberance. "I could get a peace sign shaved into one side of my head and a yin-yang sign shaved into the other!"

Yin-yang? How did Jessie even know what a yin-yang sign was? I shook my head, not because I had any issue with the idea, but because it was yet another of the multitude of daily reminders that my kids were both extraordinary.

Reid was the visionary, the ultra-sensitive who couldn't bear to even touch the grass or crawl on the floor as a baby. She was an absolutely beautiful young girl with classic features and translucent skin, who saw and felt and took in everything around her, whether she knew it or not. She could see into people. Whatever emotional current was flowing around her, she was picking it up and absorbing the jolts. It was cellular for Reid. She had no buffer. And she suffered for it.

Jessie, on the other hand, was all buffer. She had the body of a football linebacker—born with noticeable bicep, calf, and butt muscles. (That last feature did not come from either Dan or me.) In the womb, she had been so active; there were several times when I thought she would kick her way straight out through the skin of my stomach. Dan and I would watch with astonishment as this alien child would push and press and roll in my pregnant belly. I just knew the baby was a boy. I was shocked when the doctor announced I had another girl.

Jessie took no guff from nobody. Not Reid, not teachers, not friends, not her father, and certainly not me. Whatever she had in her mind she was going to do, by God, she was going to do it. If you said no to her, you were in for one of several particular reactions. Harumph! was a common one. A literal, audible "Harumph!" would emerge from her lips as she sharply turned away from you, swinging her head, red hair flying, jaw up, eyes closed, folding her arms in contempt while sticking her muscular butt in your direction. It was very hard not to laugh out loud. And harder still to stay mad at her.

One time when she was five years old, Jessie vanished off the mountain at Sugarloaf Ski Resort, where we had rented a condo for the winter. My kids learned to ski early—Reid being the graceful, fluid, natural skier in the family, able to outski anyone around her by the time she was seven. Jessie just pointed her skis downhill and went.

One afternoon Jessie did not arrive home with Reid after a ski racing lesson. Reid didn't know where she had gone; she had just disappeared from class and was nowhere to be found. Dan and I quickly spread out to search, with Reid in tow. Sugarloaf is a good-sized mountain for New England—lots of slopes and trails surrounded by woods, and dangerous, rough terrain. Not to mention that it was the middle of winter in Maine.

She was not at the snack bar, not in the ski shop, and not in the medical shack. The sun goes down very early this far north in January—dusk was creeping in on us. Skiers were finishing their last runs. It was getting colder, and the wind was picking up. I was beside myself with images of broken limbs or her head bleeding, having fallen down some backcountry ravine, crying for help. We called the Ski Patrol. Every single person on patrol that afternoon plus volunteers were out frantically looking for this lone red-headed five-year-old girl, presumably lost in the wilderness. Dan and I were told to go home and wait for a call.

The phone rang.

"Hi, Cindy? It's Sunny. I just wanted to let you know that Jessie is here with me. We're having tea." It was our neighbor from Portland, who was also renting a condo on the mountain. "Jessie dropped in about an hour ago. Such a sweet surprise!"

Perhaps *we* shouldn't have been surprised that Jessie decided on her own to leave her lesson early without telling a soul. She thought it would be "nice" to stop and see Mrs. Silverman on her way home.

We called the Ski Patrol. They were extremely relieved of course, as were we. I went to fetch my wayward child, though Jessie got a good talking to, after I too had tea with Mrs. Silverman.

Another time when she was six, she locked herself in her room.

"Jessie, open the door." I remained calm knowing there was nowhere else she could go.

"No. Leave me alone."

"Jessie! Unlock the door!"

"No! You can't come in. This is *my* room."

Fair enough, I thought. *But it's dinner time.*

"What's the matter? Why don't you want to open the door?"

"I'm going to run away."

"What? Why?" I had visions of my own six-year-old excursions. Certainly, Dan and I as parents weren't *that* bad.

"I want to do what I want to do. And I don't want anybody telling me what I *have* to do."

"OK. What is it that you *have* to do, Jessie?"

"*Everything!* I have to do *everything* that you tell me to."

Oh. Hmmm. Well, she is pretty correct on that point.

"Open the door please and we can talk about it." I don't know why I didn't just say "fine" and leave her in her room. I was fairly certain that she would have come out eventually. But now it had become a true standoff between us; only she had the advantage of a locked door.

I don't give up easily. "Jessie. Come on. Dad and Reid are waiting for us downstairs. Please unlock the door."

She finally relented with an audible sigh of resignation, unlocked her door, and retreated to sit on her bed. The look of dejection was obvious. Jessie had a classic pout that was exacerbated by her full red lips. Nothing was subtle with Jessie.

I walked in and sat down on the bed beside her. She was holding a red bandana filled with odds and ends: a few trinkets, small stones and crystals, a Q-tip, a Band-Aid, her own tiny jackknife, three marbles, and a couple of Legos.

"Where would you go?" I asked, remembering my conversation at six with my own mother after running away and hiding in my neighbor's stack of tires.

"Just away. I can take care of myself," she said with an air of absolute confidence. I didn't doubt her. Jessie paused thoughtfully, then looked me straight in the eye and said, "Mom, I need a free world."

Wow. A free world. I invisibly shook my head. *Don't we all*, I thought.

"I hear you. I get it." I bit my tongue, so I would not go into any long diatribe about how the world wasn't free, and we couldn't always get what we wanted and blah, blah, blah. "I love you so much, my baby doll." I smiled and gave her a hug. "I'll try hard to let you be as free as possible. Now let's go eat. OK?"

Jessie got up and gently placed the bandana still full of stuff on her bookshelf beside her jar of cat's-eye marbles. I took her hand, and we went downstairs to dinner.

I was so struck by her statement "I want a free world" that after she and Reid went to bed, I went down into my basement studio and wrote that song. The song never left my studio, but I've carried her words with me everywhere since.

With all her free-thinking rebelliousness, Jessie was also thoughtful, kind, and caring. She had a reverence for all life, and everything in it. Whether "living" or not, to her it was of value. She would get very upset if, while making her bed, I would let one of her stuffed animals fall to the floor.

"It's alive!" she would yell. "It has feelings!"

"OK. Fine. I'm sorry." I wasn't always sensitive to her reality.

Rocks, too, were living beings. She collected them. Meaning that no matter what it looked like, what size it was, or where it came from, she picked it up. Rocks carried a lot of weight in our family (both literally and figuratively). I used to tease her that the world's axis was going to shift if she brought any more into the house.

Jessie also made no distinction between adult humans and child humans. There was respect for both, and leeway for neither if they strayed from her sense of the way the world should be. She commanded attention from everyone because she was formidable, not because she craved it or needed it.

She befriended and defended the less popular kids at school, making sure they felt included. Jessie absolutely hated any hint of injustice and would, without hesitation, tell you so.

She had an equal number of boy and girl friends and enjoyed playing with whatever gender-normative toys and games they liked. She preferred what were then termed "boys' clothes" and hated dresses. Of course, in our house we didn't differentiate boys' anything from girls' anything. Nuh-uh. Our kids had nearly free reign on what they wore and how they played. I often reflected on how I would be different if my own parents had been as open to me.

We made an appointment for Jessie with our good friend Michael at our favorite hair salon in Portland. Most everyone around us knew by now about Jessie's illness. Like in Connecticut, we had quickly immersed ourselves in the Portland community—the kids' school, local politics and causes, and, unlike in Westport, in LGBTQ organizations as well. Maine was a much better fit for our misfit family.

Jessie's Mohawk, I think, became another kind of baptism for her—a sacrosanct act. Perhaps the term "baptism of fire" applied here—an act of not just belief, but of defiance.

Jessie was never formally christened, and this bothered her deeply. There was a reason for that. After Reid's high christening in the Episcopal Church, at Dan's mother's insistence, there was no way I would do that again. I was infuriated when Dan and I had to answer questions from the priest in his office before they would allow us to go forward (mind you, Reid was all of nine months old):

"Have you put your faith in Jesus Christ as your Lord and Savior? If so, please answer, 'Yes I have.'"

"Is it your desire to turn from sin and know, trust, and obey Jesus? If so, answer, 'Yes, it is.'" And on from there. If we didn't answer "Yes," no christening. I hated it. I was not a fan of committing myself to any one belief or form of worship, and worse, being told that if I didn't believe in this one way, I would essentially go to hell. But we did it for Mabel, Dan's mother.

On from about the age of six, after Jessie found out that Reid had been christened in the church, she demanded, pushed, and pressed Dan and me to grant her the same right. I could not understand it. How did she even know what it meant? What meaning did it have for her? Why was she so adamant about it? We were not churchgoers (we tried a few times) or even devout believers. I had to look this up: *Christians get baptized because the Bible tells them to. Baptism symbolizes new life in Christ, and it commits them to Him. Being baptized is also a way to be "filled with the Holy Spirit and experience God's power."* I was befuddled by Jessie's insistence. And what was it with my kids and Jesus?

One weekend when Jessie was eight and Reid was eleven, I took the kids to visit Santi, my best friend from the American Academy of Dramatic Arts. She was living in the Berkshires in Western Massachusetts. Santi was Reid's godmother and Jessie knew that.

"I need to be christened," she stated emphatically to Santi one afternoon.

Santi, who was by then a psychotherapist, a yoga therapist, and spiritual healer of sorts, quickly jumped at the suggestion. "Oh, this will be fun!" She laughed, excited at the idea. Reid and I had no choice but to go along with whatever was about to transpire.

"Jessie, look around the house and grab anything that calls to you to include in the ceremony." Santi continued, "I'm going to get a few things, too. We'll go out into the woods. I know the perfect place." Santi was all into it. Jessie decided upon Santi's husband's black motorcycle helmet as her ceremonial object of choice. She put it on. There was no telling what "spiritual meaning" Chris's helmet had to Jessie. But obviously, it was none of my business. I didn't ask.

Later that afternoon, the spring sun was starting its slide down the sky behind us, and the air was crisp as we walked east across the long, wet, snow-patched field toward the edge of the trees. Once into the woods, we traipsed our way along a thin piney path, boots crunching on the remaining melting snow. The burbles of a nearby river became louder as we continued toward Santi's perfect place. Finally, we could see a small structure made from bent saplings with pine branches filling in the gaps —a tarp covered the top to keep it dry. This was Santi's perfect place, her sweat lodge. Outside of the structure there was a firepit and what Santi told us was a "sacred circle" surrounding it. Jessie was ecstatic.

"Are we going to have a fire?" she asked excitedly.

"Well of course!" Santi answered. "We can't have a sacred ceremony without a fire!" Santi had brought along a small satchel with a bundle of kindling and matches. I was carrying a picnic basket with sandwiches and Juicy Juice and a surprise stash of all things s'mores.

Dusk was upon us now, and it was getting dark. But almost as if scripted, the moon, full that night, was beginning to rise. "So, Jessie, we're going to perform a short ceremony, and then we'll eat, OK?" Santi explained. Reid and I were only observers at this point, though ready for instructions if we were so called upon.

Santi prepared her "sacred circle" first. Taking a pine branch, she swept around the firepit clearing away any winter debris. Then she carefully placed the kindling in the pit and lit the fire as darkness fell. There was a ring of large stones surrounding the firepit outside the circle. Reid and I each found a stone and sat down beside each other. Jessie stood beside Santi in the circle across from us on the other side of the fire. The brightening moonlight was now streaking through the trees and into the river, creating an almost surreal sight. Whatever ritual was performed, it was short and private between Santi and the be-helmeted Jessie. Reid and I watched silently as words and motions went back and forth between them. At the end, Santi uttered a short prayer out loud for us all to hear.

"We ask whatever God is Jessie's to protect her for all her life, and to hold a space for her in the Heavenly Realm." Amen.

Then we made s'mores.

My younger daughter, my wild child, was happy and seemed relieved. Whatever internal impetus for a baptism compelled her, I guess she felt she was now complete. We never heard a word more about a christening from that day on.

I watched along with Dan and Reid, hiding my trepidation, sadness, and fear, as Michael began shaving that beautiful, thick auburn hair from my baby's head. Michael was a true artist and a good friend. He had been cutting my, Dan's, Reid's, and Jessie's hair since we moved to Maine almost five years before. He always had a big smile on his face, no matter what was going on. Slowly, gently, and carefully, he moved the shaver up from the back of Jessie's neck on each side, creating equal strips of bare head with a swath of red mane in the middle. The other stylists, one by one, as they became free, gathered round as if to witness this compelling event.

Michael continued, creating two circles on either side of her head with his shaver, and then he skillfully created Jessie's desired peace sign on the right and the yin-yang sign on the left. He then cut and sculpted the Mohawk on the top, and it was so. The growing group of stylists and customers surrounding Jessie all cheered and clapped, hooted and hollered, with love and solidarity. Me too, holding back my tears.

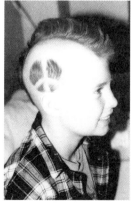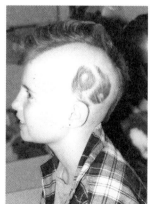

Jessie with her Mohawk. *Author's collection*

———————

Reid, Jessie, and I arrived in Key West, Florida, on February 19, 1996, and were excited to have the next six days ahead of us. The trip had been planned months before—just the three of us flying to Florida to hang in our old stomping grounds.

Jessie had just finished a round of chemotherapy in Portland and was waiting for another to begin. She had been feeling pretty good for the last couple of weeks, even going to school for a few days. She was thrilled that the doctors allowed her to come. And so was I.

When the kids were little, Dan and I owned a home in Key West where we spent much of the winter for several years in a row. We loved it. Life changed and we moved on, but still the lure of this town, the southernmost point in the United States, for me stayed put. I showed the kids their old Montessori school and our old house, the house that their father had fully renovated in Old Town, along with some other points of interest. I saved Flamingo Crossing, the best ice cream place in town, for last. They had not forgotten about it. We decided that we'd be there every single day.

This evening, we had just returned to the condo from renting a movie at Blockbuster. When we got out of the car, I took Jessie's hand—it was hot. *Oh, no*, I thought, trying not to panic inside. *Please, dear God . . .* Things can turn at any time when being treated for cancer, and it was no different in regard to my young child.

"Jessie, I need to take your temp. You're a little warm," I said calmly as we walked into our place. "Reidy, get the movie ready. We'll be out in a minute."

I had packed all the special things for Jessie that we did and might need for the trip. Her central line needed constant monitoring and cleaning. If there was an infection related to that because the line went directly into her heart, it could be fatal. My mind raced. I tried to stay focused. I found the thermometer, sat her down on the bed, and took her temperature. It was 102.5.

"You need to go to the ER," said Dr. Craig Hurwitz, one of Jessie's oncologists. He had informed me before we left Maine for this, our school vacation, that if Jessie got a fever over one hundred degrees to call him.

I hung up the phone. I tried to breathe. Dr. Hurwitz called ahead, and Jessie and I made our way over to Key West Community Hospital, leaving thirteen-year-old Reid locked in the condo with the movie, a pizza, and the phone number for the emergency room.

"Do NOT open the door for ANYBODY, do you hear me?" I commanded as I scanned the room one last time to make sure the phone was beside her, the video machine was working, and the pizza was on a plate. "*I* have a key! We'll be home as soon as we can."

For the next three nights, Jessie endured an IV drip of heavy antibiotics at the hospital. After the first night, we would arrive after Reid was in bed and stay in the ER into the wee hours. This way Jessie could at least try to enjoy a few daytime activities with her sister and me. It was noisy and chaotic. Drunks, victims of accidents and violence—we could hear them all coming and going, groaning, crying, and sometimes screaming. I was trying to stay calm—talking to Jessie, holding her, telling her everything would be all right. Here I was in the middle of the night with one brave little kid battling an infection or virus while being treated for cancer, and the other left alone and vulnerable in a rented condo in a town where we did not live. I was scared. We were all scared.

During the days we did what we could to have fun under the parameters that the doctors gave us, being mindful that Jessie wasn't feeling her best. She could not be in direct sunlight because of the chemotherapy, which made it challenging. But we did manage to have some fun, doing what activities we could, when we could.

On our fourth day at dusk, we went to a small beach off Old Town. The beach was empty, and the kids were playing quietly in the sand. I sat on a concrete block about ten feet away from them, watching intently. At one point, as I was looking at Jessie, I could suddenly see right through her, and I knew. I knew what I didn't ever, ever want to know. I knew what my mind wouldn't allow me to know. But there she was. And there she wasn't.

The next day would be Jessie's eleventh birthday, February 24, 1996. Her wish was to play miniature golf at Magic Carpet Mini Golf *at night*. That was all she wanted to do.

I had chartered an afternoon boat ride for us. Reid could snorkel, which she enjoyed, and Jessie could fish, which she loved. I was happy just to be with them both—period—now, in this moment. After a wonderful, bright, warm respite on the water, we ate a yummy meal on Duval Street complete with the requisite cupcake and candle on top for the birthday child. The air had turned cool and damp as darkness fell, and we decided to grab our jackets before heading over to Magic Carpet Mini Golf for Jessie's birthday wish.

After pulling our jackets out of the closet, I put my hand on Jessie's forehead. She was sitting on the end of the bed. Reid was standing by the door, ready to go. For several days, I had begged Jessie to consider playing miniature golf in the morning or afternoon on her birthday. She would have none of it.

"No! It's my birthday, and I want to play at night!" She was adamant.

I took my hand off her forehead. Before I said a word, Jessie burst into tears.

"I can't go. I *can't go*! I'm too tired." She started sobbing. "All I wanted was to play miniature golf *at night* on my birthday! And I can't!" Her brave veneer had cracked and was now crumbling down all around her. What this child had already gone through was more than most adults could bear. My heart was breaking.

"Oh, Jessie," I said softly. "I am so sorry. I am so very, very sorry." I put my arms around her and pulled her into me. "My baby doll, my sweet, sweet baby doll." Reid came in from the other room and put her arms around us both. We all held each other, crying. I held on for dear life to the now of her, terrified of what might be coming.

Jessie fishing in Key West,
February 23, 1996. *Author's collection*

We arrived back in Maine the day after Jessie's birthday and went straight to Maine Medical Center. After convincing us for the entire stay in Key West and for the first hours at Maine Med that Jessie most likely contracted a virus of some sort, Dr. Allegretta came into the small consultation room where Dan, Jessie, and I were all waiting. Jessie had just come back from yet another chest X-ray.

"Can I speak to you both alone?" I looked at Jessie. A feeling of dread fell over me, and I did not want to leave her in this room by herself.

"Go ahead, Mom. I'm fine." She spread her big lips apart showing her teeth in the way that she did, akin to a comic book smile, when she was proud of something she did.

I hated these shitty little consultation rooms. It seemed nothing good ever came out of being in one. My heart was racing. Dan and I sat in silence as the doctor described what they saw in the X-ray. The cancer was back, full-bore, now not only in her lungs, but also in her bones.

"The cancer seems to be extremely aggressive." Dr. Allegretta continued softly, "She's got a fifty-fifty chance now."

I lost it. "She CAN'T DIE!" I was beside myself. "She can't *die*! She's a good kid." As if being a good kid could stop her disease from killing her. "And what about Reid? What's going to happen to her if Jessie dies?" I couldn't hold back. I was shouting at the doctor. Dan sat completely still and uncharacteristically silent. I could see the terror in his eyes. He was the fixer—he could fix pretty much anything in any situation. He knew he was powerless over this.

"We'd like to see if Jessie's a candidate for a bone marrow transplant." Dr. Allegretta went on calmly. My outburst was not the first he'd heard, I am sure. "There's a hospital in Omaha, Nebraska, that specializes in pediatric stem cell transplants. There are steps we have to take first. We need to rid her body of the cancer before they'll do a transplant. That means high doses of chemotherapy. So that we will do here. I'd say you leave to go out to Nebraska in about a month."

Journal Entry—March 8, 1995, 12:10 AM

I had a hard time today. Jessie slept much of the day as I read the BMT [bone marrow transplant] *Newsletters that the social worker gave to me. I became more and more upset with each one. The magnitude of the situation gets bigger and bigger. I find it hard to cope with the prospect of anything but a complete and total recovery. But there is probably no way Jessie is going to come through this without major health problems as a result—assuming she survives. I am one of those parents who has to watch my child suffer. One of the ones I cry with on the news or in the movies. It's me this time. And Dan and Reid. My God. Jessie AND Reid! My babies. There really are no words to describe the horror, the terror. Please God, nothing else matters now. My child is in your hands.*

During the week that followed, Jessie underwent rounds of megachemo at the Maine Children's Cancer Program while staying at home at Dan's house with Reid. The treatments made her very sick. One day she was much worse—she was delirious; she had a fever. She was vomiting. She was in pain. She was admitted into the hospital. Dan and I took turns spending the night on the little cot beside her in her hospital room, the other staying with Reid.

On this morning, I woke up. Jessie was laying there quietly. It was March 21.

"Guess whose birthday it is?" I gently kissed her cheek.

"Happy Birthday, Mom." I sat down on the side of her bed, gently touching the ends of the wisps of the remaining Mohawk on the top of her head. "Mom, has the cancer gone to my brain?" She turned to me, searching my eyes for the truth.

"No, my baby doll. You were just a little disoriented from the fever." She had been hallucinating the day before.

"A *little!*" she said with her typical irreverence. I laughed. I allowed myself just for a split second to think that she was OK.

Dan came in. Jessie asked him if he would help her get up so she could brush her teeth. She could barely walk as he held her up, guiding her into the bathroom. My heart sank. I could barely hold back my tears. Dan helped her back to bed. Not a minute later, a nurse walked into the room, followed by a young female, who I presumed was a nursing student.

"Do you mind leaving the room?" the nurse asked casually. She sounded like it was routine to her. No emotion. No big deal. Nothing about my child or this experience registered as routine to me.

"What? Why?" I was incredulous. "What are you going to do?"

"We'll just give her a little sponge bath. I prefer to have a few moments of teaching without observation." I didn't like the sound of that one bit. But hospitals give off some assumption of authority. I had no energy left to fight her and neither did Dan.

I kissed Jessie on the cheek, told her I loved her, and turned to leave.

"Mom! Where are you going?" Jessie shouted, sitting up, surprised to see us leaving. Her eyes were wide, searching me. I went back and kissed her again, glaring at the nurse out of the side of my eye.

"I love you," I whispered again. "I'll be right back."

I never heard her voice again. Only moments after we left the room, she had a massive seizure and never regained consciousness. Later that day, after multiple scans and tests, as Jessie lay in the ICU, we were told by the neurologist that Jessie was "brain-dead."

On March 22, and into the wee hours of March 23, as Dan and I watched over our precious child hooked up to what looked like a thousand machines, Comet Hyakutake was above us and in view. It was now the brightest object in the sky. For some reason, this meant something to me. A blazing light, rare, and only once in this lifetime, at this moment, was streaking overhead.

After yet another consultation with doctors in a tiny room, where no good ever comes of anything, we knew we had to make the decision. There aren't any words in the dictionary to describe this "choice." Jessie was taken off life support around 2:00 AM.

She died at 7:46 AM on March 23 at Maine Medical Center in Portland as the sun, rising in spite, reached the rim of the tiny ICU window. Here comes another once in a lifetime blazing light.

Cindy and Jessie in 1996. *Photo by and courtesy of Reid Crewe*

10

SOMEWHERE BETWEEN HEAVEN AND EARTH

I curse the night I watched you slip away
Wouldn't have done no good to beg you to stay
You were here beside me and now you're gone
And I'm just trying hard to carry on
But there's no rhythm in the rain
There's no magic in the moon
There's no power in this pain
Till somewhere between heaven and earth
I can hold you again

> *"Somewhere Between Heaven and Earth" by Cindy*
> *Bullens*
> *©1997 Mommy's Geetar Music/BMI*

Journal Entry—April 8, 1996, 9:58 AM

16 days since Jessie died. I'm feeling horror, emptiness. I gasp for breath disbelieving. I cry. And I cry. My baby is dead. How could it have happened? So suddenly. So fast.

Dan and I, separated and on the verge of divorce before Jessie's diagnosis, came together now as much as we could for Reid, and for each other. Just nine days after Jessie's death, on April 2, Reid turned fourteen years old and was, like us, in disbelief and disarray.

We decided to retreat to the small cottage I had bought a couple of years before on North Haven. This island, twelve miles off the coast of Maine, felt like home to Jessie. And it was where I believed my own soul lived. We fell into the warm, embracing arms of this tiny community. Reid finished her eighth-grade school year here, and over the summer we all found some comfort in the gentle care of our island friends and from the exquisite beauty of this magical place.

Journal Entry—April 22, 1996

One foot in front of the other, I walk. I run. By the water—day and night—endlessly. I have to move.

Because I was unable to stay still, I traveled back to Portland on occasion to pick up any needed supplies and to have some crying time alone.

One day about four months after Jessie's death, I was alone in my apartment in Portland. I found myself aimlessly wandering from room to room unable to focus on any one thing. There was no point to my life, except for Reid. I had to live for her. Otherwise, there was nothing. No ambition. No future. Only a black hole of nothingness.

I see my guitar. I pick it up. It feels familiar. It's this tangible thing in my hands—wood and string. I started strumming. The sound and vibration of the strings formed in a few harmonious chords seeped under my skin and into my bloodstream. *There is some comfort here.* Suddenly a song emerged from my being, and I was horrified. I had just written a song about the death of my own child.

> *Hearts are broken and dreams are lost*
> *But I made a promise to love at any cost*
> *Little did I know the price was so high*
> *Losing forever in the blink of an eye*

"Somewhere Between Heaven and Earth" simply came through me. I heard myself singing the words, the melody predetermined. I was sobbing as I sang. I don't remember even writing down the lyrics, though I know I did. I just remember singing it over and over again, in spite of my cascading tears, as though if I sang it long enough, she would come to me.

> *If I could one more time*
> *Feel your hand in mine*
> *Hear your voice call my name*
> *And whisper sweet goodnight*

It was excruciating and energizing at the same time—horrifying because it was the *truth*. *My child is dead.* But barely perceptible, deep under the horror, I felt a tiny, tiny spark. This music was connecting me to life, and I somehow, in some way, was connecting to Jessie.

> *Somewhere between heaven and earth*
> *I will find you again*
> *And I will hold you again my baby*
> *Somewhere between heaven and earth*
> *I will see you again*

———————

Journal Entry—April 28, 1996, 10:10 AM

Sleepless night. My body hurts, of course my chest—my heart continues to bear the crush of a lost child. Oh my Jessie, my sweet joy—the earth has shifted on its axis from the loss of your 100 pounds of weight.

Days went by. Weeks went by. Inexplicably, the sun continued to rise. I heard and saw life and the world go on, but I could only feel the profound and unfathomable loss of my child. I could no longer walk down aisle seven at the supermarket where the Honey Nut Cheerios lived. It was just too painful. There were no errant pieces of clay scattered on the floor sticking to the bottom of my shoe. Bending down to pick up red cherry Tootsie Pop wrappers was no longer part of my day. Two kids were no longer bickering in the back seat of the car. There was always an empty seat at the table. The silence, as they say, was deafening.

People go on too. After a while, a bereaved parent becomes somewhat of a burden. There is little comfort one can offer, and people either know that or try to come up with something that they think will be helpful. They are good, kind, loving people. They desperately want to help. But they inevitably fail.

"God must have needed Jessie more up in Heaven."

"Thank God you had *two* children."

"There is always a reason for everything." I hated that one the most. What possible, plausible reason exists to have a child die from a horrible disease at eleven years old that would make me say, "Oh, of course! I get it now."

Listening to me was among the little that one could do. All I wanted to do was talk about my daughter. My greatest fear was that Jessie would be forgotten. I felt compelled to make sure that would never happen.

"I am *not* going to stay silent about Jessie's death!" I declared to Dan one morning. I didn't even know what I meant. But I knew that I could not pretend that she wasn't here. Or feign normalcy where absolutely none existed.

Sometime over the summer, as we discussed options for Reid's next year of school off island, she decided she wanted to attend Gould Academy, a boarding school in the mountains in Bethel, Maine. The school offered skiing as its primary sport, along with a good theater and arts program, all of which she loved. Not only that, I think she intuitively knew that it might be better for her not to be around her grieving parents every day and night. As hard as it was to let her go, I think I knew that, too. With that decision, Dan's and my strange new reality became even stranger, going from two kids underfoot to none.

My close friend Lane in New York City informed me of a studio co-op in her building on West 11th Street that was empty and for sale. It needed renovation, but she thought it could be a great investment. This was a "down" time in New York City real estate—a buyer's market.

Properties were going for much less than even a year before. She insisted that I come and look at it.

Why in the world would I want to own a place in New York City? I was living in Maine, had been "commuting" to Nashville, with an occasional trip to Los Angeles. New York was not, anymore, in any way, in my purview. But right then, so soon after Jessie's death, I was emotionally incapable of any deep rational thinking and perhaps going into the city was another excuse to get away from wherever I was.

I drove down to see it. I trusted Lane; she was a smart, savvy businesswoman and seemed to always know what she was talking about. Somewhere inside me it felt right, though I did not know why at the time. I bought it.

Three months after I wrote the song "Somewhere Between Heaven and Earth," in October 1996, I wrote another, "In Better Hands." Again, the song "emerged" from the caldera of my grieving heart.

> *I had a dream about a fire*
> *Burnin' out of control*
> *There was no way for me to stop it*
> *Till it burned through my soul*
> *There were a hundred people watchin'*
> *As the night raged on*
> *And every one of us stood helpless*
> *Through that bitter dawn*
> *But oh the sky is in your shoes tonight*
> *You can finally fly*
> *All I can do is trust that you're all right*
> *And I left you in better hands*

Also, that October, I moved out of my apartment in Portland and into Dan's house in Cumberland. We needed each other's support. We helped each other navigate the barren landscape that surrounded us now, littered with the shrapnel of our shattered souls. With Reid away at school, most of the time I had no obligations in Maine. I was free to come and go as I pleased.

The co-op in New York became 260 square feet of refuge in a city of eight million people. It was long and narrow with an eleven-foot ceiling, hardwood floors, an old nonworking brick fireplace, and two high windows facing south. It had a tiny kitchenette with a small stove, a mini-fridge, a bar-type sink, minimal counterspace, and an unusable bathroom that I had to immediately redo. The location was perfect—far enough off Sixth Avenue to avoid the traffic noise, but close to everything in Greenwich Village.

I could walk alone in the heart of my old stomping grounds of the Village where I dreamed long ago of finding my fame as an actor or musician, or down to Soho which had now become super-hip and fashionable with names of new shops that I could not pronounce. I would go across to the now bustling East Village for macrobiotic food, or down to Chinatown for dumplings. Somedays I would jog up and down the Hudson River Park and stop at Chelsea Piers, where I would watch the yachts and barges and tugs go by—the cacophony of humanity was everywhere in this city, and I never had to talk to a soul.

Here was a whole world of people going about their business as if nothing had ever happened (in my own life). Faces of despair *and* hope passing by me on the streets, sitting on the bus or the subway, each with a story. I may have been alone walking out my own hell, but I knew I was among the many there. Then I would turn the key on the lock of my very own little space on West 11th Street that I alone owned, and like on my island of North Haven, I felt safe.

Those highways and the 320 miles between Maine and New York became the breeding ground for my grieving muse. I was in motion for five and a half hours one way, alone. I had a direction in which to go, and a destination. I had cruise control.

After a few trips, when I would have to pull over somewhere and find a napkin or the back of an old receipt to write down an idea or a possible lyric line, I put my song notebook on the passenger seat beside me. Other than to write down the lyrics of the two new songs I had just written, I hadn't opened it. There was now a new split in me—creating was the life force within me, and that was good. *But* the ideas were all about my life after Jessie's death. I was always crying.

There was a technique to driving and crying, I discovered—my cry now was not just any cry—this was a different cry. The cry for Jessie was much deeper, rawer, and more visceral than any cry that I had ever experienced in my life. It was more like a guttural scream from a wounded animal. My insides wanted to come out. And once I started, I could not stop. This cry came from a place that did not exist within me before March 23, 1996. It wasn't easy to stay on the road when I erupted into one of these cries; I would have to stop. It took time to learn how to do it.

One day driving home to Maine from the city in January 1997, I thought of an old title in my notebook that I had written maybe ten years before. Sometime in 1995, prior to us knowing about Jessie's illness, I was going through old notebooks looking for ideas for cowriting in Nashville and had jotted this title down again. Now, as I was driving, I opened my notebook, leafed clumsily through the pages of past scribbles, to finally read the words "A Thousand Shades of Grey." I hadn't known what it meant when I wrote it down the first time, years before. But I did now. Between Greenwich, Connecticut, and Portland, Maine, this became the third song I wrote, and again, the music dictated itself without an instrument.

> *Oh the nights seems endless*
> *Like there never was a sun*
> *With a still pervading darkness*
> *Of all you left undone*
> *But there must be some great reward*
> *For lasting out each day*
> *For having to replace your love*
> *With a thousand shades of grey*
> *Oh can you hear me?*
> *If I shout out loud above the raging sea*
> *And oh will you know me?*
> *When winter finally frees my soul*
> *And let's you come for me*
> *And let's you come for me*

Now I had three songs. I decided to go to Nashville to record them. It would give me something productive to do—something I *knew how* to do. Like with buying the co-op in New York, there was no deep thinking involved in making this decision. My mind had no room for much thinking at all. That space was taken up by the now constant sorrow and anxiety and total devastation of my grief. The prior landscape of my mind was leveled. Those elements do not disappear quickly after the death of a child. They take up roots.

Starting with my longtime friend, guitarist George Marinelli, I reached out to several of my musician friends in Nashville. I loved and trusted George. Not to mention that he, in my mind, was one of the best guitar players on earth.

"Geohhge!" I shouted over the phone. I always said his name in my best Boston accent. It started way back when I met him with David Mansfield in the mid-'80s. They were both founding members of Bruce Hornsby and the Range. It just came out naturally one day and stuck.

"I have three songs I need to record. They are about Jessie. Will you do them with me? I need you. When are you available?"

I booked the tiny Dog Den Studio owned by engineer Bill McDermott and drove down to Nashville in March. The guys all knew why they were there. It came through their playing. Each musician took tender care of the songs and of me. They were saving me—giving me some form of purpose and keeping me going for just a bit longer. For me now, one day at a time, my recovery mantra, had taken on a whole new meaning.

After a few emotional days of recording, I went home with the rough mixes. These three songs became my constant companions—the sole disc loaded into my car CD player. Instead of me hearing the songs only when I played and sang them on my acoustic guitar, now I could listen in three dimensions, or maybe it was four—with that thump of Rick Lonow's bass drum and the crack of his snare, the low-end syncopation of David Santos's bass, the multilayered voices of Mark T. Jordan's B3 organ, and the electricity spewing out of George's guitar—all driving in, around and through my senses and soul at the same time. My good friends Mary Ann Kennedy and Bill Lloyd sang strong and soaring backing vocals. The music lifted me up and leveled me at the same time. Rock 'n' roll was my lifeblood one more time.

At Dan's house in Cumberland, my bedroom was the guest room upstairs with the now empty rooms of both my daughters. While Dan and I were together as one in our grief, and we were still married, he and I were still separated in some ways as a couple. When I was at home I hunkered down mostly in Jessie's room. Her simple pressed board computer desk became my workspace.

Nothing was changed in her room after her death. Nothing. The pale green and white patterned sheets, from which Jessie left for the hospital that day months before, remained on her bed, the blue and white patched quilt spread on top—her manhandled, motley teddy bear still propped up on her pillows. Every day I would lean down, put my face on her pillow to breathe in the fading, but ever-so-faint indescribable sweet smell of her, and kiss hello to the hollow air where she was supposed to be.

"Jessie. *Jessie!*" I'd call out her name when no one was home just to hear the sound of it. Every day I would peruse her toys, like a general surveying his troops—stuffed animals, handmade art objects, her rocks and toys, picking up one or the other, each with a memory or story attached, handling it as she would, gently and with great care. This included her bandanas and little "survival" kits with the Band-Aids and Q-tips and stones and marbles tucked or rolled up inside. Sometimes I smiled or laughed recalling a particular scenario. Many times, I cried. Each object held something of her. That was all I was looking for.

One day I found a piece of construction paper, rolled up tight, tucked under her bed and against the wall, as if she had hidden it. I opened it and gasped. It was her self-portrait in chalk and wax, made the year before when she was in fourth grade. It was astounding. She had drawn herself, red hair, full lips, blue eyes, on a piece of brown paper, *not* smiling. In fact, her look was one of sadness or uncertainty. There was a bird on top of her head, a horse on one side of her, and a wolf's head on the other. I stared at this curious piece of her for a long while, scanning every inch for clues to what I didn't know. Then I rolled it carefully back up and soon after took it to be framed. Jessie's room had become another refuge.

Jessie's self-portrait, 1993.
Author's collection

Up on North Haven, in the summer of 1997, I had agreed to resume performing my annual island summer concert that I'd started during our second summer there in 1991, after skipping the year before. Rehearsing alone with my guitar on the blue living room futon in my little house the day before the show, I found some unfinished lyrics I'd forgotten about in my notebook.

In November 1996, I flew to Paris. I had never been there, or to continental Europe for that matter. I was beginning to feel my anger at God for this unspeakable tragedy in my life. There was no panacea for this anger, so as always, I felt compelled to move, go, leave wherever I was. This time I needed to go somewhere I'd always wanted to go to but had never been.

Dan wasn't interested in going with me, so Santi happily came along for the trip. I loved Paris. It was everything I had heard or read about—dazzling, soulful, and magnificent. For four days Santi and I walked and walked and walked—up and down and across the arrondisse-ments in the grey November drizzle and rain, taking in everything we could—the Musée D'Orsay, the Louvre, a singing mass at Notre Dame, Sacré-Cœur Basilica; we rode to the top of the Eiffel Tower. We inhaled the smells at Le Marché aux Fleurs, consumed copious amounts of croissants and espresso in various cafés, lingered over the bridges on the Seine, and marveled at the beauty of this city, and . . . the lights.

Journal Entry—July 29, 1997

As I was leafing through my notebook looking for different songs, I came across some lyrics I wrote down after coming home from Paris. Suddenly I found myself furiously writing this song—the rhythm, the chords and melody just came flying out. And the rest of the lyrics. It's called "The Lights of Paris."

> *It was magnificent*
> *A city like I'd never seen*
> *The sense of history*
> *Was deeper than I could dream*
> *I walked down those tiny streets*
> *And those big beautiful boulevards*
> *With every step, I thought of you*
> *But I could not stop the pain in my heart*
> *Cause even the lights of Paris*
> *Can never shine as bright*
> *As the fire in your hair of red*
> *And the magic in your eyes*
> *And though I'll never forget it*
> *It's still you I'm dreaming of*
> *Cause even the lights of Paris*
> *Can't outshine your love*

Now I had four songs. I thought, *Oh! maybe I am going to keep writing songs.*

Soon after Jessie's death, while Dan, Reid, and I were huddled around each other on North Haven, singer and songwriter Beth Nielsen Chapman called me up from Nashville and told me I would write again.

"You will!" she told me gently, as a statement of fact. "You'll write beautiful songs." Beth had lost her young husband to cancer a few years earlier. I met her after Earnest died. She and I had a mutual friend in Bonnie Raitt, and we were getting to know each other whenever I was in Nashville. Beth was just about to release her album *Sand and Water*, the album she had written in her own grief.

"I'm going to send you an advance copy," she declared.

"OK. But I *cannot* imagine how I will write ever again!" I repeated.

The song "Sand and Water" from that album is still, I believe, one of the most beautiful songs ever written.

In the fall of 1997, I was in the grips of a deep depression. A dear friend could no longer bear the burden of my grief and told me so. It unhinged me. I broke. I felt as though I had no ground on which to stand. Everything I thought was real and true was no longer. Life had betrayed me. Reid was fourteen now and trying to find her way, something she could hold on to. I had her, but she didn't have me. I barely spoke for two months. I didn't go out of the house. I wanted to erase myself from the face of the earth.

One gray, blustery day I was sitting on the edge of my bed unable to move. I felt not despair, not anger, not loss. I felt nothing. I was void of anything.

"This is the moment," I muttered out loud to no one. "This is the moment you pull the trigger." I took a deep breath. I turned my head to look out the window. The red, yellow, and orange leaves were swirling wildly in the air, carried by the northeast wind up and down and around, each one not knowing where it would finally land. "I've got to believe in something. I have got to believe in *something*!"

I wrote "I Gotta Believe in Something" in New York a few days later.

"As Long as You Love (Scarlet Wings)" was then written in Dan's house on my grand piano that I bought with my Elton John tour money from Cherokee Studios in L.A. My father was diagnosed with Alzheimer's disease, and I wrote "Boxing with God." Each song, again, came from that sacred place in me. Now I had seven songs. Everything in me was pointing toward making an album. But how? I talked with Dan about it.

"You've got your own money." He reminded me. I had unexpectedly just around that time received a large check of back royalty payments from the *Grease* movie soundtrack. "You don't need a record deal or a label! Just go do it yourself."

Dan was right. The amount of money I got from *Grease,* along with the generous favors my friends were doing for this project, would just about cover the expenses of recording an album. I decided to go to Nashville again.

Rodney Crowell had helped produce Beth's album *Sand and Water.* I had met Rodney several times in Nashville and loved him from the start. He was kind and sensitive, along with being incredibly gifted in writing and producing music. I knew he knew that Jessie died. He and I had talked about it (he let *me* talk) for an hour one day, after bumping into each other walking around in Radnor Lake State Park, when I was in town for a brief visit a few months after. I called Beth and asked her if she thought he might be willing to help me now.

"Of course! You should absolutely call him! I'm so glad you've been writing. I told you you would! I'll tell him you're going to call." I hung up with Beth now knowing I didn't have a choice. I had to call Rodney Crowell.

I felt some kind of shift in me now. I didn't have a record deal. I had no thought of advancing my own career. Hell, I hadn't made a full original album since 1989! But this was not about me. *I will not stay silent about Jessie's death.* There was an inner force taking hold of things that I didn't seem to have any control over. That force became more powerful as time went on.

In mid-January 1998, I was in Rodney's Nashville living room playing songs for him.

"You have to do this album," he stated emphatically, leaning into me, looking me straight in the eye. "You have to. But *all* the songs must be about Jessie. All of them. You can't put any filler in there. That would ruin it. And you would regret it." My mind was reeling. Most full-length albums had at least ten songs on them. In the back of my mind, I thought that if I did record these new songs, I could stick a few old unrecorded songs of mine on the album to fill it out.

How in God's name am I supposed to write three more songs? I thought, though it felt like I was shouting back at Rodney. *Three more songs that come from that sacred place within me. They somehow come straight from my soul, unfiltered, pure, and raw. They are all moments in my grief. They come and I write. That's it. There's no thinking, no crafting. There is no way there are three more of those.**

"I'll produce a couple of the songs with you. I'll get the musicians and book the studio. You just show up. I'll call you." I left Rodney's in a daze. I got into my car and cried. I was being picked up and carried now. I didn't know where I was going to end up, but I was to discover that there were many more arms to lift me up ahead.

Cindy, Rodney Crowell, and Beth Nielsen Chapman, Nashville, 1998. *Author's collection.*

---

* Excerpted from Cid's one-person show *Somewhere Between: Not an Ordinary Life.*

11

I GOTTA BELIEVE
IN SOMETHING

I can't figure it out as if I ever could
Everything I planned didn't work out like I thought it
would
I've had my share of tragedy
I've felt the darkness cover me till I can't see
But I gotta believe in somethin'
I gotta believe in somethin'
That there's just plain nothin'
Don't sit right with me
I gotta hold on to somethin'
I gotta hold on to somethin'
Even if it's nothin'
But a little dream

> *"I Gotta Believe in Something" by Cindy Bullens*
> *©1999 Mommy's Geetar Music/BMI*

I'M DONE! THIS IS STUPID! What am I doing this for anyway? Forget it!
    I was in the bedroom that I had rented monthly from my friend Berni Nash in Green Hills after I started to come to Nashville on a regular basis in the early '90s. It had been the perfect landing spot for me when I came to town. I had a double bed, a small desk with my Apple Mac Classic II

computer, a separate phone line, and a dresser for my clothes. That was all I needed. I gave it up after Jessie's death but asked Berni if I could come back for this month of January 1998.

Berni was a songwriter now working in real estate and a perfect host and roommate. She was gone much of the day and many nights. We would cross paths at some part of the day, usually in the morning at the bathroom door, and catch up with each other. Berni was already at work this morning as I awoke contemplating what Rodney Crowell had said to me. *The album must be all about Jessie. No filler.*

> *Journal Entry—January 12, 1998, Nashville*
>
> *I'm still wandering around aimlessly knowing nothing will take away the pain. Nothing I do will replace the loss or the love of Jessie.*

The day was cold and dreary. I made myself a cup of coffee and slumped onto the soft fabric of the couch in the living room, staring out the bay window toward the backyard at the pouring winter rain. I could feel the cold and damp of the day permeating my thoughts, even as I sat there inside, warm and dry. Jessie had now been gone for a year and ten months. (I was always counting.) *What the fuck am I doing here?* The darkness was closing in on me once again. I questioned everything. My mind resembled a bug zapper—if I got hopeful about anything for the future, that hope was killed the second it flew too close to the light. There were no dreams left in me, even if life itself was hinting otherwise.

"Mom!" I jumped off the couch. It was Jessie's voice. I looked over my right shoulder as if she were right there. "Get on with it! Finish it!" She was yelling at me!

Almost immediately I felt like I had stuck my finger into a light socket. This tangible, physical shock ran all throughout my body. I was literally buzzing.

What was happening? I couldn't see her. There was no flash of light illuminating her face or vision of her floating in the air. But *she was there.* That *was* her voice!

I wrote the songs "Water on the Moon" and "Better Than I've Ever Been" that same day, with the whatever-that-feeling-of-electricity-was flowing through my veins.

The next morning, I decided to drive home to Maine. I had done what I came to do in Nashville. I had met with Rodney, and now I had written two of the three songs I needed. Plus, I had had some actual fun over the previous couple of weeks visiting with several of my good friends. I felt supported and loved, in spite of my own constant sorrow. But, as always, I couldn't stay still for very long. I had to keeping moving. And I was still buzzing from my visit from Jessie.

I was in my room gathering up my stuff when a baby cardinal started tapping at the window, fluttering in place. Cardinals had become my symbol for Jessie. Whenever I saw one, I said hello and felt her presence even more deeply. On the day of her death, several of my close friends, from Maine to Tennessee to Texas, independently reported having cardinals appear to them in various ways, and they knew that Jessie had passed.

My room was in the back of Berni's house, in the shadow of the house next door. It wasn't like this window was the most accessible. No light even came into the room. So why this little red bird was fluttering and tapping feverishly right here right now was puzzling to me. After what had happened the day before, I had to smile. This was crazy. Jessie? *Hello, my baby doll*, I thought.

A little while later, as I was packing up my Jeep in Berni's driveway, that *same* baby cardinal landed on the passenger side rearview mirror and watched me load up the car. It didn't move as I went in and out of the house. It just sat there the whole time. I couldn't help but smile again. *This is crazy!*

I finally got into the car. The little red bird flew off, and I started my drive North.

Early the next morning—as I was driving up I-95 through Baltimore, on a napkin I wrote:

> *Yesterday when I was leaving Tennessee*
> *The sweetest little redbird came to say goodbye to me*
> *And oh it made me smile for maybe it is true*
> *That the end of wishful thinking will lead me back to you*

And it's too early in the morning and too late in my life
To write another story—to hope for different lines
And I guess it's finally hit me what forever really means
That no amount of dreaming's gonna bring you back to me
And it's the end of wishful thinking

> *From "The End of Wishful Thinking" by Cindy Bullens*
> *©1998 Mommy's Geetar Music/BMI*

That's it. I now had all the songs.

Back in Maine, buoyed now by Rodney's response to the songs I played him, and by the fact that I knew I was going to indeed make an entire album, I was now on a mission. If I was going to make an album about Jessie, I wanted it to be the best, most special project I had ever done. This was all about my daughter, not about me. Rodney would coproduce "I Gotta Believe in Something" and "The Lights of Paris," so I would be back in Nashville soon. I picked up the phone and called some other friends—Bonnie Raitt, Bryan Adams, and producer Tony Berg.

For the next year and a half, I went from Maine to Nashville to Los Angeles to New York, with tapes, ADATS, assorted digital files—all forms of recorded materials from several different studios in my hands. I went anywhere and everywhere I could to get who and what I wanted for this album. I was paying for it out of my own pocket, friends were putting me up (and putting up with me), no one was looking over my shoulder, and I had no timetable. The fact was, I had no plan either. Whatever force had taken over was taking me with it. I was just following its lead.

I had sung on a couple of Bryan Adams tracks in the '80s produced by Bob Clearmountain. Bryan was a sweetheart, and I could hear his voice singing harmony with me on the song "Somewhere Between Heaven and Earth."

"Send me the tape," Bryan replied. "I'll get it done."

Tony Berg was a much sought-after record producer in Los Angeles, having produced Michael Penn, Edie Brickell, and Aimee Mann. I had met him in the early '90s when he was an A&R rep for Geffen Records, and we had become friends. Tony would agree to coproduce "As Long as You Love (Scarlet Wings)" and "Boxing with God." Bonnie, of course, I had known forever, and she and Tony both actually knew my kids. They did not hesitate to offer to help in whatever ways they could.

"Cin, of course, I will sing on something." I gave Bonnie a choice of several songs. She chose "I Gotta Believe in Something." Though I had recorded it with Rodney in Nashville, we recorded Bonnie's vocal at Tony's Zeitgeist Studios on one of my trips to L.A. Beth Nielsen Chapman, too, lent her voice to this song on a later trip to Nashville.

That very same trip to Los Angeles, at Zeitgeist, I was trying to put down the lead vocal on "As Long as You Love (Scarlet Wings)." This song was the hardest for me to write. Instead of the free-flowing, no-thinking form the other songs had taken coming out of me, this one I just could not stay with for very long. I would sit down at the piano, play the opening chords, sing the first verse, and mid-way through the chorus I'd collapse into that "different cry."

Time has a different meaning now
Since you found your scarlet wings
Forever seems like yesterday
But only angels know these things
I can hear your voice sometimes at night
And it echoes through the day
To those of us you left behind
I remember what you say
As long as you love
You will see me in the stars
As you look up at the stars
I will be there
As long as you love
I will whisper in your ear
Little whispers you will hear
As long as you love

    "As Long as You Love (Scarlet Wings)" by Cindy Bullens
    ©1998 Mommy's Geetar Music/BMI

Tony had produced a simple, spatial, gorgeously arranged track of the song. At Tony's suggestion, I played a hollow-sounding synth line of my original piano part, creating this otherworldly atmosphere. The great keyboard player from Tom Petty's band, Benmont Tench, played a haunting high single note toy piano part that dotted the track, sounding as if he was were a child poking at the keys, in a distant room. David Kemper's out-of-time percussion added a certain dimension of depth and weight, as did John Pierce's bass. All of that made it that much harder emotionally for me to sing.

Tony Berg, like Rodney Crowell, was sweet, smart, and caring. He patiently waited through each try for me to sing the chorus. I simply could not do it. I could not sing those words with any real emotion without breaking down. If I sang them without emotion, sure the notes were fine, but there was no truth in them.

"I don't know, Tony. I don't know if I'll ever be able to sing this song. Honestly, I don't. It's too much for me." I sighed, resigned to that fact.

"Why don't we take a break," Tony advised. "Let's do a rough mix. Take it home to Maine. You'll be out here again soon. We have more to do on 'Boxing with God' too. Don't worry, we will get it all done."

A week later, I was in my car running errands in Portland and popped in the disc of Tony's rough mixes. Listening, and once again crying, to "As Long as You Love," I suddenly had an epiphany—I was not *supposed* to be singing the chorus of this song. It was Jessie's part, singing to *me*—Reid should be singing it! My whole being felt light, like I was going to fly into the air right through my sunroof. I had been trying to figure out a way for Reid to be included on the album anyway. Here I was making an album with all these incredible people about her dead sister. All my attention was going into this. And yes, even though she was mostly away at school, in her mind I was going away all the time like always. She needed to be a part of it. She could always sing a backup vocal, but that didn't seem like enough to me. This was it. I knew she could do it—Reid had a beautiful voice. But more than that, this vocal would give her an actual significant part in the whole. It was late May, and Reid was home from school. I called her immediately.

"Reidy, I need to ask you something."

"OK," she replied skeptically. "What?"

"Would you be willing to sing on a song for my album? A duet with me. I really need you to do it. It's what Jessie is saying to me in the chorus. I need your sweet voice. Nobody else can do this. It's your part."

She paused for a minute. "Fine." It was as though I'd asked her if she wanted to go to PetSmart to pick up more dog food with me. It was a typical sixteen-year-old's response. But I took it.

I called Tony Berg and told him about my idea. He thought it was brilliant. Then I called my dear old friend Bob Ludwig, the multi-Grammy-winning mastering engineer who had started Gateway Mastering in Portland (originally with Dan) years before, and asked if he could set up a way for Reid to record in his studio.

Reid's performance was perfection—emotionally heart-wrenching and spot on. Listening to her voice, young and innocent and pure, playing the part of her deceased sister, singing to me from wherever and whatever Heaven is, made all the difference. Reid lifted the song into another realm. It was the right thing *and* the right thing to do.

Lucinda Williams and I had become friends over the years after we met in Austin at SXSW in 1990 when David Mansfield was sitting in on her set at the Broken Spoke. I had called her too and left a message. Somewhere along the way I asked my old friend from Rolling Thunder and the Alpha Band, Steven Soles, to come on board to coproduce "The End of Wishful Thinking." Now weeks after I left that message for Lucinda, out of the blue she called me on my cell phone in June when I was back in Los Angeles recording with Steven.

"Hi," she said in her lilting, musical voice. "I'm sorry it's taken me so long to get back to you. I've been so busy." I knew that. She had been on the road for months. "I'm in L.A. I'm doing the *Tonight Show* tomorrow."

"You're in L.A.?" I replied, my eyes opening wide. *This is not about me, ask her.*

"Listen, I'm in the studio with Soles in Santa Monica tomorrow. I have this song I would love for you to sing on. It's a song for the Jessie album I told you I was recording. Do you think there is any chance you could come over? I promise it won't take long."

"Yuh, I think I can actually," she replied to my utter surprise. "What's the address? I'll come over around noon."

I could not believe it. What were the chances that Lucinda Williams would be in L.A. at the same time as me, and I didn't even know it, when I was recording the song that I wanted *her* to sing on? Again, whatever that force was surrounding this project, it was working in a way I could never have planned or predicted myself.

That light socket energy that struck me in Nashville that rainy January day—the electrical charge that came right after Jessie's vocal push—stayed with me for six months. Now in June, after Lucinda's vocal was on tape, which was the very last of all the recording that needed to be done, it left—just as quickly as it had come.

Journal Entry—December 16, 1998

I'm done! It's finished! This album is all done! I'm in shock really. It's hard to believe. [Bob] Clearmountain mixed "Boxing with God" and "The End of Wishful Thinking" Monday. I fixed the intro on "A Thousand Shades of Grey," and Bob mixed that on Tuesday. I master with Bob Ludwig on Friday. After the holidays, I start putting the package together.

The artwork for the package of *Somewhere Between Heaven and Earth* came together as magically as the music and recording did. A friend recommended a New York photographer, Merri Cyr. She came to Maine, and we took the photos up on North Haven. My island friend and artist David Wilson, who also had an apartment in New York, painstakingly helped me design the entire elaborate CD package. Renowned North Haven artist Eric Hopkins did the lettering for the cover, for which I used a piece of Jessie's own clay artwork. Legendary rock 'n' roll writer, critic, editor, and author Dave Marsh, who had called me only weeks after Jessie's death with his own experience three years prior of losing his and Barbara Carr's daughter, Kristen Ann Carr, graciously wrote my liner notes. There were many others—musicians, engineers, friends, fans, and supporters—who took part in making this album my masterpiece. *Somewhere Between Heaven and Earth,* this great, mysterious, mystical puzzle was a completely collaborative effort. It was an entity all on its own.

Somewhere Between Heaven and Earth album cover.
Art by Jessie Bullens-Crewe, courtesy of Cidny Bullens

Journal Entry—February 1, 1999

How stress-making is it to have done the best work of your life (and spent nearly two years doing it) and be putting it out into the Universe for all to judge. Also the most deeply personal work— And of course, it's all about the most horrible thing to have ever happened.

I decided to press, sign, and sell a thousand copies for the new Jessie Bullens-Crewe Foundation that Dan and I formed after Jessie's death. Through the Foundation, I would give 100 percent of the proceeds to the Maine Children's Cancer Program. This was all I expected for the album. I had no other plans and nothing in my sights. My only wish for these songs was that they would be heard by the people who *needed* to hear them.

After pressing up one thousand CDs, I started to sell them by word of mouth. One day, I was sitting in the parking lot of the Portland post office going through my mail. I opened my first letter from a bereaved parent. The woman had lost her daughter, and someone had given her *Somewhere Between Heaven and Earth.*

"Your words and your music touched a place in me that nothing else has." I cried as I read her words. "I now know I am not alone. Thank you!" I knew in that moment that there was a purpose to this music that I could have never imagined.

———————

"I want to put out this record." It was Danny Goldberg on the phone. It was May 1999. Danny had just left Mercury Records as its chairman and CEO and was forming his own independent record label, Artemis Records. Danny Goldberg was by this time a true mogul in the music business. He had been the head of record companies, and he was the founder of Gold Mountain Entertainment where he managed Bonnie Raitt, Nirvana, and Sonic Youth among others—he had also been in public relations, and he'd been a record producer, a music journalist, and was becoming a noted author.

My old friend Jim Fouratt and I hooked up again after many years when I bought my co-op in New York. We had known each other for decades, in and out of the music business. Jim, who was one of the early leaders of the gay rights movement, also worked in the business in various roles, and had been at Mercury Records when Danny was there.

I had given a copy of my *Somewhere Between Heaven and Earth* CD to Jim soon after I finished the Limited Edition package for the Maine Children's Cancer Program. He gave it to Danny. The album then took a circuitous route through various other music business connections and ended up once again, after a few months, with Danny Goldberg. Danny called me. Thus started an incredible journey I could have never dreamed of.

———————

April 20, 1999. Columbine High School. Thirteen dead, twelve students and one teacher. In late August, a couple of weeks before *Somewhere*

Between Heaven and Earth was to be released by Danny Goldberg's new Artemis Records, I finally got up the nerve to send the CD to the few families of the victims for whom I had addresses. I had been wrestling for months as to whether it was the right thing to do. I was shocked and horrified like everyone else by this senseless tragedy. These parents were now bereaved. Yes, their circumstances were very different than mine—I could not imagine the experience of my child dying so violently—but we shared the same devastation and despair of losing a child. The bottom line was the same; they would never see their children again.

I felt compelled to connect with these parents, but I did not want to intrude. I certainly did not want to be a part of the crush of media surrounding them or one of those well-meaning folks who were trying so hard to comfort them. Yet I knew from the reactions of the growing number of grieving parents who had heard my songs that the songs might somehow be helpful to these families. The national release date for the album was September 7. It was important to me to get it to them before that. After much self-deliberation, I wrote a personal letter to each family, included the CD, stating what the music was about, a bit about me, and that I expected no response.

Ann Kechter emailed me less than a week later. Ann and Joe Kechter lost their sixteen-year-old son Matthew in the shooting. A few days later, I received an email from Tom Mauser. Tom and Linda Mauser's son Daniel was also killed that horrible day. I was humbled by their responses to my music. We began corresponding. Jessie's spirit, it appeared, was spreading far and wide. Maybe my original solitary wish for these songs—that they would be heard by the people who *needed* to hear them—was coming true.

As part of the album's release, I would be touring across the country in the fall, coast to coast. It was Danny Goldberg who suggested that I might stop in Littleton, Colorado. I regarded Danny as a sensitive and deep soul, and he and I talked a lot about grief. His mother had passed just before he signed me. He understood my concerns about promoting *Somewhere Between Heaven and Earth* as a commercial release. I wanted, no, demanded, that it be done with the utmost integrity.

"I'd rather sell this album out of the back seat of my car than have it be compromised in any way!" I stated firmly in his office in New York in our first ever face-to-face meeting about his new label, Artemis.

"I get it," he replied kindly. "I promise we will do everything we can to ensure the album gets out into the world in a way that serves you and the music in the best way possible." I believed him.

"OK," I said, taking in a deep breath. "Let's do it." Certainly, because the album would be released worldwide with all the might of a real label, and with Danny's belief in the music behind it, many more people would get the chance to hear it. I could not do that myself. Danny would license the CD as it was. *Somewhere Between Heaven and Earth* would be Artemis Records' first signing.

"Maybe do a concert in Littleton," Danny suggested one day as we were meeting in New York about the tour. I balked; I wasn't sure. Even though Ann and Tom and I were continuing our correspondence, I didn't want to insert myself into their new reality.

Finally, I acquiesced. "I'll reach out and see what they think."

I waited until I got back to Maine before contacting Ann and Tom about the possibility of going to Littleton. Sitting at Jessie's desk, which always made me feel more comfortable with anything that had to do with her, I sent an email.

———————

My cell phone rang just as we were turning onto the street in Littleton, Colorado, where Ann and Joe Kechter lived. It was late afternoon on November 7, 1999.

"I wish I were there to hold your hand," my mother's voice cracked as she continued to wish me well with the meeting I was about to have. I thought it was a little strange that my mother, who was so fearful and distant in the last hours of Jessie's life, would now make such an effort to offer me emotional support. But I was touched and grateful for her call.

Joanne Berman, my longtime good friend and now tour manager, pulled into the driveway as I read off the street number. The house was simple and attractive, in a development I thought of as western urban sprawl. I took a deep breath and got out of the car. I had no idea what to expect and what was expected of me—I only knew I had to show up.

Ann opened the door and immediately threw her arms around me. We held each other for a long time. I knew we were both wishing we didn't have a reason to be brought together.

"It's so good to finally meet you," she said when we finally let go of each other, smiling and sad at the same time.

We discussed a good time for Joanne and my drummer, Ginger, to come back for dinner. I waved to Joanne and told her to come back at six o'clock.

I followed Ann into the kitchen area, wondering if I would live up to their expectations of me. I quickly reminded myself that all I had to do was "be there" for them and listen.

Joe Kechter emerged from the adjoining den with a small smile and his hand extended. Their thirteen-year-old son Adam was lurking behind him, hesitant, and perhaps leery of who this person was, the-singer-who-made-a-record-about-the-death-of-her-daughter-that-had-affected-his-parents-so-deeply. I hugged Joe, bypassing his outstretched hand. He hugged me back. I shook Adam's hand.

We stood in the kitchen and briefly exchanged small talk about my tour and the drive from Oregon to Denver.

"Oh!" Ann exclaimed. "It's getting dark. I really want to show you the high school. We should hurry so we have time to walk around and see everything." She turned to go and suddenly stopped, turned back around, and looked at me as though she realized that I maybe I wouldn't want to see the place where a recent, horrifying American tragedy had occurred.

"Let's go," I said.

Ann was an attractive woman with intense, black eyes that nearly matched the color of her hair. As we drove, she spoke with a forcefulness and an energy that I knew well. It was as if words were our link to our missing children—we were compelled to speak of them, to tell their stories. As we reached the top of the rise in the road, Ann pointed to a familiar structure in the distance.

"There it is," she said in a flat tone. I could feel the blood pulse in my temples and my heart start to race. "There it is," she stated again, her voice rising now. "I hate that place."

We pulled into the Columbine High School parking lot and sat for a moment, silent. As soon as we got out of the car, Ann immediately started describing the events of that day. We stood in the spot in the parking lot where the first two students were gunned down. She pointed up to the library on the second floor where most of the students were killed. The windows were covered. We looked in the windows of the "common area" and walked around to the back of the school where more shootings occurred. I felt like I was holding my breath the entire time.

The sun was now falling behind the foothills of the Rocky Mountains. As we walked up the hill behind the school, thirteen crosses appeared white and stark against the fading sky—a memorial of those who fell that April day before.

There were no words. This was now a sacred place. Now and forever to be known as where the Columbine High School massacre happened. I pulled up the collar of my jacket, as the cold wind picked up, but I knew I may never shake the chill.

> *Journal Entry—November 16, 1999*
>
> *Last Monday (November 8) we played a private concert for all of the Columbine families. Believe me, it was the most profound concert I have ever done! Very powerful! I doubt if I will ever do a harder one. These people are brave and wonderful folks. Their hospitality and graciousness, their openness and honesty were extremely moving. They were so grateful that we came to do this—I can't imagine now not doing it! I felt a bond with each and every person there. There was a sadness, but also the knowledge that we will go on without these precious children—that there is a strength in knowing that we are not alone. I will never forget my visit in Littleton, Colorado.*

Joanne and Ginger Cote, who had been playing drums with me in Maine for years, accompanied me in my Chevy Suburban around the country that fall and beyond. We performed in every kind of venue from Mountain Stage and E-Town to small clubs and corporate meeting rooms. We performed on *The Today Show, CBS This Morning,* Conan O'Brien, Mitch Albom's radio show in Detroit (he was a longtime fan). We played sold-out shows and gigs that weren't promoted at all—annual conferences like the National Organization for Women and AAA Radio. We visited many mom-and-pop record stores in small towns and scores of radio stations from coast to coast. Bonnie Raitt came on stage with us in San Francisco. Emmylou Harris, Lucinda Williams, and Julie Miller came to see a show in Nashville. I eventually opened for Emmylou for a few gigs in California.

Most of the time I was in disbelief. How did this happen? I wrote some songs during the first two years after losing Jessie, only to express my own grief. When I realized the songs may not be just for me, I asked for help. Lots of friends and many, many strangers who became "Jessie-ized" came to my rescue. *They* all made this happen. And before I knew it, I was back doing what I loved, playing music, this time with a higher purpose.

I was being taken on a journey, not only around the country, the continent, and eventually the world, but more than that—into thousands of people's hearts and minds and souls.

The story of one eleven-year-old red-headed spitfire and the profound effect of her loss spread across the globe through no effort of my own. *Somewhere Between Heaven and Earth* became the biggest album of my life, and my legacy. I was not silent about the death of my daughter. Jessie herself made sure of that.

Cindy and Bonnie Raitt, San Francisco, 1999.
Photo by and courtesy of Joanne Berman

Jessie and Mom, January 1996. *Photo by and courtesy of Reid Crewe*

12

UNBOUND

Ten million miles 'cross the Universe
Dragged myself around
Searchin' for the end of thirst
Before the weight of sorrow drags me down
I saw a river in the distance
Vanished in the sand
Right there right then I knew
That where I am is where I'll take my stand
Driven by one soul desire
Follow where it leads
Break free let me be unbound
To stand just once on holy ground
Someday, somehow
Oh to be unbound

> *"Unbound" by Cindy Bullens, Wendy Waldman &*
> *Deborah Holland—The Refugees*
> *©2007 Mommy's Geetar Music/BMI, Red Hairing*
> *Music/BMI, Wendy Waldman Songs/ASCAP*

"DAN! WAKE UP!" Dan was asleep down in his bedroom. I stood over him, tugging his shoulder. "I need to go to the emergency room. I think I'm having a heart attack." It was 1:30 AM.

No one wants to be in a city ER in the middle of the night anywhere in the world. I had been there, done that with everyone else in the family.

This was the last place I wanted to be. I hated going to the doctor. Anything that had to do with anyone possibly seeing my naked body, I avoided. But tonight, I felt I had no choice.

Right before the charitable release of *Somewhere Between Heaven and Earth* in February 1999, I started having anxiety attacks. I didn't know it at the time. I just knew there were times when I could not easily catch my breath, and it scared me. I was a runner and never had an issue when I was out jogging, so I figured whatever it was wasn't that serious. But one night in my bed at Dan's house in Cumberland, I felt like I literally could not breathe at all. It had been building all day. My breaths were progressively shallower and weaker. Now I was sitting up in bed trying to breathe deeply, but the air just refused to fill my lungs. It was as if I were being buried alive, shovelful by shovelful, except there was no dirt piling up over me. I prayed. I tried to meditate. But nothing worked. I felt a heavy pressure in my chest, and I started to panic. *Shit!*

"Which hospital do you want to go to?" Dan asked as we got close to the city.

"Not Maine Med," I stated emphatically in between labored breaths. The painful images of the ICU there, those little waiting rooms where bad news was delivered, and even the particular pastel colors of the hallways were more than I could take at that moment. That meant Mercy Hospital.

After checking in, Dan, sleep-deprived but still looking for all the world like he just came from a shopping spree at Ralph Lauren, dutifully took a seat in the chair against the wall in the small incandescent cubicle. I sat on the side of the gurney, donned the requisite johnny, and laid down, feeling at once relieved and more anxious. A thin green curtain was the only thing separating us from the clinging and clanging of machines being rolled on the linoleum floor, the banter of the medical staff, and an occasional groan from a patient. The nurse came in and out taking my vitals and doing all that nurses do.

This nurse was pleasant enough. A petite, pretty blonde woman with sharp blue eyes, soft-spoken but with the definite air of a take-charge and take-no-shit kind of person.

"Your vitals are fine," she said in an almost humoring kind of way. She had this little smile on her face. I wasn't sure if I liked it or not. "*I* think you're having an anxiety attack. But the doctor will be in soon to see you."

The doctor came in shortly after and confirmed the nurse's thought. He wanted me to take a sedative, but I explained to him that I was in recovery and could not do such a thing.

"So am I," he retorted. "Fourteen years." He had the nurse give me the pill, and I took it.

In a short time, I had indeed calmed down a bit and was lying quietly on the gurney. The nurse came back in, took my vitals again, and then stood down at my feet.

"I'm not supposed to do this here," she said in a slightly hushed voice, moving a little closer to me. "But I do energy work outside of the hospital. Do you mind if I share with you some information I received?" I pushed myself up onto my elbows and looked at her quizzically.

"Information?" I looked at Dan, who was still sitting silently in the plastic hospital chair. Now, he appeared totally exhausted. I was not even sure he heard what she said.

"Um, sure," I said hesitantly, looking back at her.

"The color red is all around you. I'm not sure what it means, but did you lose someone?"

I was stunned. "My daughter. I lost my daughter almost three years ago," I blurted out—the vision of Jessie's striking auburn hair, all the cardinals, and the scarlet wings that I now deemed as hers were all swirling in my head. I didn't seem to care whether or not this was making any sense.

Even Dan, now alert, was leaning in to hear.

"Well, she's here. And she is telling you to *get a life*! That's what I'm hearing. She wants you to get a life. She wants you to be happy."

I sat up. *What? Wait a minute! Here I am in the emergency room at two-thirty in the morning, laying on a hard, Naugahyde hospital gurney with a wrinkled pale green johnny on, having an anxiety attack, and some nurse walks in and tells me that my dead daughter wants me to "get a life"?!*

"But she is not so sure about this separation between you two." The hair stood up on the back of my neck. I had just told Dan the day before that in the next year, with Reid soon graduating high school, I was going to move out. How did she know? Then she said something about Jessie being very happy where she was and that she needed to be there to do her work. I was stuck back at the separation bit. Dan started crying.

Journal Entry—February 16, 1999

This angel of a nurse basically channeled Jessie. I thought, I have been sent here tonight to meet this woman.

"How can I get hold of you? Can I book a session? How do you work?" I wanted to know more. I needed to know more. Here, standing right in front of me, seemed to be someone who could communicate with the other side. I did not swallow everything that was what I called "woo-woo." But something in me believed this nurse.

"I can't give you my number while I'm working," she said kindly. "But I can give you someone else who practices energy work here in Portland." She started to write down a number on a piece of paper.

"I don't want anybody else," I stated firmly, wide awake and without anxiety. "I want you." She cocked her head slightly and looked at me with one of the kindest expressions I have ever received. A genuine softness emanated from her eyes and smile. She gave me the other person's phone number and turned to leave.

"At least tell me your name," I said, straining to read her nametag and sitting all the way up, throwing my legs off the table, as if I might run after her given the chance.

"Maryann Russell." She smiled again and left to make the rest of her rounds.

I went home with a prescription to take when I felt an attack coming on. But I left the hospital with more than that. I couldn't stop thinking about Maryann Russell.

———————

Jessie seemed to be the prow of my ship, though I felt her come, and I felt her go. When she was around, my life was altered significantly, like she was single-handedly charting my course—usually through swirling currents and rough seas. When I was in a somewhat more stable place, she seemed to take leave of controlling the compass and let me drift in the calm waters. Of course, this is all my perception of the way things were in the years after her death, but I'm sticking with it.

Maryann Russell and I were together for five and a half years. She gave me the great gift of her love when I desperately needed something other than my grief and my sorrow. She understood me on many levels. Our relationship was intimate, sexual, and, when I was able to open enough, spiritual.

Maryann was perceived as a lesbian while with me (she wasn't), and it didn't bother her one bit. It bothered me! (In my mind I wasn't a woman.) She didn't question my feeling of being a man inside. She felt it.

"I fell in love with the essence of you," she would tell me. "Not your gender." And I loved her with all that I had working in my broken heart.

Dan and I finalized our divorce in 2001. I had moved on to the relationship with Maryann, yet it was still emotionally hard for me to let go. For twenty-seven years, Dan Crewe had been a fixture in my life. He was threaded throughout my entire adulthood, starting when I was just twenty-four years old. However much we both struggled within our twenty-two-year marriage, however flawed our love for each other may have been, together we created two beautiful human beings, and a range of experiences that helped me grow into who I have become now. We got sober together. We had two children together. Together we grieved the death of one of them. If you believe in fate, in destiny, in past lives, something brought Dan and I together and kept us together despite our differences, our issues, *my* issues. We seemed inextricably tied to one another. But the marriage now was finally over.

Journal Entry—February 26, 2006

This is not good! So what's going on? I can't do anything without a left hand. No guitar, no piano. What is the message here? What is my part in this? What is the Universe trying to tell me? Whatever it is, you have my full attention.

A couple of months after Maryann and I broke up, on Jessie's birthday, February 24, 2006, I badly broke my left pinky finger. I had stupidly wrapped the better part of my Goldendoodle's leash around my left hand to keep him close. Unbeknownst to me, the holding area door into the neighborhood dog park was not latched properly. A large German Shepard charged through the door. Jack bolted forward just as I was taking off his leash, violently twisting my hand. Snap! I heard and felt my finger break. It was now lying across my palm, unhinged.

I had surgery on my finger, pins put in and all. I had a hard cast covering my whole hand and arm up to my elbow. I would be six weeks in the cast, and who knows how long after that in physical therapy. I didn't know if I would ever be able to play guitar again.

For the next two months, I sat alone in my beautiful home in Franklin, Tennessee, surrounded by vivid green hills, lush woods, farmland, and horse country, wondering what in the hell I was going to do now? My relationship with Maryann was over. I was emotionally exhausted and physically compromised. I felt extremely isolated. Plus, I wasn't making any money. What if I really could never play guitar again? Was this it now? Finally? My newfound life in music felled by a dog leash?

Journal Entry—April 16, 2006, Easter Sunday

A small cardinal flew to and perched on the fence right in front of the kitchen window as I was making myself a cup of coffee. It stayed for about a minute ruffling her feathers (it was a female) and switching positions as if to show me every part of her. I talked out loud to her as Jessie—thanking her for letting me know today that I am never alone. My "little red bird" came back!

Neverland and *dream #29* were recorded and released after *Somewhere Between Heaven and Earth* (with the brilliant Ray Kennedy coproducing with me) in 2001 and 2005 respectively. I had gotten good gigs around the United States, all over Europe, and even Australia. I was making good headway creating a large, brand-new fanbase. But quite suddenly at the end of 2005, shortly before I broke my finger, my opportunities seemed to grind to a halt. The business was shifting to digital streaming, and no one was exactly sure where things would stand. It appeared the CD format itself was over—nobody was buying them. Both albums were "critically acclaimed." My *dream #29* album, with Sir Elton John playing on the title track and me singing duets with Delbert McClinton and Boston Red Sox starting pitcher Tim Wakefield, was dead in the water.

Yes, I could write songs, but . . .

Well, it occurred to me, *I liked to work out!*

I decided, since I loved anything having to do with sports and exercise, that I would spring for a home-study course to become a Certified Fitness Trainer. If I did nothing with it, I didn't care. I would be learning something new, learning something I was interested in. What the heck? Music be damned!

———————

"Oh Mom, what am I going to do?" Reid blurted out crying, as I sat down on the sofa beside her in her little rented apartment across from the Portland Post Office. I was spending part of the summer of 2006 in Maine. She told me earlier in the day when she and I had gone to the Maine Mall that she hadn't gotten her period yet this month. She, like me in my prime, could set her watch to it every month. Just to be cautious, we bought a pregnancy test at CVS, and I dropped her off at her place to go on with my errands. Reid was just twenty-four and dating Derek, who was a working student at University of Southern Maine. An hour later she called me in a panic.

I was back at her apartment in minutes.

"Oh, my baby, I love you so much!" I pulled her close and held her tight, welling up with the thought of a precious little being—my first grandchild. But I also knew how frightened Reid must be at this moment, feeling ill-equipped to have and care for a child. Neither Reid nor Derek had full-time jobs, and they were just getting to know each other. She hadn't told him yet.

"You have two parents who will help you, Reidy. You know that. And I am sure Derek's parents will, too. This baby will have everything it needs, and so will you. I promise." Privilege is a powerful thing. I had what I had: the house I was living in, my tiny cottage on North Haven Island, a modest flow of royalties and residuals, and whatever I could earn doing whatever I could do. I left Dan taking nothing from him, by choice. Dan had the financial means to make sure that my promise could be kept, but I was prepared to do anything I needed to do to create a safe and healthy place on this earth for this new being.

I made an offer on a little house in Cumberland that was for sale. It just happened to be across the street from Dan. It had been an old schoolhouse built in 1806 and was perfect for me—small and cozy and red. Reid was going to have this baby, and I was damn well going to be there for it. I figured my Nashville days were over anyway. Maybe my days in the music business as well.

I went home to Tennessee in August, packed up the Franklin house, and in late September, for the third time in five years, moved back to Maine.

> *Journal Entry—July 9, 2006*
>
> *So the music business is out! I have no interest—at least right now—in pursuing anything more in and from the music biz. I'm burned out. I am who I am. I have achieved what I achieved. Whatever "level" I've attained will have to remain.*

Back in Maine, I wondered, *Now what?*

I was excited about having a grandchild, but I now had nothing professionally to do, and my financial resources were dwindling fast.

Winter came, and I sank. The black-hearted demon of depression that so frequently haunted me came around again. My secretive self-loathing that was mostly disguised by my big personality was festering. Being alone with only my own voice echoing in my head was not a good thing.

I dove back into my AA meetings as though I was a newcomer. I had sober friends here in Maine, and they helped me get reoriented. I soaked up every word and interaction and tried to be of service whenever I could. I set up the chairs before meetings, did the dishes afterward. I went on commitments to speak at other meetings. I talked to people new to recovery. I started sponsoring a young woman who would, as time went on, be pivotal in me finding my truth, and now was holding my feet to the fire. "You can't give what you haven't got," the old timers used to say. But I needed even more to get out of my own house and my own head. Light is hard to come by deep in a Maine winter.

I hadn't had a real job since I was in Los Angeles in the mid '70s, pumping gas at Jerry's Phillips 66 on Santa Monica Boulevard. Thirty years later, back in Maine, and soon I'd be ready to test to become a bona fide fitness trainer.

One afternoon, in early December, putting all my inner what-if-they-know-who-I-am pretenses aside, knowing that I had more notoriety in Maine than anywhere else, I walked into the YMCA in Freeport and asked if they had any job openings.

"Aren't you Cindy Bullens?" the woman at the front desk asked me.

Ugh, I thought.

"Yup." I smiled my best smile and tried not to look too needy. "I'm looking for something to do when I'm off the road. I love the Y and what you do for the community." I said, trying to sound knowledgeable. "Have you got any positions open?"

It was true. I did love the Y. The YMCA had always held a place in my life from the time I was a kid when I could get out of the house to take swimming lessons in Haverhill, Massachusetts. Of course, this included my one night at the West 34th Street YMCA in New York when I ran away at fifteen—forever etched in my memory. But I always went wherever I lived—New York, Hollywood, Westport, Portland, Nashville. The YMCA was a grounding point for me. And I needed it now, I felt, to save my sanity.

"Well, we could use another person behind the front desk. That's all we've got right now." The woman smiled at me, seemingly happy to help. "Would you be interested in that?"

Thus began my tenure with the YMCA of Southern Maine. After a few weeks of signing up new members and checking people in at the front desk for eight bucks an hour, I officially became a Certified Fitness Trainer and moved into the wellness department. I started training people of all ages and abilities, and I loved it. Working there gave me a place to go, a new community with new people, another purpose, and kept my head out of my butt, for the most part, for a long time to come.

The first and only gig I played in all of 2006, after I somewhat regained the use of my left hand, was the songwriter's festival Tin Pan South in

Nashville. That was in May, before I moved back to Maine. (My pinkie was permanently bent. I had to relearn how to play guitar, but it was usable.)

Two old friends of mine from L.A., Deborah Holland and Wendy Waldman, were also playing the festival, together. I met Deborah in Los Angeles in 1990 when I was flying there frequently to write with other songwriters. She had been the lead singer and songwriter of the late '80s IRS Records band Animal Logic, with the Police drummer Stewart Copeland and noted jazz bassist Stanley Clarke. Wendy Waldman and I met a year later in Nashville. Wendy, who was a well-known Grammy-nominated singer-songwriter, and one of a handful of female record producers, was living in Nashville at the time. She moved back to her hometown of Los Angeles in 1992. I had become good friends with them both separately.

Wendy and Deborah didn't get to know each other until 2005, when Deborah, who was now a music professor at Cal State University L.A., asked Wendy to be a guest in a class she was teaching. Wendy then invited Deborah, who was looking to perform again, to sit in on a few gigs she was doing around Los Angeles. They arrived in Nashville for Tin Pan South and contacted me.

I attended their festival performance at the Cannery, and they came to mine at the Bluebird Cafe, after which we arranged to have breakfast on Sunday morning at Fido, one of my favorite coffee and breakfast places in Nashville. Wendy and Deborah's songwriter cohort Jenny, whom I had never met before their show together, came along as well.

"So, we are thinking of putting together a group—a kind of touring in-the-round of women," Deborah stated over our first sips of Bongo Java dark roast coffee. In-the-round means one songwriter performs a song, followed by the next writer, and the next, and so on. Usually, it includes four songwriters. Each songwriter can join in with the others, add harmonies, join in on an instrument, or just listen.

"We want to call it The California Song Girls."

I winced. I was hoping nobody saw it. The waitress slapped down our plates of various scrambles and home fries and fresh baked muffins—almost throwing the silverware wrapped in a paper napkin at each person.

"Huh. That's great," I said, unfurling my napkin and already needing more caffeine.

"Are you interested in doing it with us?" I took a long sip of my coffee, and then I took a breath. I loved Deborah. She was one of the nicest and most earnest people I knew. She was also very funny. I realized though that she wasn't joking. I was always shocked throughout my whole life, just for a split second, when people just didn't see the real me. I wasn't *really* a woman. But oh yeah, that's right, I had to remind myself, I was to them! Even still, as much as I loved Deb and Wendy, I certainly didn't want to be a part of anything called The California Song Girls.

"Um. I don't know. Maybe. I'm not sure what I'm doing right now. I'm still rehabbing my finger. I've got a way to go before I can fully play. But I'll think about it." We proceeded to eat and drink more coffee, gabbing away about what had transpired for each of us over the past umpteen years.

Deborah badgered me about joining the proposed The California Song Girls for the next seven months. In January 2007, I finally acquiesced and flew to Los Angeles to meet with Wendy, Deborah, and Jenny, partly just to get Deborah off my back.

I had started working part-time at the Y in Freeport the month before. I explained to my higher-ups prior to taking the job that there might come a time when I may have to be gone for various lengths of time for my music. After all, I was "Cindy Bullens."

I had no idea when I began the job if there would ever be another opportunity to tour or record again. Absolutely nothing was pointing toward me continuing my career, but I figured I would lay the groundwork with my bosses anyway. That ever-familiar creative urge inside me was just starting to creep in again despite the cold and dark of Maine and of my mind, and despite my declaration of disinterest back in July. When Deborah called again, I was ready.

I arrived at Wendy's house in Northridge from LAX around 11 AM. Wendy put the coffee on for me—I'd been up since 4 AM East Coast time—while Deborah was taking out her guitar and tuning her strings. There would be no time wasted in getting to a song. I opened my heavy, bright red Calton case that I had lugged around the world—from Germany to Australia to Saskatchewan to Alaska—which had been sitting for months undisturbed in an upstairs closet in my house in Cumberland, and pulled out my workhorse—my Small Jumbo single cutaway Collings guitar. As the coffee brewed, and as I wiped off the dust in between the tuning pegs on the headstock, with Deborah stretching and strumming her strings, Wendy launched into an old song of hers and started to sing. Immediately, Deborah jumped in and started singing the high part in the chorus. Jenny strummed along.

Though I knew "Plant Your Fields" from one of Wendy's solo albums years before, with its gorgeous, haunting melody and stirring lyrics, I'd never sung it. I found the third below Wendy and opened my mouth.

I had written songs with both Deborah and Wendy. I had sung with each of them while writing. But the minute the three of us sang three-part harmony *together*, it was absolute magic. I immediately felt lifted up to a place I hadn't been since maybe singing "Rocket Man" or "Don't Let the Sun Go Down on Me" with Jon Joyce and Ken Gold on tour with Elton way back in 1976. Or with Timothy B. Schmit and Claudia Lennear on Gene Clark's *No Other* album in 1974. Or maybe with Bonnie Raitt and Jackson Browne on John Prine's "Angel from Montgomery" at her show at Jones Beach, New York, in 1999. I had certainly sung with some incredible vocalists over the years, on stage and on records—Lucinda Williams, Emmylou Harris, John Hiatt, Steve Earle, Bryan Adams, Don Everly for God's sake. So many more! But now, on this day, having flown all the way cross country from Maine to Los Angeles just hours before, I was singing and *being* in harmony with these two other unique voices that exquisitely and perfectly matched mine.

"OK! I'm in!" I exclaimed after we finished the song. "But I will *not* be a California Song Girl!" A name popped into my head: *the Refugees*. We googled it. No other band with that name came up. We decided to go with it.

Jenny was soon gone. There was no room for a fourth. It was really the three of us, Deborah, Wendy, and me, who bonded and felt simpatico with each other. Our voices together told us that. We were not three individual songwriters singing on each other's songs; we were a band.

I flew back to Maine a few days later with a renewed sense of purpose and a feeling of resurrection. I also went back to the Y. I had clients to train and treadmills to clean. That black-hearted demon that had taken up residence in my head for the last few months apparently decided there was no room left for him either.

Wendy and Deborah both lived in Los Angeles, and I lived in Maine, so rehearsals and bookings were a challenge. But we were determined. Though we had disagreements as we were coalescing, we all had the same vision for this new venture.

The Refugees started small, performing some house concerts and little venues up and down California. We got ourselves out into the folk community by performing at various folk conferences. (I was never a true "folkie," so this was an interesting change for me.) We worked our way up to touring all over the United States and Canada. Over the next five years, we made three full albums.

The Refugees *Unbound* album cover, 2008.
Photo by and courtesy of Eric Staudenmaier

But here was the bottom line: the Refugees allowed me to have fun. I was no longer the only front person in charge of a band, with all the attention on me. It was a shared experience by the three of us.

Wendy took center stage introducing us each night with personal stories and vignettes augmented by her extremely dry sense of humor. She was the ringleader. Wendy's commanding smile, her Jewish earth mother presence—the deep intellectual—drew in every eye and ear. with her long wavy brown hair, her flowing blouses and multicolored scarves that accentuated her every move, and her exquisite gift for narrative.

Deborah, on stage right, was always impeccably but classically dressed—cute and canny with perfect makeup and every hair in place (whether blonde or red)—her tiny frame made a bold statement. She was not demur. Deliciously witty and super smart, Deborah's razor sharp, acerbic remarks frequently pierced Wendy's commentary, making us all erupt into laughter. Both were brilliant musicians and songwriters. Me? I was the physical humor, the clown. And the token gentile. The tall blond standing on Wendy's stage left, I just reacted to whatever was going on, on the stage or elsewhere around me. We bantered. I chimed in often, offsetting the two intellectuals with my everyman (albeit androgynous), straightforward, sometimes goofy self. I loved my role. Mostly, I laughed. Loud and hard—unhinged and unencumbered. We were each other's perfect foils. It just worked.

The singing and the harmonies, the challenge of the musicianship, and the camaraderie between three good friends was exhilarating. We raised the bar for each other in every way. We made each other better musicians, better songwriters, better parents, and ultimately better people. It really was magical. But even more than that, I allowed my spirit to fly for the first time since Jessie's death without guilt and that unbearable heaviness. The Refugees allowed me to live for myself.

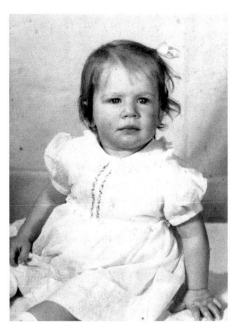

Cindy at one year old.
Author's collection.

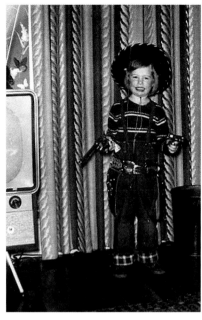

Cindy in cowboy outfit.
Author's collection.

Cindy at age seventeen.
Photo by and courtesy of Evy Nathan.

Cindy and Jon Joyce in front of the Starship, 1975.
Photo by and courtesy of Mike Hewitson

The BVs at Dodger Stadium, October 25, 1975.
Photo by and courtesy of Mike Hewitson

Elton and Cindy at Foxborough Stadium, July 4, 1976.
Photo by and courtesy of Ron Pownall.

Mom, Cindy, and Dad at the Paradise Ballroom in Boston, 1979.
Author's collection.

Cindy with 1965 Gibson SG Jr.,
1979. *Author's collection.*

Freddie Mercury, Cindy, and Billie Jean King in New York City, 1976.
Photo by and courtesy of Bob Gruen.

Cindy backstage at The Bottom Line, New York City, 1978.
Author's collection.

Cindy with Jessie,
Westport, Connecticut, 1985.
Author's collection.

Reid and Cindy, L.A., 1986.
Photo by and courtesy of Ayn Plant.

Jessie, Cindy, and Reid, North Haven, Maine, 1992. *Author's collection.*

Lucinda Williams, Cindy, and Emmylou Harris in Nashville, 2000.
Photo by and courtesy of Lawson Little.

The Refugees—Cindy, Deborah Holland, and Wendy Waldman—with Bonnie Raitt in Portland, Maine, 2008. *Author's collection.*

Cid and Tanya's wedding day, with granddaughters Tobey and Charles, New York City, 2018. *Photo by and courtesy of Dorie Hagler.*

Cid and Tanya with four grandkids, Christmas, 2018. *Photo by and courtesy of Reid Crewe.*

13

THE GENDER LINE

If you were me
What would you do?
You look in the mirror
And it's not really you
Would you think you were crazy?
And out of your mind?
You're not in your body
You're living a lie
There's a train in the station
There's a car in the drive
But they won't take me over the gender line

    "The Gender Line" by Cidny Bullens
    © 2019 Red Dragonfly Music/BMI

CALL ME, THE FACEBOOK MESSAGE said. *I need to tell you something.* It was July 14, 2011. The young woman who I had sponsored in recovery three years before had moved from Maine to New York and then back up to Boston. I hadn't seen her in two years, and, in fact, I had little communication with her at all in that time. I did know she had changed her name.

When I met Annie back in the fall of 2006, when she was in her mid-twenties, she walked up to me after a recovery meeting and asked me if I would be willing to sponsor her. Still clawing my way back to center from my hiatus from working the Twelve Steps for those few years in Nashville,

177

I figured this was a clear push from the Big Whatever to get even more involved. I felt an immediate kinship with Annie. We clicked right away.

Annie was not shy about who she was. She had struggled to be herself in a big, complicated, dysfunctional rural Maine family but had forged her own path despite all the obstacles. She was tough and contrary but sweet and kind. She walked with a swagger of someone determined to move beyond her limitations. She had a great desire to be a healthy human being. And Annie had a girlfriend. We forged a deep and honest friendship, and though I was the elder, she helped me probably more than I helped her at the time.

I called her cell phone and got her voicemail. "Hi, this is Austin. Leave a message, and I'll call you back when I can." The voice was deeper than the voice I knew. I waited by the phone, holding my breath. Austin thankfully called me back within the hour.

"I started transitioning a year ago, and I'm living my life as a man." Before the call, I had an inkling of what she, now he, was going to tell me. When I heard the deeper voice on the voicemail message, my suspicion turned to in-all-probability. But hearing those actual words come out of Austin's mouth, "I'm living my life as a man," completely and totally blew me apart. Every cell in my body was awake and alert. Wide-eyed and hanging on his every word, I talked with him for over an hour. I asked him every question I had ever wanted to ask for the last fifty years.

"What did you do? Where did you go? How does it *feel*?"

Never in all the years I had known Annie had we ever talked about being transgender. She was a lesbian (though I don't remember if she, like me, ever used that term), and to her I suppose I was too.*

After I hung up the phone, I fell to my knees and sobbed. It was uncontrollable. My body was shaking as the tears surged out of my eyes. It was almost like my Jessie cry, deep and unyielding. I laid down on the cool hardwood floor with scenes of my youth darting through my mind, certain moments: in the kitchen at four with my mother, telling her that my name was Bobby, not Cindy; Hendy Webb's lawn, when I felt that tiny little bump in my left breast; the New York Public Library.

---

* I use the female pronoun with Austin when they themselves were using the female pronoun to describe themselves before transition.

Journal Entry—July 14, 2011

It brought up EVERYTHING for me! When I say "everything," I mean my <u>whole life story</u>. The story nobody knows but <u>me</u>! The fact that I have lived my whole life "wrong" and cheated! (That's a term I have never used before, but it's right.) The fact that every single time I look in the mirror naked, I see breasts that don't belong to me. It is the CORE subject of my life.

It was indeed another soul cry.

I was crying for who I was *not*. For who I never was, and for who I never could be. I was crying for my life, now sixty-one years long, lived on a tightrope. A life of compromise and lies, of straddling the line between masculine and feminine—masculine enough to feel OK on the inside, feminine enough to not stand out *too much* as a public personality, a wife, and a mother. Of course, I had failed miserably in my attempts to fit in (though I was well-liked in most circles). People in all phases of my life thought whatever they thought of me, and as I got older, I cared less and less about it anyway. But still, I *felt* that I was compromising every single minute of my existence.

I finally pulled myself up to my feet, and for about a half an hour, I paced in my living room like a caged animal, walking in circles, dazed, and muttering to myself. There was an energy, an angst that was pushing at, out, and through my body. Sometime during that call with Austin, there was a seismic shift within me. This shift would soon lead to a 9.0 earthquake that would flatten everything I had built up to live and exist as Cindy Bullens. I finally picked up the phone and called Reid.

"Reidy, I need to talk to you."

"Is it about me?" she asked suspiciously.

"No, it is not about you! Can I come over and pick you up?"

"Now?"

"Yes, now." I had no one else I felt I could even broach this subject with, let alone bare the whole of my innards to at this moment.

Dan had built Reid and Derek a house on his property. Tobey, my first granddaughter, was now four. When Reid was pregnant with Charles, my second granddaughter, now two, Dan decided it best to give them all a "secure" place to live, moving them out from their third-floor walkup in Portland whether they liked it or not—right beside him in Cumberland. I lived across the street from them all.

"What's going on? What's the matter?" she asked, concerned, as she opened the passenger-side door and climbed into my car. I was still crying. As we drove aimlessly through the countryside on this otherwise lazy summer afternoon, I told her about Austin. She had known and liked Annie and was not shocked at the news. She also was not at all shocked when I told her how the news had affected me.

"I don't know what to do, Reidy. I don't." The tears were still flowing. My stomach hurt and my chest was heavy. I finally pulled over in the dirt parking lot of Toots, a local dairy farm in North Yarmouth, where they made our favorite ice cream. We sat in the car. I could not stop crying. Cars were driving in and out. People were getting cones and cups and milkshakes. I watched them, one by one, kids and adults, walk to and from and in and out of the old train caboose where the ice cream was served—they all seemed like regular people with regular lives. Not one of those people had an inkling that one more time, the world as I knew it was no more. It had shattered again and was gone.

"Mom, you have to do *something*! You really do have to address this now."

I had told Reid about my feelings when she was around eighteen. She didn't flinch. She had, since puberty, railed at me and questioned why she didn't have a "normal" mother—one who could show her how to put on makeup, a mother whose jewelry box she could raid, and one who resembled, even the tiniest bit, the other mothers at school. When she got older, it would have been helpful to her to have a mother who had some experience with a bra that latched in the back, that maybe had some padding and was for accentuating rather than flattening. She would have loved a mother who wouldn't rather sit in the "man chair" at Victoria's Secret while her daughter shopped.

But on this day, she was all there for me. She was supportive and empathetic. In fact, she encouraged me to look into actually transitioning. I was a little shocked, but relieved and very grateful.

We decided that I should seek out a gender therapist and start there. In all my years of recovery and therapy and whatever else I sought out to help me get through my life, I had never *fully* addressed or explored that one primary issue: my gender.

Now, with Reid's blessing, I immediately became obsessed. I started reading everything I could online about being transgender. I ordered books and memoirs. I was shocked at the amount of FTM (female-to-male) videos on YouTube—stories upon stories of (mostly) young people transitioning. *Where have I been?*

But truth be told, if Reid had not encouraged me to move forward, (at that time, it was simply to *talk* about it), I would have most likely continued on as I was, earthquake and all. In fact, only three days before Austin's call, I was sitting in my little sunroom, with my dog Jack at my feet, writing in my journal.

> *Journal Entry—July 11, 2011*
>
> *You know, honestly, I am in a good place—happy, for the most part, with my life. I feel a sense of—dare I say—peace?*

I was sixty-one years old and had lived a very interesting life. *This is it*, I thought, writing that day. *This is my life now.* I was single and a grandmother. I was still working part-time at the Y, occasionally touring, writing, and recording both on my own and with the Refugees, and I was in good health. I was me. *What you see is what you get.* I no longer had to please anyone else. I no longer was directly responsible for anyone else either. And I no longer felt that oppressive black cloud of grief that had gripped me after Jessie's death for so many years. *What could possibly change any of that?* I thought. I could relax now into the last chapters of my life. Little did I know.

Austin had given me information on where to find a gender therapist in Boston. The day after our conversation, with Reid on board, I called and made an appointment.

> *Journal Entry—July 16, 2011*
>
> *I'm only going to start a conversation. Here's the bottom line for me—I would (at this moment—it could change) be happy to live*

androgynously*—have top surgery and leave the rest alone. I don't
need my breasts. And I've been wanting to change my name for
years! I'd LOVE to get rid of "Cindy"!

I already had the legal documents in my desk for a name change. I
had gotten them months before. I hated the name "Cindy." I really didn't
know why I never changed it professionally. I had a couple of chances in
my early career, but at the time it seemed too overwhelming to me. So,
I lived with it. "Cindy Bullens" to me became just a label, an identifier,
like "Campbell's Soup" or "Starbucks." I had detached emotionally to
my given name long ago. I already knew my new name would be Cidny
Tobey Bullens.

Tobey was my father's mother's maiden name. Since I was a kid, that
was the name, had I ever changed it from Cindy, that I wanted as my own.
Reid named her daughter Tobey "after me," knowing that story. Now that
my granddaughter was the new embodiment of that name, it no longer
belonged to me as a first name. Now with Tobey as my middle name, I
would honor not only my ancestors but my granddaughter as well.

Journal Entry—July 19, 2011

In the wee hours of this morning, I was actually thinking—I'd
rather be a man and work anonymously, than continue as a public
person as "Cindy." The pure joy and excitement I feel by the very
idea of removing my breasts (I would do it tomorrow) and taking
testosterone is almost overwhelming.

I was on overdrive. On August 5, I went to see the gender therapist
in Boston. We barely said hello before I started talking.

"Most people have some questions," she stated after I blurted out my
story for almost fifty minutes. "You don't. You know who you are." By
the tone of her voice, I wasn't sure she had ever experienced someone
like me in her office before.

In 2011, a trans person had to have a letter from both a licensed
psychologist and a physician to have any kind of surgery or hormone

---

* I did not know the term *nonbinary* at the time.

replacement therapy (HRT). The therapist told me she would write a letter whenever she felt I was ready, but that it wouldn't be long. I made my second appointment for the next week.

I had also made an appointment with my longtime general practitioner, who had over the years become a family friend. Without knowledge of the reason for my visit, he took me right in. I loved Chuck. He was tall and good-natured, always trying to find the best solutions to any issues, medical or not. He knew pretty much everything about me both inside and out. I felt completely safe with him.

"Chuck, remember how you always say, I'm not one of your most boring patients?" I said, sitting on the edge of the examination table, johnny on, shoes off, looking him straight in the eye as he walked through the door.

He looked at me with his "uh oh" look. "Are you gonna tell me you're not gay?"

"No! I am NOT gay!" Chuck was also Dan's doctor and had been through my time with Maryann, and a couple of my other short-lived attempts at relationships with women. "Do you know anything about transgender people?" His eyes opened wide.

"Yes, as a matter of fact, I do! My partner, Dr. Jim Bradley—you know Jim—treats most of the Portland transgender community. I'd say at least thirty to fifty trans people are treated right here at North Star Medical."

What?! I couldn't believe it.

I told Chuck about the phone call with Austin, a bit of my hidden internal history, and that I had seen a gender therapist the day before. He was genuinely excited for me.

"It must be so liberating for you," he said lovingly. *Yes,* liberating *is the word*, I thought.

Chuck set up an appointment for me to see Dr. Bradley for the next week, just to talk. He would be the one to prescribe testosterone and write a letter recommending top surgery, should those times come. The fact that I could come to my own doctor's office for *all* my medical needs now was beyond belief. Something had indeed cracked open in the Universe. The torrent of energy flooding through that crack now seemed unstoppable.

Journal Entry—August 10, 2011, North Haven

I woke up around 5 AM to the sound of heavy rain and wind and with the absolute thought that I should do NOTHING about transitioning. I was as clear as I could be. I even questioned changing my name! I think it's because last night I finally read some very clear info, both scientific and personal, about the realities of transitioning. So waking up with the opposite feeling of what I had just yesterday gave me a real indication that this is all a process. And that I do need therapy through it all. I do think that I will not tell anyone else about my process that I've not already told—even about the name change. I need to go through this myself. As I write now, I would love to have top surgery and take hormones. But socially and sociologically—that's the tough and uncertain part for me—a HUGE deal! I may put off my name change until October. I actually had the thought, "What will be on my gravestone?" I mean I'd have to ask the question if I kept "Cynthia"—which I won't—would "Cindy" be on there at all?

"I think you should start testosterone as soon as possible," said Dr. Bradley after I told him my whole story, including that after this fall, I potentially wouldn't be singing again until spring. It was August 12, 2011.

"*Now?!*" A flood of fear and excitement simultaneously shot through my body. I was not prepared for that scenario at all. I was still teetering on the edge of doing nothing, just two days before having woken up with that idea in my head. The deep green leaves of the maple trees outside the window of Dr. Bradley's tiny office rippled in the breeze. Puffs of fair-weather clouds highlighted the specific bright blue of the August Maine sky.

My gaze was fixed on the natural beauty beyond his desk as he went on to explain what he expected the changes in my body to be, muscle gain and the shifting of fat. But I was his first post-menopausal biological woman transgender patient, so he was essentially guessing. I would not need copious amounts of testosterone, he continued, to "stem the tide" of estrogen.

"Your voice won't likely change at all for the next few months, and it should be settled in again by April." My head was spinning. "I think I'd like to start you with a normal dose that I would give to a younger transman just to see how you react."

"Let me think about it," I said, glancing out the window again as I got up to leave. "I'll let you know soon." I had an appointment on August 16 to see the gender therapist again, this time with Reid. It was very important to me to make sure, no matter what I did, that Reid was part of the process.

The trees and the clouds and the sky were the constants in this moment and in my life. They were still and always just there. But what about me? Where was I? *Who am I?* That single question would become another constant in the months ahead.

Reid had specifically asked me to tell her father what was going on. It was too much for her to keep it to herself when she was essentially living with him. I called him just a day before my appointment with Dr. Bradley and simply told him that I was seeing a gender therapist.

"You mean it's only taken you sixty-one years?" he replied with his usual sarcasm. I was relieved, as much for Reid as for me. (Dan and I still could be very critical of each other.) I was grateful to have his support. I needed as much of that as I could get.

Before I even drove out of the North Star Medical parking lot after seeing Dr. Bradley, I called Reid and Dan and told them I was coming over to talk.

"What's the downside?" Dan asked me when I told him about starting with a high dose of testosterone that Dr. Bradley had suggested. I could feel the sweat forming on the back side of my legs as I sat in my shorts on the dark brown leather chair across from Dan and Reid. They sat side by side on the matching leather couch in Dan's den, looking at me intently.

The "downside" flipped through my mind like a celebrity's Rolodex—meaning there were a *ton* of little white index cards with names and faces and situations in bold, black ink that I could see very clearly. Scrolling was the list of people I cared about, friends and family and supporters, who might fall away or even outright reject me, and the hazards of navigating through my constantly vacillating career. Certainly, my opportunities to work with bereaved parents and my charitable causes would come to a screeching halt. What about the Refugees? We were "three acclaimed *women* singer-songwriters." And even my clients at the Y? Would they want to continue to work with me? How was I going to address all of this? Life was already hard enough. Did I really want to throw a bomb into my shaky status quo? The unknown perils of transitioning and the uncertainty that lay ahead was as daunting as it was exhilarating to think about taking testosterone and having top surgery.

Journal Entry—August 14, 2011

It's the SOCIAL aspects that I question. The fear of losing the people that I love. On the other hand, who knows what opportunities will come from this—if I do. Hey—my life has never been boring! But I have to make sure I am ready. Again, there is that excitement about the possibility of being and feeling like what I've missed—my true self.

I had yet to tell my siblings anything. Both my parents and my older sister Nancy had passed. They all would have had the most difficult time with my transition, I believed. But my brother too, I thought, would have a hard time. I idolized my brother growing up. The five years between us, and his tall frame, meant that I was literally looking up to him for a good part of my life. And he had always been protective of his sisters. Though he and my sister-in-law Diane totally accepted Maryann into their lives in the years we were a couple, being seen as gay and changing one's gender were two completely different things.

My brother followed my parents' political views as old-school conservatives. At this point, he and I were diametrically opposed to each other in our beliefs of how and what the social constructs of the world should be.

I wasn't sure about how my sisters Debbie and Suki would feel. Suki had just recently had major surgery from which she was recovering, and I would be going to Massachusetts in a few days to help her while her husband, Kevin, drove their older daughter to college.

Suki and I had always confided honestly in each other. We called on each other when we needed support or advice. I would speak to her about all this when I was there.

My plan was to tell them all only that I was coming out as a transgender person, not that I was thinking about transitioning from me to a man. Somehow there was a delineation in my own mind. As much as I wanted to be male, it was all coming at me so fast that I needed a middle ground.

"Cin! You could lose half the people in your life!" Suki's voice rose quickly from her supine position in bed, strong and loud. She did not sound like someone who had just gotten out of the hospital. This was not encouraging.

"I'm only *thinking* about it!" I tried to back up after I had told her more than I intended and added the possibility of transitioning. "But I feel like I have to at least *say* who I truly am. *What* I truly am!"

"Why? You're sixty-one years old!"

"I *know!* Who am I living for now? And what if I did lose half the people in my life?" I tried to reason with myself. Suki was just saying and asking the same things I was repeating over and over in my own mind.

"Look," I said, taking on a serious tone. "Just like I went out there for all those years after Jessie died to speak to and for bereaved parents—I did that for me but also to be of service. What if I come out as a transgender person and it helps just one other person?" I knew I was sounding pedantic, but it was true. I knew that besides being true to myself, maybe I could be an example to someone else, and that was *because* I was my age and had lived a full life. It was *because* I was respected in the community, both locally and in the music business. People who knew me knew I wasn't somebody on the fringe. Just maybe this was another way for me to show up for the Greater Good.

"But you could go bald! Do you want to be a fat, bald old man?"

This is not going well, I thought, as I sighed and covered my face with my hands.

"Suki, you know me," I sighed, sliding my hands down my cheeks. "I'm vain. I promise, no matter what, I will not let myself go. OK?" I wanted it all to stop. "I'm going to get some ice cream."

My conversation with Debbie was not any easier. Nor was it with my brother Rick, my close cousin Mardi, or anyone else in the family. I knew all their concerns were out of love as much as they were out of fear. But the can of worms was now all the way open.

Journal Entry—August 16, 2011

Reid and I drove into Boston to see the therapist yesterday in the pouring rain. Let me say that my daughter is an incredible human

*being, and I am so grateful that we have a strong relationship.
One couldn't have a better advocate!*

I wanted Reid to come and talk about her own views, concerns, and feelings about my possible transition. She waited on a lone wooden chair in the small, dark, nondescript corridor outside the office as I spent the first half of the session alone with the therapist.

"Maybe you should live as a man for a year. Just to try it out. And then see how you feel," she said, seeming to backpedal from our previous session where she acknowledged that I "know who I am."

I exploded. "Are you kidding? I am sixty-one years old! I'm either doing this or I'm not. I've spent my whole life living out of my body. Plus, I live in Portland, Maine! Everybody knows me there!" Something shifted in me as I was responding to her.

Suddenly I saw myself as *me*. Just me. No gender. No pronouns. I hated pronouns. Like my name, "she" was a moniker, a convenience for others in my life. I wasn't really interested in being grouped into another category. But I was interested in experiencing my own true self. Of course I knew I would never be a biological male. I would be a "transman." But at least maybe I could walk through this world for the last years of my life *feeling* the truth of who I knew I was.

The rain was still coming down hard as we slogged our way through the narrow streets of Back Bay in Boston and onto Route 1 North toward Maine. Reid interrupted me as I was going on about all of this. "Mom, here's the gender line." She held up her right hand perpendicular to the ground like she was about to do a karate chop. "You've always been on just this side," she moved her left hand over the top of her right hand, "the female side. Now you're moving over to just this side," she moved her hand across the other again, "to the other side of the gender line. You'll always be you."

Within the next two weeks, the gender therapist wrote a letter to Dr. Bradley stating that I was a good candidate for hormone replacement therapy, and on September 1, 2011, a little nervous and very excited, I took my first shot of testosterone.

14

LITTLE PIECES

Flat on the floor my face to the ground
I grumble a word but I make no sound
Haven't you noticed that I disappeared
I'm not here
Boxes of photos are strewn on the bed
Snapshots of memories fall out of my head
Someone's existence has gone up in smoke
It's my own
Little Pieces falling away
Every day, every day
Little Pieces Little Pieces
Falling away

> *"Little Pieces" by Cidny Bullens*
> *©2019 Red Dragonfly Music/BMI*

Journal Entry—September 1, 2011, Day 1

So the surrealness of it—the phone rings—it says BLOCKED—and
I'm thinking why is Wolfgang [my old friend from Germany]
calling me now? I answer in my "Who is this?" low voice—and I
hear "BLANCHE!" It's Elton.

"Really?" The emphasis was down at the end of the word. "Well, I'm
not shocked, and you know I love and support you no matter what." I

had called Elton's office the week before and asked them to have him call me when and if he could. Elton being Elton, he did.

"I wanted you to hear it directly from me," I said after explaining what happened and that I planned to declare publicly who I was and that I was moving toward fully transitioning. Rumors would start flying fast in the music business. He was very kind and loving about it all. We went on talking about his new son, Zachary, and how wonderful it was to have a child.

"Of course, I could go bald," I said as we were saying our goodbyes.

"No, you will NOT!" Elton barked emphatically. We both laughed. I thanked him for calling, and we wished each other well.

There were a few people who I regarded as foundational to my life, meaning they were like the individual concrete blocks that were laid before one could build an entire structure. Elton John was one of them. Without my experience with him, my life would not have unfolded as it did. Though we rarely saw each other, he held a place in my heart that was his alone. He *had* always been there for me over the years, publicly promoting my music and answering the call of my occasional asks. Privately, he always wanted to know if I was OK, or why something wasn't working in my life; he was happy to know if something was and would encourage me to keep moving forward. I was not in his inner circle, I was not in the top tier of his list of friends, I was not a confidant, but there was something special between us that I cherished. He was arguably the most famous person in the world—all I could do for him in return for his friendship was love him and keep that place in my heart open and available.

I thought it was wild that he called me on *the* day I would be getting my first shot of testosterone. Not only that, only days before, I made a deal to sell my baby grand piano that I bought with the money I was paid from Elton's *Rock of the Westies* tour. I was only willing to let go of my long-time possession to pay for my probable upcoming top surgery. (Luckily, I sold it to a close friend who would sell it back to me should the time ever come.) The movers were just walking out the door with the piano when the phone rang.

For all my doubts about whether to completely transition or not, there was a fully paved road in front of me, and I seemed to be in the fast lane. Only I felt like a crazy person trying to steer a rally car in an arcade game with a blindfold on. The mental machinations were constantly pinging and crashing through my brain. One moment I was all for it—everything, all of it—complete and total transformation, consequences be damned. The next moment, I would do nothing at all and live out my life as I was. And then there was the in-between place: maybe I could stay "Cindy" and "she" but take testosterone and have a flat chest. But Pandora's Box, the can of worms, a hornet's nest, or any idiom or analogy that meant *You've done it now and there is no turning back* was the new reality I was facing. Maybe destiny was doing the real driving. Maybe this was out of my hands entirely. All I knew was, above everything, my curiosity alone was too much to counter.

I had already contacted a few surgeons about top surgery, both in Maine and elsewhere. This was not a procedure that was widely advertised. Simply described, chest reconstruction consisted of removing the nipples and most of the tissue of both breasts, plus any excess skin, then sizing, placing, and attaching the nipples back on the now flat chest.

I had already had a conversation with a specialist in Cleveland. I scheduled two consultations in Portland in the coming days, though I found that no one so far had ever done this specific surgery in Maine.

There was one surgeon in Florida I discovered from the FTM videos on YouTube that performed *only* female-to-male chest surgery, Dr. Charles Garramone. After looking all through his website—the explanations, the photos, the testimonials—I was pretty sure he would be the one when and if the time came. I made an appointment for a consultation.

"Mom, it's not like anybody's gonna know the difference," Reid remarked dryly when I told her about my surgery consultations.

"Very funny," I responded. "Well, *I* will!"

Meanwhile, the people in my life were starting to understand that this was not a passing fancy of mine. Reid was having dreams about her mother dying. My sisters were rebelling with emails and calls. Over time, I could not contain myself and told a few more close friends about my plan to come out as transgender.

"You can't do this to Reid—after all she's been through?" said one good family friend from our former Connecticut Montessori community trying to reason with me.

"You're much cooler as a woman. Your androgyny—it's part of your charm," said a close musician friend of mine. "Don't do the obvious and become a man."

I decided I would not tell anyone but Reid, Dan, my Refugees cohorts Wendy and Deborah, a couple of other close friends, and of course Austin, that I was starting hormone replacement therapy—taking "T." Surely, nothing much would change in the next few months. I would be on a lower dose than younger trans men. I would not be growing any facial hair in the next few weeks. (However, I secretly wished I would—the Bullens family were essentially genetically hairless. Hell, even my brother couldn't grow a full beard!) My voice shouldn't change much if at all according to Dr. Bradley. There should be no dramatic outer changes or signs of transitioning in my understanding. If I wanted to stop it all, I could. No one would be the wiser.

Other than an enhanced libido (I had none before) and a slightly scratchy throat, the first few weeks on the "high" doses of testosterone were not particularly eventful. I was hyper focused day by day, watching, waiting, trying to feel or sense the tiniest effect, recording every single nuance in my journal. I was a little nervous about my throat—I had Refugees gigs coming up soon—but it didn't seem to affect my singing, at least when I was rehearsing by myself at home. Dr. Bradley was discussing different doses and shot cycles with me during that time, and finally we decided that after my Refugees tour, we would start with a quarter of the "normal" dose once per week.

What I did start to feel after a few weeks was a sense of *being* that I had not felt ever before. It was a sense of "rightness" in my body and in my brain. Like a big "YES" was emanating from within. I felt like I had discovered my magical missing ingredient. Estrogen, I realized, had been the bane of my life.

Journal Entry—September 27, 2011, Northridge, California, Day 27

Obsessed now with the name change. Last night (late again—in bed) thinking no, no, I'll put it off and suddenly my brain shifted and said YES! DO IT NOW—CIDNY TOBEY BULLENS. Just like that! I couldn't find the thought thread that got me there—there was none. It was like someone came and turned off the negative switch—BOOM! So at this moment, I'm going to do it next week.

The Refugees shows in Alberta, Canada, and Alaska went very well. We hadn't played together in several months, but as usual, the minute the three of us got into the same room (or on stage) we melded beautifully. I was still "Cindy." We were still "three women singer-songwriters" to our venue hosts and our audiences. But I was different. For one thing, I swore my voice was changing already. Only days before, in Maine, I felt no vocal affect from the scratchiness, but now singing live on stage, my throat felt thick, and my voice sounded just a bit rough. Dr. Bradley was wrong, I feared.

No one seemed to notice any variation in my voice, but I knew more than that was about to change. The Refugees, as bands do when on the road, were making plans into the far future—recordings and tours. I didn't know what my future would look like. I didn't know who I would *be* in the future. All I knew was that we had more gigs coming up in just a couple of weeks and my voice was already changing.

Deborah and Wendy knew exactly what I was doing. They knew I was now taking testosterone. I had to tell them. Wendy was starting to make clever cracks onstage about my gender "ambiguity," with me reacting with a comical it-is-what-it-is shoulder shrug. We laughed. I laughed. The audience loved it. Yet, I was surprised that they didn't seem to be concerned in the least bit with the possibility of my total transformation and what it might mean for us as a band.

"There's no time to waste now," Wendy said, walking in front of me, bags in hand, craning her neck side to side looking for our assigned seats on our Alaska Airlines flight from Anchorage to Los Angeles. Wendy and I were the same age, Deborah a few years younger. We had all been successful in music to some degree. But we had all also struggled with career and compromise, husbands and motherhood, and a lack of self-worth. "It's all about finding our own personal power and with it, our freedom."

Wendy frequently sounded like she was being interviewed on NPR by Diane Rehm or by Terry Gross on *Fresh Air*.

"I feel more expansive just by even exploring my gender," I said, shoving my over-stuffed backpack under my seat, mentally cursing the lack of room for my feet. "By the way, you know my voice could get lower. And . . . I could lose my hair." I didn't sound like I was on NPR. But I knew that was all true.

We talked for the whole flight to L.A., which was unusual because Wendy liked to sleep when we were traveling, any chance she could get. The subject of power and place kept us both awake, and for me, the lack of room to stretch my legs.

Journal Entry—October 7, 2011, Day 37

Got it! And changed my driver's license and SS card! And I was more excited when I left the courthouse than I thought I would be. REALLY excited! My name is official! My NAME! Wow!

I immediately sent out a letter in an email to my friends and extended family announcing that I had legally changed my name to Cidny Tobey Bullens. I received a few "Happy Birthdays" and "Welcome to the World" responses over the next few days, along with the general acknowledgments. No one seemed to be too upset, or surprised. Of course, this was about my name change only, not my so-far subversive transition tryout. I had a hunch that more than a few of those who had known me for my lifetime wondered if this announcement about my name was only a precursor to a bigger change.

Journal Entry—October 10, 2011, Day 40

Well, on Day 40 my voice is starting to crack—ever so slightly. I've been feeling the rawness in my throat for a while now, and it seems to be getting worse. Today I sang to "Three" [the new unreleased Refugees CD] in the car—I could feel a difference in reaching notes even from yesterday! Tonight it actually completely cracked, and it scared me. I have three solid weeks, almost four, of having to be able to sing! So suddenly, after all of my enthusiasm and joy for what I am doing—reality hits like a ton of bricks. I know I've been rolling the dice—walking on the edge—I may be about to fall off.

I got through the Refugees gigs in Colorado and the Northeast without any noticeable vocal issues, though I became acutely aware that I had to think about every single note I was singing. It was as though I couldn't trust what note I would end up on. It was a very strange feeling.

Wendy was no longer using "three women" in her intro and was now openly talking to the audience about me being transgender. She was on her own as usual, paving the road ahead, whether I was on it or not. Though it was all through humor and I didn't mind at all, I had not publicly come out.

The name issue was a bit more challenging. I had posted about it on Facebook and sent out a blog to my website email list, and I was informing folks one by one as I met them. But of course, all the marketing and advertising for the shows was done weeks and months before the performances. I let it slide.

Saying I was a trans person was still conceptual at this point. People still saw a masculine or androgynous female when they looked at me, same as before. There were no outer signs of physical maleness. The changing of my name, on the other hand, was a hard fact now. Yes, I could refrain from correcting someone if they called me "Cindy," but I had a license in my pocket that said otherwise. Sooner or later, male or female, I would become "Cid."

I had one "Jessie gig" coming up in Danville, Pennsylvania, at the Geisinger Medical Center that had been booked for over a year. I knew it could be my last. I wouldn't be able to tell my story as Jessie's mother if I came out as a transgender man. I figured I would only be able to manage one subject at a time, and so would my audience.

I was asked to do my workshop *Somewhere Between Heaven and Earth: Grieving Out Loud*, by Dr. Neil Ellison, an oncologist and the founder of the Palliative Care Program at Geisinger. Back in early 1999, I happened to sit next to Dr. Ellison on a flight from Philadelphia to Los Angeles. We were just random strangers traveling east to west—seatmates in 7A and 7B.

Once in the air, I pulled out some photos of Jessie, our family, and me, plus possible CD booklet designs for the upcoming release of my *Somewhere Between Heaven and Earth* album and started going through them on my tray table.

"What's that you're working on?" he asked me. "What do you do?"

I was surprised by his sudden directness. I don't always engage with whoever is sitting next to me on a plane. But this man, handsome and neatly dressed in a jacket and tie, was clearly interested in the pictures in front of me. I looked at him, trying to assess whether to reveal anything about me and the photos or not. Certainly, once I started talking about Jessie, the whole story would come out. Did I want to do that now, here with this stranger? But I could plainly see from the softness in his eyes that there was no threat there. There was an invitation.

"Well," I started sheepishly, knowing I would be imposing the weight of my personal life on a stranger. I looked at him again. He was waiting patiently for more. "Um, I lost my daughter to cancer almost three years ago. I'm a songwriter, and I am making an album about it." I didn't look up.

"Oh, I'm sorry." He said sincerely. "I'm an oncologist. What kind of cancer did she have?"

Our friendship began at that moment. He wanted to know everything. For the next four hours Dr. Neil Ellison explained more to me about Jessie's illness and the probable reasons for her sudden death than anyone before him. He alone alleviated my still nightly haunting about the decision to take Jessie off life support.

"No parent should *ever* have to make that choice," he stated emphatically. "We have to fix that in our system. The doctor should be telling the parents that it's the reasonable and humane decision. That way a parent like you doesn't carry all of that responsibility around for the rest of your life."

He told me he was on his way to a conference of palliative care physicians in L.A. and that he would be in touch. He wanted me to come to another conference in Utah in a few months to tell my story and play the songs from the album. He hadn't even heard them yet.

I gave him my contact info and a CD copy of the rough mixes I had on me. We hugged each other warmly as we left the baggage claim area to go our separate ways. He went off to his conference, and I went onto mix a few of the songs with Bob Clearmountain. As I was walking away from him, I realized I left something on the plane—a big, heavy bag full of questions and a huge burden of guilt.

Through Dr. Ellison, I was invited to the American Academy of Palliative Care Physicians conference that year in Snowbird, Utah. It was the first of many, many conference appearances and workshops I would do as a bereaved parent. Now in November 2011, twelve years later, this conference at Geisinger Medical Center, through Dr. Ellison, would most likely be the last.

Journal Entry—November 22, 2011, Day 83

I'm feeling uneasy today, not comfortable in my own skin. Maybe partly "dysphoric"—a word I hear and see a lot from transmen on YouTube who are transitioning—the struggle between who you are and who you are not. My upper body is bigger, making my shirts and bras feel tight and uncomfortable. It makes me want to be rid of my breasts even more. For a moment this morning, I actually felt like crying. I'm not sure why, but maybe because I'm literally "out of sorts" with myself.

After my fall gigs were over, I went back to work at the Y for the winter. I had no gigs until February, and right then I really needed the respite and grounding of a schedule, my clients and the staff, and the place itself. I was still mentally all over the place. I was still split about transitioning fully, even though I was already taking all the steps to do just that. Plus, there were also changes happening to my body and my voice, as subtle as they were. Some would change back if I stopped testosterone, like the fat and muscle distribution. But others would be permanent, hair gain and hair loss. More importantly, the thickening of my vocal cords was irreversible.

———————

Journal Entry—November 29, 2011, Day 90

Day 90! Hard to believe 90 days have gone by since starting T. With all my questions and quandaries, I continue to move forward. I just spent 20 minutes going over the calendar to see when I could squeeze in 6-8 weeks for top surgery. Maybe early June?

I sat in the chair in the middle of the small, beige room, waiting. Austin stood quietly in the corner, iPad in hand, ready to film. The full-length mirror on the wall in front of me was about to reflect an image of my future. What that future would be, I did not know. I only knew that now there was no going back.

A thick bandage wrapped tightly around my chest, soon to be unraveled, would reveal part of the long-hidden essence of who I knew myself to be.

After about ten minutes, Dr. Charles Garramone and his assistant walked in.

"Hi! Are you ready? Are you excited?" he smiled and immediately started taking off my bandages, already knowing the answer to both questions.

"Yes!" I said. That was the only word I could utter at that moment.

Austin pressed record.

Dr. Charles Garramone performed this one specific surgery—female-to-male (FTM) chest reconstruction—his entire career. It was his sole mission to give his transmen patients, young and old, a second life—a life where they could see themselves, finally, as they physically always should have been.

As he walked around me again and again, with more and more of the bandage unwinding, he made a few comments, but I couldn't hear him. I was fixated on the revelation in the mirror that was about to take place.

My mind snapped back to that lazy August afternoon on Chebeague Island in Maine when I was twelve years old, to the moment when there was a different kind of revelation—that cruel moment that revealed that I was not in reality a boy. That fateful day, I would put on my shirt, never to show my chest again in public for what I thought was forever.

Dr. Garramone unwound the last of the long, wide, cloth bandage, and carefully, slowly tore off the soiled, bloody gauze covering my fragile, newly placed nipples. He stood behind me as I stared into the mirror, breastless, and smiled again.

In the six days between the surgery and my post-op appointment, I had little to no emotion about the fact that I had just had a double mastectomy. I had no negative feelings about losing my breasts. It was as if nothing could be real until I actually saw the results.

Both Austin and Reid flew down to Ft. Lauderdale to be with me through the surgery. Reid would fly back to Maine the day after, while Austin would stay with me for the full eight days.

The morning of the surgery, after I took my shower, Reid came into my room in our hotel suite. We both had decided that we needed to celebrate the one significant act that my breasts had performed in my life. Ironically, I had loved each tender moment of breastfeeding both of my children. The opportunity was a gift that I cherished then, and I cherish now. In those precious times, I thrived as a mother, as did my babies on my milk.

It was a brief, but poignant ceremony, blessing the source of Reid's first nourishment as a baby. We honored my breasts for their service and sent them off with a fond, final farewell.

Now, looking into the mirror in front of me, I could not contain my joy.

"Oh my God! Holy crap!" I wanted to laugh and cry at the same time. I had a man's chest! It was red and rashy, irritated by being bound up tight for a week in the humid Florida heat, but it was beautiful and finally, *finally* right. I was sixty-two years old, but I was staring at a much younger body, and a brand-new person.

As I stared into the mirror in a near ecstatic daze, Dr. Garramone leaned down and whispered gently into my right ear. "Well," he said softly, "I decided to give you a twenty-five-year-old chest."

Journal Entry—May 30, 2012, Newark Airport, Day 275

I'm not sure I can express my joy and awe in words. It feels SO natural to be flat-chested. And I feel different than I did this morning before I got my bandages off. And I just went into the MEN'S room for the first time here at the airport! Luckily, I walked straight into a stall and straight out as fast as I could without encountering anyone. I didn't even wash my hands. It was strange and a bit scary. But—onward!

Cid with his new chest, June 2012.
Photo by and courtesy of Reid Crewe

15

PURGATORY ROAD

Did I leave myself stranded?
Did I get myself lost?
There's no going back over
All those lines I've crossed
There's nothing I can do now
'Cept carry my own load
And just keep on walking down
Purgatory Road

> *"Purgatory Road" by Cidny Bullens*
> *©2019 Red Dragonfly Music/BMI*

Journal Entry—May 13, 2012, Day 258

In many ways, I am feeling increasingly empowered as I get closer to revealing my truth. And less afraid. I will be relieved when it's all said and done.

"You'll be doing a lot of good." Said Dave Marsh, as we visited in his writing den in Norwalk, Connecticut.

Only ten days before flying to Ft. Lauderdale for my scheduled surgery, I was driving to Falls Church, Virginia, to meet Deborah and Wendy for some mid-Atlantic Refugees shows. I stopped in to see Dave on my way down from Maine. I had called him a few days before and told him about my transition, but there was something else I wanted to discuss with him. I felt it was best to do it in person.

Dave Marsh was not only a brilliant music writer and author, but he was also the epitome of someone who called something like he saw it. He had caused many a ruffled feather over his years as a well-known journalist, author, music critic, radio host, and social commentator. I trusted him implicitly.

Dave had been present for me only weeks after Jessie died when he called me out of the blue and shared his experience of losing his step-daughter, Kristen Ann Carr. He helped guide me forward with kindness and resolve. Without his belief and encouragement around those songs inspired by Jessie, and my need to express my grief of losing her through them, I'm not sure my album *Somewhere Between Heaven and Earth* would have ever been made.

Now sixteen years later, I again sought his counsel and expertise. I was in the process of writing an essay, an article, publicly declaring myself as transgender. I had been working on it for weeks and wanted to make sure it was exactly right—that it said precisely what I wanted it to say. I asked Dave to read it.

"This is extremely well-written," he said, looking across his desk at me with his piercing blue eyes. The early afternoon sunlight bounced through the two double-hung, small-paned windows on the far side of the room. The den in Dave and Barbara's 1700s colonial house was painted white, with dark brown pine beams across the ceiling and a wide-planked hardwood floor. In it were his desk, floor-to-ceiling bookshelves, a few odd chairs, several Persian rugs of various colors and sizes, and a warmth that made me feel very safe and comfortable.

"Thanks," I replied with a mixture of pride and gratitude. "I've been working on it for a while now." He pointed out a couple of small things he felt needed clarifying and a few grammatical errors. "I'll help you in any way I can. I think you're going to get some good publicity out of this."

I wasn't sure I wanted publicity exactly. But I did want to have a legitimate journalistic vehicle which would get my article out to the public in the best possible way.

I arrived in Falls Church later that day and was greeted by my friend Mark Potts and his wife Jane, with whom we were staying. Wendy and Deborah had not yet arrived.

Mark was like a brother to me. I loved him. He was another person in my life who pulled no punches. He was honest and straightforward while being completely supportive. Mark was also a journalist and an author.

I had been keeping my transition a secret for now almost nine months. I was a little amazed at myself that I had managed to keep quiet about it even to some of my closest friends, Mark being one.

Jane was upstairs making up the Refugees' bedrooms. Mark and I were standing in the kitchen as he began to prepare a batch of his fresh *pico de gallo* that he knew I loved so much.

"I need to tell you something," I blurted out, ripping open the fresh bag of tortilla chips. "I've been taking testosterone, I'm getting chest surgery next week, and I'm going to transition to a man."

Mark, a big, tall teddy bear of a man—kind, generous, and always looking at the bright side of things—stopped cutting up the tomatoes, turned, knife in hand, and looked at me straight in the eye. Then he smiled, put down the knife, and pulled me in for a long hug.

"I'm so proud of you! I guess I knew this was coming for a while now."

Yet another person not shocked, I thought. I was once again relieved.

"You know what you have to do now, don't you?" He said in his brotherly I-mean-it kind of way.

"What?" I said, thinking I knew full well what was coming next. Mark had been nudging me for a long time.

"Write your book!"

I nodded. "Yup, I know." I could not even fathom such a task at that moment, though I knew now at some point I would have to write about my life in some form.

"Before writing a book," I said with a mouth full of chips, "I need you to read my coming out essay. Maybe you can suggest an outlet that would publish it."

Mark had been a longtime journalist at the *Washington Post*, *Chicago Tribune*, and other news organizations. A digital news pioneer, he jump-started the *Washington Post*'s online efforts in the early '90s, which led to washingtonpost.com. He knew a lot of people in the media.

On June 16, 2012, my essay was published in the *Daily Beast*. Mark Potts sent an email to his friend, CNN's *Reliable Source*s host Howard Kurtz, who was also working for the *Daily Beast*. Within minutes, Howard responded to Mark, and eight days later, after a few emails back and forth between Howard and me, my piece was published—"Singer Cindy Bullens Goes Public: She's Becoming Cidny, a Man."

OK, not my favorite title, but who was I to complain? There it was. And now here I was—out.

> *Journal Entry—June 17, 2012, Day 293*
>
> *Well, word is out, and so am I! It's all over the net. Believe it or not, since the article, I've had second thoughts again about all of it. It's just fear of course. It's like wanting to get pregnant and then <u>getting</u> pregnant—you're gonna have that baby!*

There was no going back now. I had to show up wherever I went. I had to face any and all circumstances now knowing that I would not ever again be viewed the same way.

Portland, Maine, was a safe place for me. I knew so many people in so many different circles. The local media had been doing stories on me since I moved there in 1991—first about me as a musician, then about me as a bereaved parent, the Jessie Foundation, and of course, the *Somewhere Between Heaven and Earth* album.

I was active in political campaigns and state referendum issues. I even ran for State Senate at one point. (I withdrew in a three-way race so my neighbor, who was the Independent, could win. He did.) I had been interviewed dozens of times for television and radio all over Maine. I called several local news anchors and media-personality friends.

Before the release of *Somewhere Between Heaven and Earth,* anchor Cindy Williams from the Portland NBC affiliate relayed her story about the album to the higher-ups at Rockefeller Center. That effort landed me an appearance and story on *The Today Show* in September 1999. The same thing happened with the local CBS anchor Kim Block. I wound up with an appearance on *CBS This Morning* in October of that year. Now they would tell this story, too. Both channels would broadcast statewide.

Another media friend, Rob Caldwell, who hosted the local television news magazine *207*, where I'd made many an appearance as Cindy, would feature me for a segment. My transition would be portrayed as a positive thing, as an uplifting story of someone becoming their authentic self.

This was Maine. I would be safe. *Nobody would care here, would they?* I've been a good citizen, a conscientious resident, a contributing member of society in this state. But there was a question in the back of my mind that started to pierce my thoughts: *What happens when I go somewhere else? What happens when I go on the road?*

Journal Entry—July 16, 2012, Day 319

I'm floundering a bit, rudderless in an open sea. I am in between genders. It's starting to cross my mind that I should have kept it all to myself. (But I still love my chest.)

I started working at the YMCA again for a few hours per week. It was a safe space within a safe place. I had a thought that the Y would be the perfect place to start changing my pronoun. All my friends and siblings were referring to me as "she/her" still because I hadn't been asking them to do otherwise. I was extremely hesitant to start that process. This was, after all, in my mind, the step that sealed the deal.

I asked for a meeting with the Freeport Y branch director. Everyone at the Y had been extremely supportive of my transition and I knew everyone would honor whatever I wanted to do in this regard. My Y name had always been "CB." When I started back in 2006, I didn't want "Cindy" on my nametag. I wanted to be anonymous, even though at the time, that really didn't work anyway. "CB" stuck then and still worked now.

"Scott, I've been thinking a lot about this, and I think it's time for me to change my pronoun. Could you tell the staff to start using 'he/him/his'?" I heard my own words squeaking through my throat. My stomach was in knots. *Why is this so hard?*

"Of course!" he said, pushing away from his desk and sitting straight up in his office chair. "Absolutely. You know how proud we are to have you here." Scott Krouse was a kind and gentle soul. A tall, slender man somewhere around forty, with tiny hints of gray in his short, cropped hair. I never saw him without a smile.

The consensus from the Y leadership was that not only would my pronoun be changed, but they suggested that I also change my nametag to "Cid."

Even though I had changed my name ten months earlier, almost no one except my recovery friends were consistently calling me "Cid." I would remind my siblings and those friends closest to me on occasion, but I didn't push it. I knew it was hard enough for them to process all the other changes in me. What they probably didn't realize was that it was extremely difficult for me to process too.

The restroom issue was a whole other kettle of fish. At the Y, I would go into the pool area "family changing rooms." But out in the real world, the need to pee felt extremely precarious. Now I had a flat chest, and my upper body was starting to fill out, but my face was just as ambiguous as it was before transition.

"Can I help you, sir?" This was the repeating refrain of my entire adult life—as a woman. The response I would give, if any, depended on my mood or the day or my energy level or who I was with.

"It's ma'am," I retorted at times when I simply wanted to challenge their perception of gender.

"Oh, I didn't really look. I mean, I didn't see you. I just . . . "

The words would trail off, and the quizzical look would transform into either an apologetic smile or avoidance all together. I didn't blame them. I wasn't angry. It was my fact of life. Nobody could see me. Now it was happening again, only my response, if any, was the opposite. "It's sir." I said, challenging not only them but myself.

Using the men's room, at this in-between time, and at my age, was a different story. I was very nervous. Of course, as a teenager and an early twenty-something, I didn't care at all. Nobody else did either. The mid-1960s to the mid-1970s was a time when the gender-specific appearance of half the younger population was questionable.

Now, I took a cautionary pause when I stood between the men's and women's restroom entrances. The decision to go into one or the other was based on my location, how many people were around, and my general comfort level at that moment. If someone else was in there, which I tried to avoid, I would usually get a look either way.

"If a man sits down to pee," Dan offered one night, driving to our regular Friday night AA meeting, "the sound of the stream is different than a woman's."

We were discussing the nuances of male behavior. My eyes widened. Of course! That made total sense to me. I had to go into a stall no matter what and sit. There could be no standing up at the urinals for me. "Don't make eye contact either," he advised. "Usually, men don't look at each other."

I listened intently. I had to learn how to be a regular guy. Plus, I did not want to draw any attention to myself in that situation, ever.

"Look straight ahead when you walk in. If you have to wait for a stall, look down or gaze into nowhere," Dan continued as we pulled into the parking lot of St. Ansgar's Lutheran Church. "You can't go around complimenting cute babies, either, like you did as a mother. Women do not want strange men lurking around their children."

Wow, I thought. *This is not going to be easy.* I had been nearly sequestered in Maine since my surgery in May—in Portland, at the Y, and on the island. I was also visiting Bob Crewe a few nights a week as a kind of a personal aide. Bob was now in an assisted-living facility in Scarborough with dementia. I didn't really have to act any different than when I was Cindy; at least I didn't think about it all that much.

Sixty-one years of socialization as a woman, a female, regardless of how I felt inside, was the reality. Being *seen* as a man would be a completely different reality. I had better keep my eyes wide open and take nothing for granted.

———

The Refugees had kept our scheduled short run of shows in and around Chicago in mid-September. *Why not?* I thought when we parted ways back in the spring. I'd be fine. My voice was a bit scratchy, but I could sing. I did not project any issues between the spring and those gigs. Yes, I would have my top surgery, but as Reid said, it was not like anyone would know the difference.

The Americana Music Conference in Nashville was the week before Chicago. I decided to attend, thinking that it would be a good public testing ground for my new persona outside of Maine. I'd know a bunch of people, and, after all, these were musicians and music businesspeople, *my* people. I was publicly out now. Who better to test my new gender on? I'd drive down to Nashville and then up to Chicago, after the conference, to meet Wendy and Deborah.

"Terry, this is Cindy Bullens. She's a great singer-songwriter. You should definitely hook up and write with her." It didn't seem important or necessary for me to correct the person introducing us. She was only an acquaintance, and somehow I knew I would not hook up with this guy.

The hallway of the Nashville Sheraton Downtown Hotel was filled with other singers, songwriters, and musicians from all over the country and the world. I recognized the kinetic energy that was permeating this time and space. I had experienced it many times over the years.

The people attending conferences like these were hoping for a chance, any chance, a random connection in the hallway that led to a radio show invitation or a cowriting opportunity, or a showcase that led to a new manager or a gig or a recording contract.

As I glanced around at all the intense faces walking past me, huddled in bunches or hunched over in the lobby chairs, digging through their swag bags, I was surprised that I barely knew a soul. This was only the beginning of the first day of the conference, but I began to get a bad feeling. I felt utterly alone.

After forcing myself to stay, I wandered into a couple of the morning and afternoon workshops and encountered a few people I knew, only one of whom knew of my current situation. The feeling of isolation grew as the day went on. Finally, before the afternoon sessions were over, I left.

"Hey Michael! It's Cid. I'm here in Nashville. You wanna come into town and grab a bite with me?" My good friend Michael Kelsh lived about forty-five minutes out of town in Fairview, Tennessee. I knew he didn't come in much unless he was rehearsing or playing somewhere. But I was desperate for some solid, trusted company, with someone who knew me well. Michael knew everything—we had been in touch just before I left Maine. I'm sure he could hear the underlying panic now in my voice.

This trip was the first time anyone I knew outside of Maine was seeing me fully transitioned. And contrary to my confidence prior to coming, I now felt totally out of place. Driving away from the Sheraton, I felt something very, very familiar starting to overtake me. What was it? What was this feeling? It was grief.

What the FUCK did I do? What did I DO? Where is Cindy!?

I started to sob. I held on tight to the steering wheel as the black veil I knew so well descended deep down into my whole body and being. The hot sun was glaring through the windshield, westward in the late-afternoon September sky. I could barely see the road between the sun and my tears. *Cindy is dead.* I started to shake. She was gone. I was no longer her. I had killed her. I was grieving the death of myself.

Who was Cid? I had no answer. *Nobody* knew who he was! I certainly didn't. He had not revealed himself yet. At this moment, I wasn't sure I wanted to hold out long enough for that to happen.

I called Reid on my cell phone. "Mom, it's going to be all right. I promise. If you have to come home, come home. But you're going to be all right." I took a breath. We chatted about the kids for another few minutes, and then I thanked her and hung up. I felt better. I took another breath. I had a daughter. If I had no one else, I had a living daughter. She came out of *my* body. *I* had birthed her. She was proof that Cindy had existed.

I decided to drive to Radnor Lake to take a walk before getting together with Michael. It was one of my go-to places in town where I felt close to nature and could think. I had run into Rodney Crowell there, all those years ago, after Jessie died. It was that conversation that led me, months later, to want to work with him on *Somewhere Between Heaven and Earth*.

The fresh air and the sight of the lake water calmed me as I climbed the hill up from the parking lot and past the ever-present box turtles sunning themselves on the fallen trees. When I got back to my car, I grabbed my notebook. A sudden breakout of words erupted from the emotion of the day.

> *I felt the hot, black tar*
> *Beneath my shiftin' feet*
> *I heard the rumble of the fire*
> *Before I felt the heat*

Like a moth to a flame
I felt my wings explode
Now I find myself stumblin'
Down Purgatory Road
I got a hole in my pocket
And it's drivin' me mad
I've lost every little bit
Of any sense I had
I'm in a whole lotta trouble
It's a fact I know
Cause I can't see what's comin'
Down Purgatory Road

Journal Entry—September 13, 2012

On my walk I thought, I MUST come through this place—this mental, emotional, spiritual place—myself. In other words, hoping that a job, money, relationship is gonna save me, is not gonna happen—shouldn't happen! I'm afraid. I feel groundless, lost, floating in space. The sense of having everything blow up in my face—that nothing is as it once was—is present now as it was when Jessie died. This time I did it to myself!

Michael met me at Fido in Hillsboro Village. I could not have been happier to see him. A good-looking man of average height and weight. Michael was wearing his usual checkered flannel shirt, faded jeans, and his old, seriously scuffed hiking boots. He was also sporting his usual shaggy hair and his ever-present salt-and-pepper goatee. He looked like he lived in an old cabin in the woods, which was exactly where he lived. Michael was one the most kind, loving, authentic people I knew, and he was also one hell of a musician and songwriter.

"What's up, Cid?" Michael gave me his "I've got you" smile and threw his arms around me.

I had several more days in Nashville before I could drive up to Chicago. I never went back to the conference at the hotel. Michael, being the angel that he is, spent the better part of those few days being my companion, my rock, my friend. He kept me close as we bounced from music venue to music venue, coffee shop to coffee shop, restaurant to restaurant. We even played a few songs together to a small crowd at a friend's Americana showcase. He didn't seem to mind hanging out with Cid, even if Cid didn't know who he was yet.

Journal Entry—September 21, 2012, Chicago

Well I guess you couldn't get too much more bizarre than where I am right now. Deb and I are staying in the convent WITH the Polish nuns at St. Ferdinand's Parish in Chicago. I am "Cindy" here. Since no men are allowed anywhere near the convent.

"I'd like to welcome these three lovely ladies to the station, Wendy Waldman, Deborah Holland, and Cindy Bullens—the Refugees." *Oh no*, I thought. *Here we go again.* I said nothing. Neither did Wendy or Deborah. We were live on the radio. Let it go. We then traveled to Ann Arbor, Michigan, for a day to tape the longtime syndicated radio show *Acoustic Café*. Again, we were three women. Nothing was said. I was invisible. Weren't we just joking about me on stage in the spring before I officially came out? These were live radio broadcasts, not venue gigs like in the spring. Hundreds if not thousands of people were listening. We were there on our hosts' terms. We were expected to play our music, as a band, on their shows about music, not tread into the territory of gender or politics or societal norms. But I felt like I was moving backward.

Wendy had arranged a private concert for the St. Ferdinand's Church parishioners in Chicago through her Polish friend who was the pastor, hence Deb's and my sleeping arrangements. That particular experience would have been fine if not for my current state of mind. The nuns seemed nice enough when we encountered one. But our time together for this little group of gigs was fraught with various little professional snags and individual personal issues, though we always performed at our highest level. The icing on the cake for me was the fact that on these shows, I discovered that I truly could not sing some of the high notes of my songs in the set at all.

After my experience in Nashville and now Chicago—with nobody knowing exactly who or what I was—I now felt like a machete had sliced my being in two, leaving nothing in the center. I was in Purgatory. I had no definitive me to hold on to.

We decided to cancel the few coming dates we had booked over the fall and winter and take a break from the Refugees. After our last concert that week, I couldn't drive home to Maine fast enough.

Journal Entry—September 27, 2012

Catching up. Today I'm going to work in the yard. I've seen the kids twice already, and that's always good for the soul. I feel better being home—it was truly an unsettling trip!

I had sold my little red schoolhouse in Cumberland to Dan a few months before. I needed the cash, and he thought he could renovate and sell it. I moved into the upstairs apartment of a duplex that Dan had also purchased recently as an investment, in a quiet neighborhood just west of the downtown peninsula in Portland. Ever the "fixer," Dan decided to house both me and my now former son-in-law Derek in the same house. Derek got the bigger apartment downstairs, so he could have my granddaughters stay when it was his turn.

I was very happy with the plan. If Dan wanted to interject himself into my life again, so be it. I was grateful. I did not have a clue what my future would hold now. I was an old transman. I had just dipped my toe into the waters of my profession, and the results, for me, were disastrous. The less fiscal and outside responsibilities I had now, the better. I needed to close in on myself and hide away—at least for a while.

————————

- Bend, lift, grab, reach and squat, repeatedly
- Stand and walk entire 8-hour shift (approx. 9 miles)
- Lift to 50 lbs. overhead frequently

- Strong attention to detail and accuracy
- Comfortable working in a fast-paced, physically demanding environment

Anyone who has lived in Maine for any length of time has either worked or thought of working at or for L.L. Bean. That's what they said anyway. At this point, I was so devoid of any sense of self that I didn't even want to go back to work at the Y, as accommodating as it was. I wanted absolutely zero interactions with the public, any public. And with winter coming on, I knew that if I didn't have a schedule, somewhere specific to go, and a little extra cash coming in, I would descend rapidly into my all-too-familiar den of darkness. I was already in a very fragile state.

A job in the fulfillment warehouse at L.L. Bean, which was just a few miles up the road in Freeport, sounded like the perfect fit. I'd be just one of the many signing on for the season from all over southern Maine. Surely, I would be anonymous there. The warehouse was huge. I could easily hide. And if I were hired, I would start soon, in mid-October.

"I love your music," said a middle-aged, blonde, bespectacled woman walking by as I hung up my coat on one of the large temporary coatracks just inside the entrance of the warehouse. She said it almost under her breath as if she didn't want anyone else to hear her. Surprised, I glanced at the nametag on her forest-green year-round employee shirt: supervisor. It was only a few days after I had started the job. She didn't stop walking. She just smiled and kept going.

"Thanks," I replied hesitantly as she passed. I decided I'd better smile back, not yet knowing how the hierarchal system worked within the company. *Shit!* I looked around hoping no one else heard the exchange. No one did. The swishing sound of the new employees' nylon parkas rubbing together and metal hangers clinking on the metal racks filled the large foyer. There was little conversation anywhere. None of us knew each other yet.

It doesn't matter, I reassured myself. *It's just one person, and you won't be working on the floor with her.*

None of my seasonal coworkers seemed to think I was anyone other than another random guy working the second shift. At least that was what I was hoping. I *was* a guy now, wasn't I?

We were "pickers," picking any and all of L.L. Bean's merchandise off the miles of shelves stacked high in dozens of rows on the shiny, gray concrete floor of the 980,000 square foot structure, throwing the items into oversized carts and dumping them down the giant chutes to be shipped off around the world in time for Christmas.

My orientation class was a diverse bunch. Seasonal workers came from every walk of life. They ranged from college kids to housewives to retirees, laid-off construction workers and teachers, immigrants from Somalia and Ethiopia. Someone was starting over after a divorce, another just out of rehab. There were a few local artists and other musicians. I worked alongside a former doctor who wanted a respite from his stressful life.

The company policies were taught to us in our orientation class, along with the proper way to reach and grab, squat, and bend. I was grateful to learn that the company had a strict diversity and inclusion policy—absolutely no bias would be tolerated at any time, in any form, for any reason.

In the beginning, I was always on high alert. I watched myself as I interacted with my coworkers, both men and women.

I must have walked an extra few miles on every shift going to the farthest, most remote men's rooms in the facility, all to avoid close personal contact with the other male workers. Most of the warehouse men's restrooms had only one stall, and the one or two urinals were right up against it.

Watch the tone of your voice and try not to reveal too much, I reminded myself over and over. My voice had a tendency to move into a higher range when I was excited or talking intensely about something. When I was conversing with women on a break, if they mentioned their children, I had to remember that *men have never been pregnant and do not have babies! They aren't mothers! Try not to reveal anything!*

"You see the game last night?"

"Jeezus, friggin' Jets! We shoulda crushed 'em."

The men were easier. As a lifelong New England sports fan, I knew facts and statistics I didn't even know I knew. I could talk about old cars and new home renovations. I hate to say it, but the gender topic divides were fairly typical, at least there at the L.L. Bean warehouse. However, cooking was a subject almost everybody loved. This was something about which I knew very little. I listened.

It was hard, physical work, and I loved it. I loved being present and, in the moment, being anonymous and a regular guy. I showed up for whatever the job required of me that particular day. All I had to think about was picking the correct count and SKU number of flannel shirts or backpacks or wool socks in a timely fashion and send them down the right chute.

Ironically, now free from any outside obligation or public pressure, I started to think about writing a one-person show. The thought had been in the back of my mind even years before I transitioned. I liked the idea of telling my story on stage in a theatrical setting. Writing a book still seemed too daunting to me. A solo show might be less of an effort, but I would still have control over telling my own story my own way. I knew I had the beginning and the middle of the story when I first thought of the idea: the old rock 'n' roll days, my marriage, kids, and the loss of Jessie. But where to after that?

Oh! Wait a minute. The thought occurred to me one day as I was getting ready for work. *Now I have the story!* With my transition, the arc of the story was complete. Furthermore, maybe now a solo show could be a "bridge" to help people understand my decision to change from Cindy to Cidny.

On my own in the huge concrete hangar-like space of the L.L. Bean warehouse, from 2:30 PM to midnight, my mind was free to wander. Day after day, I walked twelve to fifteen miles pushing a large, heavy aluminum cart, filling it with every item in their famous catalog, and now I was recalling my own personal catalog of life-changing moments and memories.

Sometimes when I was given the task of sorting different L.L. Bean signature crochet-like Christmas stockings—the deer, the Santa Claus, the candy cane house, the Christmas tree—I would be sorting through my own life stories and scenarios. I slowly started piecing together a concept.

I decided I would begin the story in 1973, when I arrived in Los Angeles, and I would end in the present. But how in the hell would I stick forty years' worth of living, *plus* I figured at least eight live songs, into ninety minutes? I needed help.

16

CALL ME BY MY NAME

Oh are you there? In the sky?
Or wherever your grace lives
I pray for some time—Just to breathe
And find where my place is
And please, please
Call me by my name

> *"Call Me by My Name" by Cidny Bullens*
> *©2019 Red Dragonfly Music/BMI*

I COULD SMELL THE SAGE and piñon as I drove slowly up the dusty, dirt-ribbed road off Old Las Vegas Highway just outside the city of Santa Fe, New Mexico. I was glad I rented an SUV as the ruts and ridges in the road continued to deepen the farther in I drove. It was April 28, 2014.

I had loved Santa Fe from the first time I went, way back with Dan in 1974. I had been there a bunch of times since, with the Alpha Band in 1977, on my own to visit friends, with Reid after Jessie's death, and a few times for gigs with the Refugees. I had been drawn to the place since I was a teenager, always wanting to travel there. The minute I crossed the border from Colorado that first trip with Dan driving south down US Route 285, full rainbow aloft, I felt an unusual, deep bond with the land and the light.

I flew in a couple of days early just so I could drive the "high road" from Santa Fe to Taos, through the small mountain villages, stopping at the sacred Santuario de Chimayo, and then back down over the Rio Grande Gorge Bridge on US Route 64. I marveled as always at the breathtaking grand vistas of mountains and high desert, and in the tiny details in the windows and doors of the pueblo-style homes.

I pulled into a driveway hoping it was the correct address. The GPS had ceased to work once I turned off the main road onto Apache Ridge. I took a deep breath and opened the car door. I took another nervous breath as I grabbed my guitar out of the back seat. I had no idea what I was walking into.

"Hi, Cid. Welcome." The woman across the threshold of the opening door smiled warmly as I walked up to the entrance of her modest two-story house.

She was tall and attractive, with blonde shoulder-length hair complimenting her flawless, almost opaque complexion. The pattern on her summer dress reminded me that I was not in Maine. This was the Southwest. Everything was brightly colored. Her piercing, blue-green eyes pulled me in, and I felt a sudden stir as I walked into her pleasant, wood-framed, rustic home. I made a quick mental note of that feeling. The wooden door closed behind me.

Since the idea of a one-person show firmly took hold of me a year and a half before, I had been looking for someone, some thing, some process to sort through the wide and varied spectrum of my life, so I could tell it in a short form.

Tanya Taylor Rubinstein was a story coach. I found her after months of periodically searching the internet for solo show classes and courses. I couldn't go to New York for a yearlong course at the New School, or to courses in San Francisco or London or Chicago or even Boston. I almost gave up.

One day early in the year, after watching parts of various one-man and one-woman shows on YouTube, I again googled "solo show courses." This time I saw something I hadn't seen before—Solo Performance Coach. I clicked on tanyataylorrubinstein.com.

A Pepto-Bismol pink website popped up. I almost clicked off. But just then my eye caught the word "bootcamp." *Sign up for my solo performance bootcamp! After four days with me in Santa Fe, you'll leave with a full outline of your show.*

Wow, I thought, surprised. *One-on-one. I'd have an outline. And she's in Santa Fe!* Still, I hesitated. Was I truly ready to commit to writing this? Finally, in late February, I looked her up again. I watched Tanya performing some of her own one-woman show "Honeymoon in India" on YouTube. It was funny, and she was good. There was only one other story coach that I could find online anywhere, and he didn't offer what Tanya Taylor Rubinstein was offering. I sent her a short message through her pink website:

> Hi Tanya. My name is Cidny Bullens. I am a singer-songwriter and a two-time Grammy nominee. I toured with Elton John and sang lead vocals on the *Grease* movie soundtrack. I am also a bereaved parent, and I transitioned recently from female to male. I am interested in talking with you about your solo show bootcamp.

In this winter of 2014, I was still moving through my transition as quietly as possible. Deborah Holland had gotten me to step out of my shell for a week in mid-February to do a short northeastern tour backing her on guitar and vocals. Otherwise, I continued to be a seasonal employee at L.L. Bean. I had been asked to work at the warehouse through the summer of 2013 and now into the new winter season. I agreed to do all that, still not convinced of any future in music.

Just an hour after I sent the message to Tanya, I received an email. "I'd be happy to talk with you, Cidny. Let's set up a time for a call."

A couple of weeks later, Tanya Taylor Rubinstein and I talked on the phone for well over an hour. Her niche was helping people flesh out the true meat and essence of their stories to be performed as solo shows. That's what I needed. Plus, my idea was not just in my own head now; there was someone else affirming it. More than that, Tanya seemed to get me.

"Would you like a cup of coffee?" Tanya asked as I laid my guitar case down on the terracotta-tiled floor of her studio. The room was bright and airy, surrounded by pinewood framed windows and walls. Outside, as far as one could see, juniper bushes covered the hills of rocky, light brown desert sand. There was a woodstove in the southeast corner, a dark red sofa where Tanya would sit and a high-backed stool in the middle of the room, waiting ominously for me.

The first day was relatively easy. We chatted a bit about my current life, and I told her about the bigger points of my past—my career beginnings, marriage, kids, Jessie's illness and death, and my transition in more detail. Tanya took copious notes. After we shared a big, fresh green salad for lunch, I played some songs that I thought should be in the show: "Boxing with God," "The End of Wishful Thinking," "Gravity and Grace," and "Better Than I've Even Been."

Toward the end of our session, as we were wrapping up the day, Tanya casually said something that would scare the hell out of me.

"Cid, you can tell your story, and it will be good. Or you can embody your story, and it will be great." I stared at her, frozen. "You need to tell it in the present tense, like it's happening right now."

My mind flashed through all the same stories I had just told her in the past tense. Did she mean that I had to *relive* each scene as I spoke it? I could only envision the telling of Jessie's death on stage during each performance *in the present.* No. Fucking. Way.

I went back to the Residence Inn terrified and exhausted. But I also knew I had been challenged.

Journal Entry—April 28, 2014

I had had this idea of doing a show for a long time. I would tell my story with a few songs mixed in. I thought Tanya was going to help me figure out what to tell and in which order. It was all cerebral and abstract. What did I know? I'll have to work! Dig deep! Feel and care about it all! Shit!

Unsure that I could do what Tanya was asking of me, I decided to switch off my head and switch on the television. The channel that popped on was HBO. There in front of me, just minutes after it had begun, was Billy Crystal's one-man show *700 Sundays.* I had been dying to see his show, but I didn't have HBO. And now? On this night? Was it a coincidence?

I pulled up the beige fabric-covered chair by the pull-out sofa and pulled it close to the TV. For the next two hours, I sat totally absorbed by the funny, poignant, and very real performance by Billy Crystal in his brilliant show.

That's how you do it, I thought. *But can I?*

"I don't think I can do this, Tanya." I said deadly serious as I walked into her studio the next morning and set my coffee down on the little table by my stool. I had had little sleep. "Honestly. It will be too much for me to actually be in the moment with my whole story."

"OK. Let's not worry too much about it right now," Tanya said with a calm, steady voice, picking up her large white notepad, placing it on her lap, and then taking a sip of water. But there was also a tone of resolve I heard underneath the words. She placed her glass back on the side table. "Why don't you just sit down on your stool, and let's take a few deep breaths together." I did as she told me with my whole body resisting. "Now close your eyes and tell me your story. Start with meeting Bob Crewe. But this time imagine it's happening now."

My mind couldn't think of a way out of it, except to get up and walk out.

OK, I thought. *I paid real money to be here. I need help. I can't do this by myself.*

Plus, I absolutely knew two things: 1) I knew down deep she was right and 2) Whatever I did creatively, I had no desire for it to be just good. If this show had the slightest potential to be better than good, I had to go for it.

I pressed record on my iPhone voice memo app as instructed, took a deep breath, closed my eyes, and started talking. Tanya would ask a question every now and then, but for the most part, I talked.

That afternoon after lunch, we continued. I cried through the telling of Jessie's illness and death, eyes still closed, visualizing all the details of that time that were seared into my very soul. I could hear Tanya sniffling and pulling tissue after tissue out of the box. She was crying, too.

The present was powerful. Over the next two days, wherever I was in my own story, it all became real, like removing the old dusty covers from precious antiques in a house that hadn't been lived in for decades. Each detail, in each scene, played like a movie on the back of my wet and swollen eyelids.

Tanya had been taking notes and was making a rough outline of the show for me, and I had been recording the whole time. By the end of the last day, I knew I had had gotten what I came for.

Journal Entry—May 2, 2014, on the plane from ABQ

By Day 4, I got it. I committed to the project and trusted (I have to trust) the process. And by the time we left each other today at breakfast, we knew the show was going to happen. And maybe more than that. Tanya is amazing. I love her energy. She is spiritual and down to earth at the same time—real. She's honest, open, and sincere. I am almost afraid to say this, but this week may have been life-changing.

———————

On Sunday August 30, 2015, fifteen months after I returned from Santa Fe, I did the very first reading of my show for around thirty friends and acquaintances.

Tanya had taken the train up to Maine from Boston two nights before, where she had just left her daughter Chloe, who was entering her freshman year at Boston University.

Usually, Tanya did not attend the first readings of her clients—I didn't know that when I asked her to come. I mean, she would be nearby in Boston anyway, and she did agree to be my director. We had been working together on Skype quite a bit lately going through the latest script edits and additions. It seemed to me like the natural, right thing for her to come up for the reading. Right? That almost didn't happen.

"I don't think I can come." I was startled awake by my cell phone ringing early on the Friday before. I could barely make out the words through the crying. I sat up on the edge of my bed. It was Tanya.

"I've been up since three o'clock with a panic attack. It's so hard to leave my daughter." Tanya was an only child with an only child. She had been a single mother since her former husband had a schizophrenic break when Chloe was four years old. It hadn't been an easy time for her in the years since.

"I don't think I can be there one hundred percent for you this weekend," she continued. "I'm so sorry. I think I'm just going to take the first flight home to New Mexico."

My head was going in a hundred directions. I wasn't sure how to respond. Here was my coach, my director, who had been steady as a rock through the entire process of me writing my show, sobbing into the phone, clearly in a great deal of distress.

"Just come, Tanya," I said, trying to speak as softly as I could. "You'll be staying in a beautiful home in the country with gardens and trees all around. You can come and just relax. You don't have to do anything. You don't even have to go to the reading." I meant every word. I knew I would be fine without her. But I really wanted her to come. I knew already, even through Skype, that her physical presence would make me feel more settled and confident.

I was a little nervous when I picked her up at the Transportation Center in Portland that evening. But I didn't show it. I wanted her to feel comfortable and safe. I certainly didn't want her to feel any more stressed than she already was.

I couldn't help but smile when I saw Tanya walking toward me up the ramp from the train. She smiled back. We hugged our hellos, and I took her bag as we headed toward my car. She thanked me for being so kind to her over the phone and said that after we talked, she booked a massage in Boston before getting on the train. She was still feeling fragile but better. I was glad she came.

Dan had just moved into a new house he had renovated in Cumberland overlooking Casco Bay, around the corner from his place where Tanya and I were going to stay. Over the years he had built several houses on these twenty-two acres, along with donating land for a nature center in Jessie's name.

Seventeen Jessie's Lane consisted of several acres of woods with landscaped lawn and gardens, two houses, Dan's and Reid's, and a large "barn" that now displayed all of Bob Crewe's fine art. The barn, with its space, light, and high ceilings, would serve as the perfect venue for the reading. Because the property was unique, it was taking a while to sell. Fortunately for me, Dan offered all of it to us for this weekend.

I took Tanya to dinner at one of my favorite local restaurants in Portland, and then we headed up to Jessie's Lane. We were both worn-out. I gave Tanya the large master suite with the king bed and its own bathroom. I took the guest room across the hall. The multimedia tech I had hired, who arrived late from New York, had the second house all to herself.

Saturday turned out to be a twelve-hour day—most of it spent on the multimedia, getting the pictures and images to project in the right order, inserting the home video I had edited to go with "Mockingbird Hill," my song about my life as a young mother in Westport, the soundbites from *Grease,* and the collage at the end.

At around 9:30 PM I started a full run-through of the show with the multimedia and the eight live songs I would sing throughout. Tanya sat on a high stool in the back of the large room, took notes, and cried. We turned in just before midnight.

Sunday morning, the day of the reading, as soon as the coffee pot was on, Tanya gave me an hour's worth of notes. It was all good, and I was ready.

> *Journal Entry—August 31, 2015, 8:39 AM*
>
> *It's done! It happened! I did it! It was fantastic—at least according to the audience and Tanya. I did my best, "embodying" the script. The songs worked seamlessly and were placed right. Anyway, I'm still a bit numb from the whole thing! The audience gave me a long standing ovation, and it was genuine and heartfelt. OMG! I have a show!*

"I need to tell you something," Tanya said around midnight on Sunday, as we sat in Dan's den chatting about anything and everything. My brain instantaneously became alert. I braced for what might be coming.

"I have feelings for you. I've felt a connection since we met." I was sitting in the very same brown leather chair in Dan's den where almost exactly four years before, the reality took hold that I was about to take my first shot of testosterone. Once again, my adrenaline surged, and the sweat started accumulating on the back of my legs.

Tanya looked at me with a little smile, soft eyes, and a look of relief. But then her expression turned more serious. "And there is something else."

I held my breath.

"Jessie visited me in the bathtub on the second night you were in Santa Fe and said . . ." I continued holding my breath . . . "'You're going to be with my mom.'"

I felt the blood drain out of my face. *Oh no! Not again!* I wasn't ready for this.

Tanya went on to explain that only two or three times in her life had she ever had an experience like this, but that when it had happened to her, whatever message was conveyed proved true.

"I couldn't shake it," she continued as I sat more upright in the brown leather chair, shifting my legs off the leather, listening. "It felt impossible to me. No way would I ever be with a client, or in a long-distance relationship, or with another musician, or I'm sorry but with," she paused, "an *Aries!*"

I could feel my eyebrows raise with this last point.

"And, as you know, I'm still in a relationship. It's not working, and it will end, but we are still living together." She paused again.

My mind felt like all the circuits were blowing at once. "Come sit down over here beside me." Tanya patted her hand on the leather sofa seat next to hers. Completely numb at this point, I did as I was told.

She took my hand. Tanya had held all of this in check for the whole time she worked with me on my show, never once giving any hint of her feelings for me, or the prophecy from my own daughter she felt would come to be.

The show was real now. It would happen with or without her. The question was, what else was going to happen with or without her? The ball was now in my court. But at that moment, spent and depleted, I could not take in one more ounce of anything, let alone the thought of another relationship. After a few minutes of silence, I squeezed Tanya's hand and let it go.

"I really have to go to bed," I said softly, standing up. "Thank you for everything."

"Me too," she said in almost a whisper. I held out my hand to help her up from the sofa, and we went upstairs to our separate bedrooms.

Two days before Tanya arrived in Maine, the woman I had been dating on and off for about a year ended it. I had met her simply walking into my local Starbucks, back in the summer of 2013, as I did often for my afternoon shot of caffeine.

"Hi, Cid."

It was odd to hear my new name being called out randomly in public. Even two and a half years after changing it to Cidny, I was still being called Cindy by almost everyone except at the Y and at L.L. Bean.

"How did you know my name?" I asked, perplexed, as I turned to see a preppy, nice-looking, middle-aged woman behind the counter, smiling at me.

"I'm on your mailing list. I read all your blogs. And I've seen you play a few times over the years." The woman said as I ordered my tall dark roast coffee. In all the times I had been in that particular Starbucks store, I had never seen her before.

"I know Reid, too," she said, handing me my cup, "We chat when she comes through the drive-through with the kids."

"Oh, cool," I said, detecting a slight smirk on her face, and still wondering who this person was. "What's your name?" I asked.

"Darcy." She smiled again as she turned to take another order.

"Nice to meet you, Darcy," I nodded. "Take care. I'm sure I'll see you again sometime."

As it turned out, Darcy was a divorced, single mother of three children, one out of college, one in college, and one in high school. She lived in Cumberland, a few miles from my old house.

"She likes you mom," Reid said when I told her about meeting Darcy. "You should ask her out." Just hearing those words made me recoil in fear.

"But I'm a transman!" I replied. "I can't just go around asking women out!"

"Mom, she liked you as Cindy, and now she likes you as Cid. Just ask her to coffee."

After a few more conversations with Darcy over the Starbucks counter, and a few more nudges from Reid, I did indeed ask her to coffee—at a different place.

Darcy was smart, kind, good-hearted, and made me laugh a lot. She helped me through some hard moments with Reid, who was going through her own difficult times. She accepted me fully for who I was becoming as Cid. She helped me *feel* like Cid when I was with her. We had a lot of fun together. We had sex. But ultimately, I could not love her in the way she wanted. I honestly didn't feel that I could love anyone. My heart would always be broken after all. And almost all my energy was still going into simply becoming. It *was* all about me, as she often accused me. And now it was about doing my show too. After my characteristic in and out attempts at a relationship, Darcy finally, and rightly, let me go.

Before Darcy, I didn't think I would ever again have a partner after Maryann anyway, but then as an *old transman*? Forget it! Darcy had challenged that notion.

Little by little, Cid was being formed, molded into a full person like a big piece of clay by events, time, and circumstance.

Journal Entry—September 1, 2015, 10:38 AM

Tanya and I just talked. It's all OK. I told her I didn't have the space to even think about a relationship with her. And we agreed, we couldn't let anything get in the way of the progress of my show. Of course, I am attracted to Tanya, but it was the last thing I expected to hear. If anything were to happen—it would have to be in the future.

"You really should wait until after you do the show, Cid," Wendy said firmly in her best exhortative voice. Wendy had summoned Deborah and I out to Los Angeles to write and record new Refugees music right after I got back from Tanya's bootcamp in Santa Fe in May 2014. We agreed immediately, got together in June, and started a new record. Now it was the end of January in 2016, and I was in L.A. for another few days of recording with them.

I had driven to Santa Fe from Maine the week before to spend a month preparing for the premiere of my one-person show, now called *Somewhere Between: Not an Ordinary Life*, which would open on February 26. Tanya was producing two weekends at the Railyard Performance Space. I figured

I'd leave the car at the Albuquerque airport and take the short flight to L.A. and back before starting my mental and emotional show prep.

I had been telling Wendy and Deborah about my dilemma with Tanya. By this time, we had seen each other twice, once in Maine and once in Santa Fe, since the first reading. We had flirted, cuddled, and kissed, fully clothed, but we had not had sex. I was still, as always, keeping my options open and thus, some space between us.

"Yes, totally," I replied affirmatively, as we walked out into the parking lot of Outback Steakhouse in Northridge after dinner. "You're right. That's what I think. Because once we sleep together, forget it."

I had told Wendy and Deborah everything of course. They were both my confidants. They knew all about my split inclinations: my impulsive gotta-have-it-all-now side and my run-away-from-anything-that-even-hints-at-commitment side.

Just then my cell phone rang. It was Tanya. "Hi!" she started, in a lilting voice, as if the word "hi" were two syllables. "I just wanted to tell you that I booked us a private tub at Ten Thousand Waves when you get here. But there's just one thing." She paused. I stopped walking. I waited. Wendy and Deborah waited. "We have to get naked. I just wanted to see if that was OK with you."

Ten Thousand Waves, the famous mountain spa resort, was one of my favorite places on earth. I had been going there on every trip to New Mexico since 1988. It was yet another invitation. Tanya was relentless.

"OK." I could feel my lips forming a devilish smile that I could not control. My body was responding before my brain. I couldn't resist her any longer.

"Well, so much for waiting!" Wendy and Deborah said in unison, as if they had rehearsed it together. I shrugged my shoulders, still smiling. We continued walking to Wendy's car. But I knew then that I was about to walk into a whole new world.

––––––––––––

The house lights in the Railyard Performance Center slowly faded to black. I walked out from behind the tall, black flat, stage right, that bordered the stage area, in the darkness and silence. I picked up my trusty Collings guitar and walked to the center of the stage. I stood there now as all of who I was, as Cidny Tobey Bullens, about to tell my own unique story, in word and song.

As a transgender man, a mother, and a grandparent, I would begin the story by calling up the "sweat and skin and fever" of my rock 'n' roll past. But at this moment, guitar slung on, fingers poised on the strings, ready to slice into the first power chord of my own anthem "Sensible Shoes," as the spotlight hit my face, there was no need to recall. It was happening now.

I *am* a rock star.

All the electricity, the fire, the power, the very essence of me was surging through my body as my voice, strong and clear, carried out into the performance space, surrounding the audience as I sang my song.

"I am a girl. I am twenty-three years old."

I saw the faces in the first few rows, open and receiving, as I spoke the opening lines of my show. The current flowed from me to them and right back to me. In the shadows in the very back of the room there stood the figure of the woman who would become my wife. I realized then, at that very moment, onstage with my story as the spark—*I am the lightning bolt. I am transelectric.*

Epilogue

LUCKY FOR ME
(IN SPITE OF MYSELF)

Call of wild
Luck of the draw
Never did I think I'd get this far
Tweedle dee dum
Tweedle dee dee
Alive and kickin'
Lucky for me

> "Lucky for Me" by Cidny Bullens & Ray Kennedy
> ©2019 Red Dragonfly Music/BMI/Me Own Songs/
> ASCAP

IT'S BEEN OVER A DECADE since I made that decision to come out publicly as a transgender man. I've been lauded, praised, and honored, and I've been castigated, chastened, and condemned. I am dead to a few.

As luck (or the Divine) would have it, Tanya Taylor Rubinstein married me in January 2018. We said our short vows in New York City Hall surrounded by our daughters Reid and Chloe, my granddaughters Tobey and Charles, and Tanya's dear friend, Dorie. It was the perfect place for Tanya and me, as a queer couple, marginalized in our culture by gender and sexuality, to be that day. We were surrounded by other brides and grooms, or however they identified themselves, in the wide margins of society.

Much has transpired in those ten plus years. The first five you've read much about in this book. The last five have been more complex and subtle; the reality of changing genders after a lifetime in one has taken somewhat of a toll.

Like my show, I knew I had to write a memoir. My wife Tanya is a story coach. Her entire method is about getting down into not just the truth, but the *roots* of the truth. She made me do that with *Somewhere Between: Not an Ordinary Life*. She makes me and us as a couple do that in our marriage. It's fucking hard.

I've been keeping journals for fifty years. I have them in boxes. The old volumes are those lined cardboard school notebooks, and they're tattered and torn and smudged. I worked my way up over the years to black bound unlined sketchbooks, dozens of them. I dated each entry with the exact time of day.

Some of the boxes my journals are kept in are thirty years old and have been moved from place to place, house to house, without being opened. After my most recent moves from Maine to New Mexico to Nashville, the boxes were sitting in a storage space in Nashville waiting for retrieval. The day finally came in October 2020 when I tore off the yellowed packing tape and began to dive into my past. Reading the oldest ones nearly killed me: I am the same person I have always been.

At twenty and twenty-one years old, I had the same issues I still have today. I have forty-six years of sobriety and recovery as I write this, and yet here I am—still the same wounded soul.

Of course, now I have the perspective of age and experience. But while reading these entries by the young me, I sank. Everything I had to be grateful for in the present, and there was of course a *ton*, went out the window along with my will to live. I couldn't stop the train from tumbling off the broken rail. And if I had jumped, it would have run over me.

Maybe all this was partially due to the pandemic and all the death and displacement and horror within it. Maybe I had just reached my limit of insanity from people who are hell-bent on bringing the human race back to the Middle Ages (or the Cave Man) and accelerating the destruction of our Mother Earth. Maybe it was just brain chemistry. My perception of reality, true or not, was dark and hopeless. In a matter of weeks, I became nothing. Depression is real and monstrous. It can devour one's very soul.

When Jessie died, every cell of my being changed. I changed. I grasped for many years after some tiny shred of trust in Something. I still believed in some kind of divine energy, but the trust had evaporated. Trust is entirely different than belief or even faith. Trust is an action. And if you don't have it in something, anything, nothing works. Trust in yourself, a process, a person, or the Divine. You gotta trust *something*! Me? Nada.

Jessie's been gone for twenty-six years. I break down in tears now as I write. I've now turned the corner into my seventies. I changed my gender at sixty-one years old and tried to become "all of who I am." I've resurrected myself from the brink (with help) all too many times. Here it all was in black and white, on the old, yellowed pages of my journals. But all the "whos" and "whats" I'd ever been fell away, and I had become a blank sheet.

The descent into nothingness served a purpose. (Though I can tell you it has left debris in its wake.)

In the writing of this book, I have had to face that I had unrecognized trauma, some of which is in my story here and some I am still uncovering. I'm challenged every single day to be more of who I am, even if I don't believe it. I have to practice "acting as if" I trust a power greater than myself—something I learned in the early days of recovery. Tanya calls it radical faith. (And radical acceptance.) I fail still on many days. But I am gathering more bits of steam and resolve as I go. I have a wealth of support. I have no choice now but to face all my demons if I want to *actually* be all of who I am, no gender required.

They tell you in the recovery rooms in early sobriety, "Don't drink even if your ass falls off." Mine now, after decades of being clean, is "Don't *die* even if your ass falls off!" Don't die until you're struck dead. Dead is dead. There's no coming back.

I lost a friend to suicide in August 2021. Someone kind and insightful, loving and soulful. She was fifty-three years old. It hit me hard, and I grieve. But along with what it is for her husband, her children, her family, and her many friends, Sylvie's loss is humanity's loss.

She was a transgender woman. A woman who hid in a man's body for fifty years. For most of the years, Sylvie, her husband Skip, and I were friends, I knew her as a gay man. I didn't see her. As most people did not see me when I was a woman.

She and Skip came to that first show reading of mine in Dan's barn in 2015. Sylvie was not yet Sylvie then. They were both longtime supporters of me and my music.

I remember the day a few years ago she told me that she was indeed a woman and wanted to explore transitioning. We talked about the fear, the challenges, the possible consequences personally, professionally, and socially. But as I have experienced myself, once the window opens and you start to envision yourself becoming who you really are, the fresh air of freedom comes rushing in, filling all your senses with possibility. It's nearly impossible to stop it. Soon you begin to fly, lifted up by that very breeze—clean and new.

With the full support of her husband Skip, Sylvie blossomed. The Maine-issued flannel shirts became flowing floral prints. Her face glowed with a hint of blush and a simple stroke of eyebrow pencil. Her words bounced when she spoke. Sylvie beamed.

But transitioning is hard. No, brutal. Especially for a transgender woman. It is exponentially more difficult for an older transwoman. I have been lucky. I have been supported throughout my transition for the most part, by friends and family (but no, not all). I pass, as they say, as a man in the world now. And even so, with all that support and the fact that I can go unnoticed now in any men's room, I have felt the deep pain of cultural annihilation on the grand scale—and on a smaller scale, the fear of being found out.

Only the indigenous cultures hold a space for us. They ceremonially raise up those of us born as more than one gender, the opposite gender, or the people who feel they have no gender at all.

Sylvie, because of our incredibly myopic culture, finally could not *see herself* as the woman she was because *we* as a culture could not or *would not* see her.

Humanity has squandered the great gift of Sylvie, along with untold numbers of other transwomen and transmen who have been lost to murder and suicide. Why are we so threatened by human beings wanting only to be their true selves?

If we are the most evolved species on earth (which I highly doubt right now), then wouldn't we by nature be the most diverse? In my mind, the answer is yes. Can we accept that? I do not know. I grieve for my friend, my fellow traveler. And I deeply grieve for humanity.

There is a plaque on the wall of every dingy church basement or grand hall that holds a recovery meeting: LIVE AND LET LIVE. Maybe just maybe it's time we try to understand what that phrase really means.

Tanya has a force of will that cannot be moved. It's a mountain. At the same time, she is capable of "holding" space, a place for anyone and everyone with whom she relates. She bends and sways like a great oak with strong outstretched branches—arms full of you, whoever has the good fortune to work with her, while she helps shape your unique story into sheer power. That's her gig. That's her heart. That's her soul's work. And . . . don't fuck with her.

I've become a fighter in my later years. I react fiercely if I feel pushed. Sometimes I rage. It is not pretty or attractive. I hate it in myself. Even as I sat up in bed many a night the winter of 2020–21, silently crying and wishing I could disappear from the face of the earth, even though I did not tell Tanya how bad it really was for me, she knew. She held a space for it all. It wasn't easy in the least. But, with her deep support and encouragement, I started to write this book—all without trust, all without faith.

But now, here at the end of this endeavor, having read, thought, and felt through every circumstance, action, and opportunity—both taken and lost—every bold move and backpedaling retreat in my extraordinary life, I am not only alive, but I am once again being reborn. I realize now that the emptiness of depression was the new womb; the kicking and screaming of my rage was the hitting of the fresh, cold air of a new beginning.

There is unbounding love around me. My wife, my family, my wide circle of friends, and others—fans and supporters, whom I do not know well or at all—surround me with love every day. As challenging as life has been for me, there is nowhere I truly want to be other than where I am today. I have been bestowed more grace than any one person should be allowed. The Divine has *always* provided. As Tanya would say, "Baby, there is magic everywhere."

I have witnessed and experienced that magic with Tanya, my children, my grandchildren, and my music throughout my now long life. I just forget, all the time. Tanya and I like to say we are on a spectacular adventure. My practice is to remember that. I must remind myself every day to open my eyes and look all around me—past the blare and bluster, through the growing waves of discord and vitriol—to open my heart and let the Love in. If I do that, it is absolutely evident—there *is* magic everywhere.

Tanya and Cid, Nashville, Tennessee, 2022.
Author's collection

AUTHOR'S NOTE

In Alcoholics Anonymous the Eleventh Tradition states in part: *We need always to maintain personal anonymity at the level of press, radio, and films.*

After adhering to this very principle for my entire sobriety, I felt I had to break my own anonymity in this memoir. (As for the five others mentioned in this book regarding AA, three people are deceased. The fourth has given me permission. Another person's name was changed.)

I've been clean and sober, one day at a time, for over four and a half decades. Early on the Fellowship became part of the fabric of my being and it is interwoven throughout my life. I cannot tell the truth of my story without stating that fact out loud.

Alcoholics Anonymous is "a program of attraction rather than promotion." And I respectfully believe in that. I believe I would not be here on earth now without the Twelve Steps and Traditions of recovery. But my program is personal to me. And in this memoir, I represent only *my own* sobriety, just as the rest of my story is unique and mine alone.

ACKNOWLEDGMENTS

Special thanks to my literary agent Irene Goodman for scooping me up and paving the way. To my editor Jerry Pohlen and all at Chicago Review Press for their belief, expertise, and enthusiasm in releasing this book.
To Perdita Finn for helping me walk my very first baby steps in writing this book.

To my many dear friends, cohorts, and colleagues in music, recovery, community, and life past and present— in Maine, Nashville, Los Angeles, New York, and all over the world— who have lifted me up, held my hand, pushed me along, held me back, kept me safe, told me the truth, lied when necessary, carried the message, built a bridge, taken me in, taken a chance, created a space, donated time and talent, invested in me, inspired me, listened to me, cared about my truth, and loved me through it all.
(Too many to list—I'm sorry, I tried. I know who you are, and you really do know who you are.)
Thank you!

To my siblings Rick, Deb, Suki, my late sister Nancy, my sib-cousin Mardi, and all my extended family, young and old—deepest thanks for your love and support through all of it!

Infinite thanks to Dan Crewe, Tony Berg, Lane Berkwit,
Joanne Berman, Ken Bernstein, Bill Brimm and Andrew Krichels,
Frank Brooks, Bob Clearmountain, Pam Crewson, Rodney Crowell,
Kye Fleming, Bob Halley, Mike Hewitson, Deborah Holland,
Mark Islam, Dallas James, Peter Jason and Eileen Rosaly,
Ray and Siobhan Kennedy, Billie Jean King and Ilana Kloss,
Tracey and Kris Latshaw and the entire Nelson family, Bob and
Gail Ludwig, David Mansfield, Dave Marsh, Santi Meunier,
Mary Noyes, T.J. Parsell, Mark and Jane Potts, Bonnie Raitt, Rob Roth,
Maryann B. Russell, Rosemary and Luther Smith, Tim and
Stacy Wakefield, Wendy Waldman, and all my dear friends in and
around the community of
North Haven, Maine,
for going beyond the bounds of friendship.

A very, very special thanks to Sir Elton John and David Furnish
for their love and generosity throughout the years, xoxox.

To my beautiful daughters Reid Crewe and angel Jessie Bullens-Crewe,
my stepdaughter Chloe,
and to my grandchildren Tobey, Charles, Hunter, and Rhys
Thank you for lighting up my life. I love you!

Thanks to
Helen Brena and YMCA of Southern Maine and
L.L. Bean, Freeport, Maine

There are many people who have passed briefly through my life
who have touched me deeply. There are people I have never met
who have greatly affected me. To all of you, thank you.

Heartfelt hugs to my bereaved-parent family around the world.

In honor of my late mother and father
Mary Jane and Richard S. Bullens
and the late

Jamie Andrews, Bill Aucoin, Bobby Brooks, Bobbie Callahan,
Beth Canning, Bob Crewe, Robert Hicks, Jack Kissell,
Sylvie Markiewicz,
Tena Taylor Rone,
Lu Ann Simms, Dicy Waters, Kristine Watson, Jerry Wexler,
Timothy White, John Wulp
and

In memory of
Bobby Neuwirth

*For my trans and nonbinary community,
seen and unseen, present, past, and future.*

LGBTQ AND TRANSGENDER RESOURCES

Transgender Legal Defense & Education Fund

A national legal advocacy organization focused on advancing equity for transgender and nonbinary people through impact litigation, legal services, policy, and public education.
https://transgenderlegal.org/

National Center for Transgender Equality

A national transgender rights organization based in Washington, DC, that advocates for inclusive federal policies.
https://transequality.org/

Stand with Trans

Empowerment and support for transgender youth and their loved ones.
https://standwithtrans.org/

Gender Spectrum

Educational resources and events for parents, educators, medical and mental health providers providing support to transgender children and young adults.

https://www.genderspectrum.org/

Transgender Law Center

A national transgender organization rooted in community-driven strategies to keep transgender and nonbinary people alive, thriving, and fighting for liberation.

https://transgenderlawcenter.org/

The Trevor Project

The world's largest suicide prevention and crisis intervention organization for LGBTQ people.

https://www.thetrevorproject.org/resources/

Trans Lifeline

A twenty-four-hour confidential hotline by and for transgender people in crisis and in need of support.

https://translifeline.org/

Trans Justice Funding Project

A "by-and-for" community-led funding initiative providing financial support to grassroots transgender groups across the country.

https://www.transjusticefundingproject.org/

GLAAD

An organization that has been at the forefront of cultural change for more than thirty years, working to accelerate acceptance for the LGBTQ community.

https://www.glaad.org/resourcelist

Camp Aranu'tiq

The first-ever summer camp established for transgender young people in New Hampshire.
https://www.camparanutiq.org/

Gender Infinity

The largest conference in the South for transgender young people and their families.
https://genderinfinity.org/

Trans Tech Social

An incubator focused on providing skills, training, and career opportunities for transgender people.
https://transtechsocial.org/

PFLAG

Founded in 1973, PFLAG is the first and largest organization dedicated to supporting, educating, and advocating for LGBTQ+ people and their families. PFLAG's network of hundreds of chapters and more than 325,000 members and supporters works to create a caring, just, and affirming world for LGBTQ+ people and those who love them.
https://pflag.org/

DISCOGRAPHY (1974–2022)

YEAR	ARTIST	ALBUM	LABEL	CREDIT
1974	Steve Eaton	*Hey, Mr. Dreamer*	Capitol	Background Vocals
1974	Gene Clark	*No Other*	Asylum	Background Vocals
1974	Eleventh Hour	*The Eleventh Hour*	20th Century	Songwriter/ Vocals
1975	Don Everly	*Sunset Towers*	Ode	Background Vocals
1975	Disco Tex & the Sex-O-Lettes	*Disco Tex & the Sex-O-Lettes*	Chelsea	Background Vocals
1975	Rod Stewart	*Atlantic Crossing*	Warner Bros.	Background Vocals
1976	Elton John	*Blue Moves*	MCA	Background Vocals
1976	Elton John	"Don't Go Breaking My Heart" (single)	MCA	Background Vocals
1976	Geoff Muldaur	*Motion*	Wounded Bird	Background Vocals

YEAR	ARTIST	ALBUM	LABEL	CREDIT
1976	Bob Crewe Generation	*Street Talk*	20th Century	Songwriter/ Vocals
1977	Bruce Johnston	*Going Public*	Columbia	Background Vocals
1977	Rory Block	*Intoxication So Bitter Sweet*	Chrysalis	Background Vocals
1977	Bill Quateman	*Night After Night*	RCA	Background Vocals
1977	The Alpha Band	*Spark in the Dark*	Arista	Background Vocals
1978	Various Artists	*Grease: Original Motion Picture Soundtrack*	RSO	Three Lead Vocals
1978	Jerry Corbetta	*Jerry Corbetta*	Warner Bros.	Background Vocals
1978	The Alpha Band	*Statue Makers of Hollywood*	Arista	Background Vocals
1978	Cindy Bullens	*Desire Wire*	United Artists	Artist, Songwriter
1979	Cindy Bullens	*Steal the Night*	Casablanca	Artist, Songwriter, Producer
1980	Nitty Gritty Dirt Band	*Make a Little Magic*	United Artists	Songwriter
1981	Mickey Thomas	*Alive Alone*	Elektra	Songwriter
1981	Bryan Adams	*You Want It You Got It*	A & M	Background Vocals
1989	Cindy Bullens	*Cindy Bullens*	MCA	Artist, Songwriter, Producer
1992	Radney Foster	*Del Rio, TX 1959*	Arista	Songwriter

YEAR	ARTIST	ALBUM	LABEL	CREDIT
1993	Dixie Chicks	*Shouldn't a Told You That*	Crystal Clear Sound	Songwriter
1994	Bill Lloyd	*Set to Pop*	East Side Digital	Songwriter, Vocals
1994	Cindy Bullens	*Why Not?*	Blue Lobster	Artist, Songwriter, Producer
1995	Radney Foster	*Labor of Love*	Arista	Songwriter, Vocals
1996	Bob Neuwirth	*Look Up*	Watermelon	Vocals
1996	MidSouth	*MidSouth*	Warner Alliance	Songwriter
1996	Sarah Brown	*Sayin' What I'm Thinking*	Blind Pig	Songwriter, Vocals, Guitar
1997	Irma Thomas	*The Story of My Life*	Rounder	Songwriter
1999	Cindy Bullens	*Somewhere Between Heaven and Earth*	Artemis	Artist, Songwriter, Producer
2000	Shane McAnally	*Shane McAnally*	Curb	Songwriter
2001	Cindy Bullens	*Neverland*	Artemis	Artist, Songwriter, Producer
2003	Various Artists	*Light of Day: A Tribute to Bruce Springsteen*	Revolver	Artist, Vocals, Guitar
2003	Elliott Murphy	*Strings of the Storm*	Blue Rose	Vocals, Guitar
2004	Malibu Storm	*Malibu Storm*	Rounder	Songwriter
2005	Cindy Bullens	*dream #29*	Blue Lobster/ LetsPlay	Artist, Songwriter, Producer

YEAR	ARTIST	ALBUM	LABEL	CREDIT
2006	Cindy Bullens	*Live*	Blue Rose	Artist, Songwriter, Producer
2006	T Bone Burnett	*Twenty Twenty: The Essential T Bone Burnett*	Sony	Background Vocals
2008	Katy Lied	*Late Arrival*	Katy Lied UK	Background Vocals
2009	The Refugees	*Unbound*	Wabuho	Artist, Songwriter, Producer
2010	Cindy Bullens	*Howling Trains and Barking Dogs*	MC Records	Artist, Songwriter, Producer
2012	The Refugees	*Three*	Wabuho	Artist, Songwriter, Producer
2019	The Refugees	*How Far It Goes*	Wabuho	Artist, Songwriter, Producer
2020	Elton John	*Jewel Box*	Universal	Backing Vocals
2020	Cidny Bullens	*Walkin' Through This World*	Blue Lobster	Artist, Songwriter, Producer
2022	Beth Nielsen Chapman	*Crazy Town*	Cooking Vinyl	Background Vocals

ALBUM CREDITS

1978   *Desire Wire*   Cindy Bullens   United Artists
Produced by Tony Bongiovi, Lance Quinn (with Cindy Bullens), Engineered by Bob Clearmountain at Power Station, NYC, Dee Robb at Cherokee Studios, Los Angeles, Mixed by Bob Clearmountain at Power Station, NYC, Mastered by Bob Ludwig, Masterdisk, NYC, Guitars: Cindy Bullens, Mark Doyle, David Mansfield, Danny Gatton, Jeff Mironov, Lance Quinn, Keyboards: Cindy Bullens, Paul Shaffer, Rob Mounsey, Leon Pendarvis, Jr., Billy Mernit, Synthesizer: Leon Pendarvis, Jr., Kenny Bishell, Bass: Bob Babbitt, Neil Jason
Drums: Jerry Marotta, Allen Swartzberg, Percussion: Jimmy Maelen, Background Vocals: Cindy Bullens, Jon Joyce, Billy Mernit, Saxophones: Lou Marini, George Young, Jerry Petersen

1979   *Steal the Night*   Cindy Bullens   Casablanca
Produced by Cindy Bullens and Mark Doyle, Engineered by Neil Brody at United Western, Village Recorders, Allen Zentz Recording, Los Angeles, Mixed by Neil Brody, Mark Doyle, and Cindy Bullens
Mastered by Brian Gardner at Allen Zentz Recording, Guitars: Cindy Bullens, Mark Doyle, Keyboards: Trantham Whitley, Cindy Bullens, Mark Doyle, Synthesizer: Trantham Whitley, Mark Doyle, Bass: Roger Freeland, Mark Doyle, Drums: Thom Mooney, Percussion: Thom Mooney, Cindy Bullens, Mark Doyle

Background Vocals: Cindy Bullens, Jon Joyce, Mark Doyle, Harmonica: Cindy Bullens

1989   *Cindy Bullens*   Cindy Bullens   MCA
Produced by Bob Clearmountain, Cindy Bullens, and David Mansfield, Engineered & Mixed by Bob Clearmountain at Hit Factory, NYC, Mastered by Bob Ludwig at Masterdisk, NYC, Guitars: David Mansfield, Cindy Bullens, Mark Doyle, Bobby Messano, Keyboards: Nick Bariluk, Bass: Jeremy Alsop, Drums: Tom Devino, Background Vocals: Cindy Bullens, Holly Sherwood, Mark Doyle, and Bryan Adams on "Don't Let This Love Go Down," Horns: Jon Faddis, Danny Marouse, Tom Malone, Violin: David Mansfield, Harmonica: Cindy Bullens

1994   *Why Not? EP*   Cindy Bullens   Blue Lobster
Produced and Mixed by Cindy Bullens and David Mansfield, Recorded at House of Bugs, NYC, Engineered by David Mansfield, Mastered by Bob Ludwig at Gateway Mastering, Portland, Maine, Guitars: David Mansfield, Cindy Bullens, Piano: Trantham Whitley, Organ, Synthesizer, Dobro, Accordion, Drum programming: David Mansfield, Mandolin: David Mansfield, Cindy Bullens, Bass: David Santos, David Miner, Drums: Tom Devino
"On Broken Wings" Produced by Cindy Bullens and Mary Ann Kennedy, Recorded at Lombardy Studio, Nashville, Engineered by Bill McDermott, Guitars: Cindy Bullens, Drums: Mary Ann Kennedy, Bass: Mark Hill

1999   *Somewhere Between*   Cindy Bullens   Artemis
        Heaven and Earth
Produced by Cindy Bullens with Rodney Crowell, Steven Soles, Tony Berg, Recorded at Dog Den, Hum Depot, Nashville, TN, Zeitgeist, Los Angeles, Twin Palms, Santa Monica, CA, Engineered by Bill McDermott, David Thoener, Larry Hirsch, John Paterno, Glenn Spinner, Mixed by Bob Clearmountain, MixThis, L.A. and David Thoener, Sound Kitchen, Nashville, TN, Mastered by Bob Ludwig at Gateway Mastering, Portland, Maine Guitars: Cindy Bullens, George Marinelli, Keyboards: Benmont Tench III, Mark T. Jordan, Steve Conn, Jeff Levine

Bass: Michael Rhodes, David Santos, Kenny Edwards, John Pierce, Drums: Greg Morrow, Rick Lonow, David Kemper, Violin: David Mansfield, Harmonica: Cindy Bullens. Featuring vocals by Bonnie Raitt, Lucinda Williams, Bryan Adams, Beth Nielsen Chapman, Reid Bullens-Crewe, Mary Ann Kennedy, Bill Lloyd

2001   *Neverland*   Cindy Bullens   Artemis
Produced by Ray Kennedy and Cindy Bullens, Recorded at Room and Board, Nashville, TN.
Engineered by Ray Kennedy and John Hurley, Mixed by Ray Kennedy, Cindy Bullens, and John Hurley
Mastered by Bob Ludwig, Gateway Mastering, Portland, Maine,
Guitars: Cindy Bullens, George Marinelli, Ray Kennedy, Keyboards: Steve Conn, Benmont Tench III,
Bass: Michael Rhodes, Drums: Ginger Cote, Percussion: Ray Kennedy, Cindy Bullens, Mandolin: Ray Kennedy, Harmonica: Cindy Bullens, Cello: John Catchings, Background vocals: Mary Ann Kennedy, Bill Lloyd, Tom Littlefield, Reid Bullens-Crewe. Featured vocals by Steve Earle, Emmylou Harris, and John Hiatt

2005   *dream #29*   Cindy Bullens   LetsPlay/
                                                      Blue Lobster
Produced by Ray Kennedy and Cindy Bullens, Recorded at Room and Board, Hermitage, TN,
Engineered by Ray Kennedy, Mixed by Ray Kennedy and Cindy Bullens, Mastered by Bob Ludwig, Gateway Mastering, Portland, Maine, Guitars: Cindy Bullens, George Marinelli, Keyboards: Dennis Burnside, Bass: Garry Tallent, Justin Maxwell, Drums: Ginger Cote, Percussion: Ray Kennedy, Featuring Elton John on piano,
Featured vocals by Delbert McClinton, Reid Bullens-Crewe, and Red Sox Hall of Fame pitcher Tim Wakefield

| 2010 | *Howling Trains and Barking Dogs* | Cindy Bullens | MC Records |

Produced by Cindy Bullens, Recorded at Root Cellar, Hallowell, Maine, Engineered by Bob Colwell,

Mixed by Bob Colwell and Cindy Bullens, Mastered by Ray Kennedy, Zen Mastering, Nashville, TN

Guitars: Stephen B. Jones, Cindy Bullens, Keyboards: Bob Colwell, Bass: Justin Maxwell, Stephen B. Jones, Bob Colwell, Drums and Percussion: Ginger Cote, Mandolin and Harmonica: Cindy Bullens, Dobro: Stephen B. Jones, Fiddle: David Mansfield, Featured vocals by Radney Foster, Wendy Waldman, Deborah Holland, and Reid Bullens-Crewe

| 2020 | *Walkin' Through This World* | Cidny Bullens | Blue Lobster |

Produced by Ray Kennedy and Cidny Bullens, Recorded at Room and Board, Nashville, TN, Engineered by Ray Kennedy, Mixed by Ray Kennedy with Cidny Bullens, Mastered by Ray Kennedy at Zen Mastering, Guitars: George Marinelli, Cidny Bullens, Ray Kennedy, Stanton Edward, Keyboards: Mark T. Jordan, Bass: Steve Mackay, Drums: Lynn Williams, Harmonica, Electric Sitar, and Synthesizer: Cidny Bullens,

Featured vocals by Rodney Crowell, Deborah Holland, Reid Crewe, Siobhan Kennedy, Beth Nielsen Chapman, Harry Stinson, Mary Gauthier, Bill Lloyd, Michael Kelsh, Jess Leary

INDEX

Entries in *italics* refer to images.